On Being Mindless

On Being Mindless: Buddhist Meditation And The Mind-Body Problem

Paul J. Griffiths

Open Court
La Salle, Illinois

Printed and bound in the United States of America.
OC879 Cloth 10 9 8 7 6 5 4 3 2 1
ISBN: 0-8126-9006-0
OC880 Paper 10 9 8 7 6 5 4 3 2 1
ISBN: 0-8126-9007-9

Library of Congress Cataloging-in-Publication Data

Griffiths, Paul J.
On being mindless.

Bibliography: p.
Includes index.
1. Nirodhasamāpatti. 2. Consciousness—Religious aspects—Buddhism. 3. Meditation (Buddhism)—Psychology. I. Title.
BQ4327.G75 1986 294.3′422 86-845
ISBN 0-8126-9006-0
ISBN 0-8126-9007-9 (pbk.)

For my father

CONTENTS

On Being Mindless

ACKNOWLEDGEMENTS

In completing this work I accumulated intellectual debts to so many people and institutions that it is now beyond my powers to remember what I learned from whom, much less to fully acknowledge all of it. The acknowledgements that follow are therefore necessarily incomplete.

Trinity College, Oxford, provided me with a stimulating intellectual environment for five crucial years (1975–80), and gave me training in both Theology and Sanskrit, skills which were instrumental in making this work possible. The Buddhist Studies Program at the University of Wisconsin gave me the freedom to develop my interests in Buddhism in my own way during 1980–83. I am grateful to the Harkness Foundation for generous financial support during 1980–82, and to the University of Wisconsin for providing me with a University Fellowship in 1982–83. It was this financial support which made possible the speedy completion of my PhD dissertation, on which this book is largely based. Finally, the Department of South Asian Languages and Civilizations at the University of Chicago has, since August 1984, provided me with an intellectual setting that is both relaxed and exciting: an ideal place for the completion of this study. I am especially grateful to Frank Reynolds, Wendy O'Flaherty and A. K. Ramanujan, all of whom have gone out of their way to make me feel at home in Chicago.

My intellectual and spiritual debts are more numerous. Trevor Williams showed me long ago in Oxford that it is possible to both be religious and study religion. Richard Gombrich introduced me to both Sanskrit and Buddhism, and gave me substantial encouragement during my early studies. When I first came to the US Frances Wilson acted as my *kalyāṇamitra* and guided me through the administrative complexities of a large American university. Minoru

Kiyota was gracious enough to act as my dissertation advisor at the University of Wisconsin in a field far from his own, and to allow me an unusual degree of freedom in pursuing my goals. He also opened my eyes to the range and quality of the work on Indian Buddhism currently being produced in Japan. To him I owe a special personal debt. From Geshe Sopa I learned what Tibetan I know, and learned something also of the depth and range of traditional Tibetan scholarship. Keith Yandell has provided me with continuous philosophical challenges and a personal friendship that has shaped my intellectual outlook in very important ways. Noriaki Hakamaya has been consistently generous in giving me both time and advice, and first showed me, in a series of seminars on the *Mahāyānasaṃgraha* from 1981 to 1983, how best to study Indian Buddhist texts. Stephan Beyer may recognize many of the ideas in this study as closely related to his own. John Keenan will recognize that our fruitful disagreements about both Buddhism and philosophy continue. Finally, a special debt of gratitude goes to Delmas Lewis; without his conversation and friendship this book would not exist in its present form.

My thanks are also due to W. W. Bartley III for reading the manuscript of this work and making helpful comments, and to David Ramsay Steele, Sue Olson and Lisa Zimmerman of Open Court for agreeing to publish this work and for doing so in such an expeditious and helpful manner.

Portions of the first chapter of this work (in very different form) have appeared in the *Journal of the American Academy of Religion* (1981) and *Religion* (1983). A portion of the second chapter appeared in *Philosophy East and West* (1983).

My wife has neither typed nor proofread this book; my daughter is not yet in a condition to type or proofread anything; but I am indebted to them both for almost everything else.

Chicago
October 1985

INTRODUCTION

This book is about the philosophical implications of meditative practice. More specifically, it is a case-study of certain intra-Buddhist controversies about the nature and implications of a particular, precisely defined altered state of consciousness,[1] attained by way of an equally well defined set of meditational practices. It may seem at the outset as though this has rather little to do with philosophy as understood in the analytical traditions of the West: it may be suggested that we are instead dealing here, as Louis de La Vallée Poussin put it, with:

> . . . Indian 'philosophumena' concocted by ascetics . . . men exhausted by a severe diet and often stupified by the practice of ecstacy. Indians do not make a clear distinction between facts and ideas, between ideas and words; they have never clearly recognized the principle of contradiction.[2]

Poussin was one of the greatest historians of Indian Buddhism the West has yet produced, and while he was clearly correct in his view that the practice of meditation was and is of fundamental importance for Buddhism, he was equally clearly incorrect, as I hope to show, in thinking that this resulted in any lack of clarity in philosophical argumentation, much less in a failure to recognize the 'principle of contradiction'.

It is upon meditative practice that the religious life of the Buddhist virtuoso is based and from such practice that systematic Buddhist philosophical and soteriological theory begins. The experiences produced as a result of meditative practice have therefore historically been of great importance to Buddhist philosophical theory; it would hardly be an exaggeration to say that the whole of the magnificently complex edifice of Buddhist philosophy is a drawing out and systematization of the implications of such experience. The Buddha himself (insofar as we can say anything about him; the historical problems associated with making judgements about the teaching of the historical Buddha are great) seems to have placed great emphasis on the significance of meditative experience and to have regarded it as both the origin and guarantee of his more strictly philosophical teaching.[3]

Rather than judging the significance of meditational practice in Buddhism to allow no place for clear philosophical analysis, a useful method of gaining access to the rationale and significance of some key Buddhist doctrines might be to examine their connections with those meditative practices with which they almost always operate in symbiosis. It is not that specific meditative practices straightforwardly give rise to specific doctrines, though this kind of simple and direct causal relationship is sometimes suggested both by Western critics of Buddhism and by Buddhist scholars working from within the tradition.[4] Rather, philosophical beliefs shape meditative techniques, provide specific expectations, and thus have a formative influence on the kinds of experience which are actually produced, as well as on the philosophical conclusions which are drawn from these experiences.[5] Similarly, the results of meditative practice inform the philosophical views of practicing Buddhists with new experiences, and thus suggest new ways in which the philosophical system can be modified and developed. To examine the philosophical use made of (the results of) a specific set or sets of meditative practices may therefore provide useful insights into both the origins of Buddhist philosophical doctrine and the functions of Buddhist psychotropic technique.[6] This work is therefore intended as a case study in the relationship between philosophical theory and soteriological practice in Indian Buddhism. It takes as its presupposition the idea that there is indeed such a relationship—something which is not always obvious from a reading of the works of students and critics of Buddhism from both within and without the tradition—and applies the presupposition to a particular case: that of the 'attainment of cessation' *(nirodhasamāpatti)* as this was described, recommended, analyzed and discussed in the philosophical texts of early Indian Buddhism.

The attainment of cessation is a particularly interesting case for the kind of study envisaged here. The term, and its equivalent, 'cessation of sensation and conceptualization' *(saṃjñāvedayitanirodha)*,[7] denote a specific very precisely defined altered state of consciousness, one which occurs as the direct result of specified meditative techniques. While the term is rooted in the earliest strata of the texts available to us, and though the altered state of consciousness denoted by it is attributed by such texts to the Buddha himself,[8] its unusual nature, coupled with the fact that it has no obvious connections with mainstream Buddhist soteriology, meant that from the beginning it produced a set of problems for Buddhist theoreticians. These problems arise from the fact that the term 'cessation of sensation and conceptualization' denotes a state of (un)consciousness in which no mental functions occur, and that such a condition is frequently given high recommendation in the texts, and sometimes seems to be equated with Nirvana, the ultimate goal of all virtuoso Buddhist soteriological practice. Given that this is the case (and the evidence for it will be presented in the body of this work) a number of interesting philosophical problems arise.

The first set of problems has to do with the nature of salvation, the ultimate goal of virtuoso religious practice as this was conceived by Indian Buddhists. There appears to be some tension between a view which regards dispassionate knowledge of the way things are[9] as a *sine qua non* and constituent factor of enlightenment, and a view which sees complete unconsciousness, the cessation of all mental functions, as essential to, or even identical with, enlightenment. This is, therefore, a problem for Buddhist soteriological theory, a problem created by a witness within the tradition to variant and even contradictory sets of soteriological practices. Some of the significant elements of this debate will be presented and analyzed in what follows.

The second set of problems has to do with the relationship between mind and body—or, more precisely, between the mental and the physical—as this was conceived by Buddhist thinkers. If there is indeed a condition in which all mental events come to a halt (as the canonical texts say), and if this condition is sometimes temporary and reversible (that is, if mental events can sometimes, as it were, start up once again from a condition of cessation), then some explanation of the mechanism by which this occurs is called for. The canonical definitions of the condition denoted by the term 'attainment of cessation' make it clear that no mental events—and thus by extension only physical events—occur when any given individual is in this state. How then is it that the stream of mental events (brought to a halt by the meditative techniques which produce the attainment of cessation) can begin once again when there exist only physical events from which they can arise? Almost all the possible answers to this question were suggested by Buddhist philosophers in the course of the early Indian debates on the issue, and the examination of these debates will provide an interesting set of perspectives on Buddhist views of the mind–body problem.

My study will restrict itself to an analysis of the debates on the attainment of cessation in early Indian Buddhism. I shall therefore consider mostly material from the systematic philosophical texts of Indian scholastic Buddhism,[10] beginning with the discussions in the Pali *Collections (Nikāyā)* as representative of the earliest available traditions. The *Collections* are a body of texts which present themselves as verbatim reports of the discourses of the historical figure now given the honorific title of 'Buddha' (enlightened one). Historical research makes it clear that these texts do not in fact give us access to the *ipsissima verba* of the Buddha, but they do preserve a witness to a reasonably early stage in the development of the Buddhist tradition, and thus make a useful starting point for the investigation.

In addition to this material I shall also make use of Buddhaghosa's commentarial discussions of the *Collections* together with his systematization of the material contained in them in the influential text called *Path to Purity (Visuddhimagga).* The comments by Dhammapāla, the author of a large commentary on the *Path to Purity,*[11] will also be discussed. An examination of the material on the attainment of cessation in these texts should thus provide an historically accurate overview of the understanding of this phenomenon arrived at by the Theravāda[12] tradition, a tradition to which all these texts belong.

The Theravāda tradition was not the only one of the early schools to carry on extensive discussions of the attainment of cessation. With the Theravāda view I shall compare the extensive discussions found in Vasubandhu's important text called *Commentary on the Treasury of Metaphysics (Abhidharmakośabhāṣya),* a work which sets forth the views of the Vaibhāṣika[13] school, and which offers in addition a critique of these views from the Sautrāntika viewpoint.[14] Use will also be made of the major Indian commentaries to this work, especially those of Sthiramati and Yaśomitra.[15] These texts contain full discussions of the views of all the major Indian Buddhist schools on the issue.

Finally, I shall analyze the discussion of the same issue found in some key Yogācāra texts; in these works the same issue is treated from the standpoint of the Yogācāra school,[16] a perspective which results in a radically different philosophical solution to the problem.

The intentions of this study as a whole, therefore, are (at least) threefold: 1) to shed some light on the history of Buddhist views about a specific altered state of consciousness and its relationship to specified soteriological goals; 2) by analyzing the philosophical discussions surrounding this altered state, to increase our understanding of the way in which the relationship between the physical and the mental was conceived in early Indian Buddhism; and 3) to ask and attempt to answer some questions about the adequacy of the Buddhist view of the causal relations between the mental and the physical.

This third goal, the asking of questions about the adequacy of Buddhist views on the relations between mental and physical, raises some philosophical difficulties, which require some methodological remarks. I originally conceived this work as a historical and exegetical study of a set of Indian Buddhist controversies about certain kinds of meditational practice. In the process of research and writing it has come to be something both less and more than that. In addition to the planned descriptive and historical study it is now also an exercise in cross-cultural philosophizing; the philosophizing found in this work both rests upon and illustrates an important general thesis about rationality. Briefly stated, this thesis is that philosophy is a trans-cultural human activity, which in all essentials operates within the same conventions and by the same norms in all cultures. These are, broadly speaking, the conventions and norms which demarcate what in the West has sometimes been called 'rationality'. This is not an uncontroversial view; it is probably true to say that the current intellectual orthodoxy in the Western academic disciplines of philosophy, anthropology, sociology, history (especially history of religions) and literary criticism is opposed to it. The development of a sociology of knowledge,[17] superficial understandings (and misunderstandings) of the late Wittgenstein and the classical Quine,[18] the pervasive adherence to varieties of relativism in the work of important anthropological theorists,[19] the fuss in philosophy of science over the early Kuhn's incommensurability thesis and Feyerabend's fulminations against method,[20] and the vogue for deconstructionist readings of any and all genres of text[21]—all these have combined to create an intellectual climate in which it is problematic even to suggest that rational discourse may be a phenomenon which operates by recognizably similar rules and with effectively identical goals cross-culturally, and is thus a tool available in a relatively straightforward manner for cross-cultural communication and assessment.

The view that the functions, nature, and limits of rationality are conceived similarly in all cultures has as its corollary the idea that cross-cultural assessment of philosophical views and arguments is possible. It suggests that I, as a twentieth-century English-speaking Westerner, am theoretically capable of both understanding and passing judgement upon philosophical arguments and conclusions presented by fifth-century Indian Buddhists writing and thinking in Sanskrit. This too is problematic, given the current intellectual climate in which terms such as 'pluralism' and 'dialogue' have become almost numinous, denoting an orthodoxy in the direction of which it is necessary to make at least a ritual obeisance.[22] Even if such cross-cultural attempts at normative judgement can avoid offending against one or more of the intellectual orthodoxies just mentioned, they tend to be regarded as symptoms of cultural imperialism and intellectual triumphalism.

Clearly, then, there are important systematic problems involved with the view that it is legitimate to move from historical and expository writing about philosophical debates located in a culture distant in space and time from one's own, to an analytical and critical study of such debates which is in part concerned to pass judgement upon them. Among these systematic problems are the questions of whether the functions, goals and limits of rationality are understood in essentially similar ways cross-culturally; whether cross-cultural assessments of truth (in propositions) and validity (in arguments) can escape the pitfalls of parochialism and arrogance; and whether, *pace* the sociologists of knowledge,[23] there are distinctions to be made between the contingent causes for the holding of a particular belief, and the non-contingent grounds for holding that belief. Ideally, such systematic problems should be resolved systematically; only thus can the objections of the adherents of the pluralistic view be properly answered. Such a systematic enterprise is possible, I think, but is a task too large for this study. Instead, the presence of attempts at critical assessment of the arguments and conclusions of the sources with which I deal in this work, are best understood as an attempt to provide some indirect evidence for the truth of the thesis that rationally grounded normative discourse is an appropriate tool for undertaking the activity of cross-cultural philosophizing. At the very least, the effective completion of a case-study of the kind essayed here requires (logically) the falsity of the thesis that cultures (and their norms of rationality) are radically incommensurable. Its effective completion does not, of course, demonstrate the truth of the proposition that they are straightforwardly commensurable, much less that rationality operates under much the same rules in all cultures. At most it provides contributory evidence for the truth of a limited version of that thesis.

I shall, then, undertake in what follows the analysis of a set of (rational) arguments from the Indian Buddhist traditions about the nature of the relationship between the mental and the physical. Where it seems appropriate I shall not hesitate to offer critical assessments of both the arguments presented in those traditions and of the truth of the premisses involved therein. I undertake this enterprise with the humility appropriate to all philosophical enterprises—the knowledge, among other things, that I am likely to be frequently wrong. But I reject that humility which, all too often in those Western academic circles where the study of Buddhist thought is carried on, refuses to take its material with philosophical seriousness. As I hope will become clear, this material presents interesting and complex arguments which claim to be valid and which also claim therefore (given the truth of their premisses) to lead to true conclusions. We do the tradition a disservice if we refuse to move beyond the exegetical mode of academic discourse to the normative, the judgemental.

A close study of the material discussed in this work makes it increasingly apparent that the authors of these texts took themselves to be engaging in a normative enterprise, and one, moreover, that they thought to be capable of support by persuasive, and at times demonstrative, rational arguments. To ignore, as is so often done by historians of religion, this fundamentally important dimension of the material is a failure to seriously consider the intentions of the texts' authors in their own terms, and such a failure necessarily results in partial and inadequate views about the importance of normative discourse in almost all religious and philosophical traditions. It was, in part, an increasingly strong desire to avoid such a partial and inadequate representation of my sources that reshaped what was originally conceived as a historico-exegetical study into what is now also a philosophico-critical study. The presence in the following study of normative elements—of the putting to my sources such potentially unpleasant questions as: 'Is that a good argument?' or 'What reason do we have to think that the premisses of that argument are true?'—proceeds, then, from the logic of the sources themselves.

A full defence and explanation of asking (and the theoretical possibility of answering) such normative questions of texts (or persons) from different cultures and different periods would require the elaboration of (negatively) a critique of the varieties of relativism, and (positively) a theory of rationality and a theory of truth. Aside from these prefatory remarks I shall offer neither, but will content myself for the moment with a utilitarian and hermeneutical defence:

on the first (utilitarian) ground the directing of normative questions to philosophical and religious traditions foreign to those of the questioner is almost certain to result in an increased awareness on the part of the questioner of the weaknesses and strengths of his own position, something which I take to be an intrinsic good; also, this approach makes it possible to ask questions which, by using traditional history of religions methodology, simply cannot be asked. And this also is an intrinsic good, even if the questions should turn out finally to have been misconceived. On the second (hermeneutical) ground, a serious listening to our sources, a genuine fusion of horizons (to use Gadamer's phrase in a sense of which he would be unlikely to approve),[24] requires that when those sources are explicitly normative in their claims and methods we, as interpreters, take that aspect of them seriously and deal with them on that level. Neither the utilitarian nor the hermeneutical defence will serve for long as a justification of this way of doing cross-cultural philosophy; they are stated here only as pointers toward what needs to be done, and as a stop-gap rationale for the undertaking of a study in what is very close to being a new field of enquiry: the attempt to address, in a cross-cultural mode, normative questions as these relate to large-scale and sophisticated conceptual systems, and to elaborate and state cross-culturally valid norms of rationality on the basis of which such assessment can properly take place.[25]

I intend that this work should be of use and interest to at least three groups which do not communicate with each other as often as might be hoped. First, I hope that the philosophical discussions of the mind–body issue, as these arise from the historical and textual analyses of the work, will be of interest to those philosophers concerned with the same issue in the Western traditions, and to that (happily increasing) group of Western philosophers interested in Indian philosophical thought in its own right. Second, I hope also that the discussions given here of a particular type of Buddhist soteriological practice and its resultant altered state(s) of consciousness will be of interest to those trained in the history of religions; we have here a case study of an especially interesting type of virtuoso religious technique, one, moreover, which has interesting connections with techniques fostered and recommended in other traditions. Finally, on the technical and historical level this monograph is intended to be of use to Buddhologists, those who are professionally concerned with the history of Buddhist thought and practice. It is at this group that the textual, historical and linguistic discussions in the extensive notes are aimed.

Since this work is written with the intention that it will be accessible and useful to those who are not specialists in the history of Buddhism and not competent in the major Buddhist canonical languages, the use of technical terminology in the original languages (principally Pali and Sanskrit, but also occasionally Tibetan) in the body of the text has been kept to an (unavoidable) minimum. Where technical Buddhist philosophical terminology is concerned, my practice is generally to give the original term, in parentheses, upon its first occurrence in the text, to establish my preferred translation, and thereafter to use only English. A glossary is provided at the end, giving my standardized English equivalents and the terms which they translate. A similar practice is followed for text-names in the body of this study: they are given consistently in English with the original provided in parentheses upon the first occurrence of the text-name in question. In the notes, in contrast, extensive use is made of (sometimes untranslated) technical terms in the relevant languages, and of abbreviations for text-names. Most of these technical terms and abbreviations will be familiar to those professionally concerned with the history of Buddhism—at whom the notes are primarily aimed—but a complete listing of all abbreviations is to be found at the end of the work. Brief bibliographical essays on the texts which have been of major importance for this study are also included in the bibliography; these essays describe the editions I have used, discuss any major problems, and explain the system of reference adopted.

There are three types of exception to this practice of eschewing the use of Sanskrit in the body of the text: the first concerns technical terms (in Sanskrit) which have become effectively naturalized into English: the obvious examples are Buddha, dharma, karma and Nirvana. These will generally be given (as here) without italicization or diacritics and with a somewhat inconsistent set of practices in regard to initial capitalization. The second concerns names of persons, which will be left in the original without comment or translation. (The non-Sanskritist, sadly, will miss a great deal here since Indian Buddhist philosophers tend to have delightful names. For example, Jñānaśrīmitra means 'he whose beloved friend is knowledge' and Sthiramati means 'he whose intellect is firm'.) The third exception concerns school and sect names which will also be left in the original in the body of the text (largely because of the difficulty of finding English equivalents which stop short of polysyllabic multi-hyphenated chaos), but which will be discussed in full where relevant, either in the notes or in the body of the text.

All discussions that have to do primarily with technical matters, textual, philological or historical, have been relegated to the notes. All translations are my own unless a specific translation credit is given, although where I provide translations of previously-translated texts I am, of course, indebted to and dependent upon the work of my predecessors, even in cases where I have chosen not to follow them. Full details of all translations consulted will be found in the bibliography. I have supplied in the notes the full original text of all extracts translated from canonical Buddhist languages; this, as anyone who works in this field is aware, is a courtesy verging upon the essential, since few of us have access to libraries in which all these texts are easily available. For the representation of Sanskrit and Pali in roman type I follow the systems introduced at the end of the last century and now universally accepted among scholars;[26] for the representation of Tibetan I follow the system developed by Turrell V. Wylie and other scholars of the Inner Asia Project at the University of Washington:[27] this system is simple and consistent and has been gaining ground as the standard in the West, though sadly it is less frequently used by Japanese scholars; for the representation of Japanese I follow the system used in Andrew Nelson's dictionary;[28] finally, in the (rare) cases in which Chinese characters are represented in roman type, the Pinyin system has been used.

CHAPTER ONE

THE ATTAINMENT OF CESSATION IN THE THERAVĀDA TRADITION

1.1 THE THERAVĀDA TRADITION

Theravāda is that form of Buddhism which takes as canonical an extensive body of Pali literature and which is now dominant in the countries of South and South-East Asia, especially Burma, Thailand, and Sri Lanka; it is one of the major forms of Buddhism still currently active and influential. Its canonical texts are written (and chanted) in the Pali language and consist of a large and heterogeneous body of literature, the earliest parts of which date (in their written form) from around the beginning of the Christian era. Both before and after the reduction of the canonical texts to writing, they were preserved and handed on by a complex system of memorization and public recitation, and there is little doubt that some of the early orally preserved traditions upon which the written texts are based go back to a very early period indeed, perhaps even a period close to the time of the Buddha himself, whose words the texts often represent themselves as preserving.

The canonical literature of Theravāda Buddhism is usually described in the West as 'the Pali canon' in an attempt to differentiate it from the considerably more extensive collections of canonical literature preserved in, for example, Tibetan, Chinese and Japanese. It is not precisely defined and delimited; the borders between the canonical and the non-canonical are fuzzy, and some texts which usually appear in our contemporary canonical collections have at various times had their canonical status debated.[1] But both the core texts and the broad outline of the collection are the same in all cases. The collection is traditionally divided into three sections: the first purports to preserve the words of the Buddha himself in the form of sermons and discourses; the second contains material pertaining to monastic discipline and early Buddhist history; and the third lists and classifies the major terms and concepts of Buddhist doctrine, using more or less well-developed organizational schemata. There is little doubt that the material preserved in the first two sections of the canonical collection is for the most part older than that contained in the third. It is in the discourses and sermons and in the regulations governing monastic conduct that we can approach most closely the shape, both intellectual and institutional, of primitive[2] Indian Buddhism. My remarks in what follows will be based largely upon material from the first section of the tripartite canonical collection, largely because it is this section, the collection of discourses and sermons, which preserves material most appropriate for my purposes. Also, using this section of the Pali canon will allow me to root my analysis of the attainment of cessation in an early stage of the development of the Buddhist tradition, since much of the material contained in the first section of the canonical collection reaches back beyond the limits of our knowledge of primitive Buddhism and brings us close to the origins of the tradition.[3]

The first section of the tripartite canon is itself subdivided into five parts, called *Collections*.[4] The first four of these—the *Long Collection*, the *Intermediate Collection*, the *Linked Collection* and the *Gradual Collection*—contain material which is comparatively homogeneous in form and style, and which undoubtedly preserves the core content of normative Theravāda Buddhist doctrine. The fifth collection is considerably more heterogeneous. Although it contains extremely old material it also contains some of the latest and most problematic books of the entire tripartite canonical collection. Because of the heterogeneity of this fifth collection and its concomitant historical-critical problems, I shall not make use of it in the study that follows.

Even restricting the first part of this study to the first four *Collections*, a very substantial body of literature must be dealt with. In the romanized editions produced by the Pali Text Society, it runs to something over 4500 pages. Fortunately, this bulk is largely the result of extensive repetition of stereotyped formulae and lists—repetition which is itself a direct result of the way in which the canonical texts came to take their present form—and it is possible to give an accurate and coherent presentation of early Theravāda doctrine by considering in detail a comparatively small number of text-places. This is the approach that will be taken in what follows.

In addition to the tripartite canonical collection, there is also an enormous later commentarial and systematic philosophical literature, the production of which continues among Theravādin intellectuals up to the present day. While much of this literature was composed in Pali from the fifth century AD onwards, there is also a substantial body of Buddhist texts available in vernacular languages of the major Theravāda cultures—Burmese, Thai, Sinhala and so forth. Clearly, no attempt will be made in this study to survey all discussions of the attainment of cessation produced in all of this literature. Nevertheless, the fact that the material in the four *Collections* is not, for the most part, systematic and precise in its discussion of the problem of the attainment of cessation makes it necessary to go beyond it in order to gain an accurate idea of what the tradition has to say on this subject. Therefore, I shall make some use of the interpretations and glosses given to it by Buddhaghosa—perhaps the most influential intellectual figure in the history of Theravāda Buddhism—in his commentarial works. This does not suggest that Buddhaghosa's interpretation of the canonical material is either the only possible one or, necessarily, historically reliable. There are often alternative ways of understanding the canonical material and Buddhaghosa, living 800 years or more after the earlier parts of the canon had taken something like their present form, was in many instances in no better position than we are to understand historical and doctrinal oddities. Nevertheless, Buddhaghosa's interpretations are the most thorough and comprehensive available, and they do represent the orthodox views of the developed Theravāda tradition. I shall therefore treat them with the respect they deserve.

Buddhaghosa's commentaries probably date from the fifth century AD[5] and thus represent a much later stage in the development of the Theravāda tradition than does the material from the *Collections* which will form the basis of my exposition. A very extensive opus is attributed to Buddhaghosa by the tradition, including complete commentaries extending to many thousands of pages on all of the first four *Collections* of the discourse section of the canon, although it remains unclear to what extent Buddhaghosa was the author of these commentaries and to what extent a redactor and translator of earlier material in language(s) other than Pali.[6] But Buddhaghosa was not merely a commentator; he was also a creative philosophical thinker and a comprehensive systematizer of the tradition as he found it.

This creative philosophizing and systematization is especially apparent in Buddhaghosa's magnum opus, the *Path to Purity*, a text which, more than any other, defines doctrinal orthodoxy for the Theravāda tradition in all its cultural variants. Much of what is said in the following study will be based, more or less explicitly, upon Buddhaghosa's intellectual contribution to the systematization of his tradition as this is visible in the *Path to Purity* and in his commentaries to the four *Collections*.

A still later stage may be seen in the commentarial and systematic works of Dhammapāla, a Theravādin scholastic whose dates are even more uncertain than those of Buddhaghosa, but who certainly lived later than Buddhaghosa—perhaps as late as the ninth and tenth centuries AD—and who wrote sub-commentaries on some of his works.[7]

One of Dhammapāla's most important works is a large sub-commentary on the *Path to Purity*, Buddhaghosa's main systematic work, called *Casket of the Supreme Meaning (Paramatthamañjūsā)*. This work analyzes and systematizes Buddhaghosa's already systematic study of the issue still further and often contains useful clarifications of Buddhaghosa's comments from which I have profited greatly. The *Casket* has not yet (so far as I am aware) been translated into any Western language (nor, I think, even into Japanese) and deserves much more systematic treatment than I have been able to give it in this study.

It needs to be said that the attainment of cessation was not an issue of major significance for the scholastic thinkers of the Theravāda tradition; for reasons that will become apparent, the altered state of consciousness denoted by this term was not regarded by the orthodox as of central soteriological value, and the discussions accorded it thus remained on the margins, as it were, of the complex intellectual edifice developed by the architects and systematizers of Theravāda Buddhism. But just as it is often the marginal annotations to a text which hold the most interest for the scholar, and often the stones which do not quite fit into their allotted places in a carefully planned building which reveal the points of stress and weakness in an architectural scheme, so also the study of this particular piece of Buddhist psychotropic marginalia sheds light on some key points in the conceptual system of Buddhism as a whole.

I should point out, by way of warning to those who think that the only proper way to study Buddhism—or indeed any other religious tradition—is through the practices of living Buddhists,[8] that this study will treat the Theravāda tradition almost exclusively from the perspective of the history of ideas. Whether or not there actually are or were virtuoso practitioners who claim to be able to enter the interestingly altered state of consciousness denoted by the term 'attainment of cessation' is not an issue that will be discussed here; the sociological and anthropological implications and dimensions of the ideas analyzed here will not be considered. Instead, Theravāda tradition will be treated as a set of more-or-less clearly expressed ideas set down in texts and will be discussed exclusively on that level. Whether this involves excessive distortion of the tradition, and whether indeed this is a valid method of undertaking the study of any tradition whatever, are large philosophical issues which I cannot discuss here. It should be obvious, though, even if not quite obvious enough to go without saying, that the kind of intellectual programme being undertaken here carries with it a large number of philosophical and hermeneutical presuppositions, among which are the following: that the texts of the Theravāda (or any other) tradition express meanings which are accessible to readers from drastically different religious and cultural groups; that these meanings can, in appropriate cases, properly be analyzed, considered and judged simply as meanings in isolation from the socio-cultural contexts which gave them birth (though of course a proper understanding of the appropriate socio-cultural context is desirable when possible and will, in many cases, be a necessary condition for the consideration of meaning), and finally that such cross-cultural intellectual evaluation is likely to have positive effects upon both those undertaking the evaluation and those being evaluated.

In summary, therefore, a range of diachronic textual data representing what I take to be Theravādin orthodoxy (and, at least as important, what the intellectual representatives of the tradition took to be orthodoxy) on the matter of the attainment of cessation will be set forth and critically considered in what follows.

1.2 THE NATURE OF THE ATTAINMENT OF CESSATION

At the outset, it is important to get a precise idea of the nature of the attainment of cessation, initially as it was perceived and described in the Buddhist texts devoted to it and then as it might be described in the psychological idiom of the West. This will involve some exposition of texts and an attempt to restate the meanings of those texts in a more accessible form. A purely phenomenological approach, in which an altered state of consciousness is described without a highly ramified set of interpretive concepts[9] in terms that hope to capture the way it appears to the experiencing subject, is not likely to be of much use for the analysis of the attainment of cessation since the central point about this altered state is that it permits no experience while it endures. The reasons for this, and its implications, should become clearer as the investigation proceeds.

I shall begin with an interesting passage in the *Intermediate Collection* which discusses whether, and in what way, the attainment of cessation can be distinguished from death. The general context is a discussion between Koṭṭhita and Sāriputta, two prominent disciples of the Buddha, on a number of doctrinal issues.[10] The passage runs thus:

> What is the difference, Reverend, between a dead person who has passed away and a monk who has attained the cessation of sensation and conceptualization? Reverend, the physical, verbal and mental functions of the dead person who has passed away have ceased and subsided; his vitality is destroyed, his heat is extinguished and his sense organs are scattered. But although the physical, verbal and mental functions of the monk who has attained the cessation of sensation and conceptualization have ceased and subsided, his vitality is not destroyed, his heat is not extinguished, and his sense organs are purified. This, Reverend, is the difference between a dead person who has passed away and a monk who has attained the cessation of sensation and conceptualization.[11]

The key terms here are 'physical functions' *(kāya-sankhārā)*, 'verbal functions' *(vacī-sankhārā)*, 'mental functions' *(citta-sankhārā)*, 'vitality' *(āyu)* and 'heat' *(usmā)*. The passage states that both a dead man and one in the attainment of cessation no longer possess the first three of these, physical, verbal and mental functions. The difference between the two lies in the fact that the dead man has also lost vitality and heat, whereas the person who has reached cessation is still in possession of these. Finally, the sense-organs of the dead man are 'scattered', whereas those of the man in cessation are 'purified'. Buddhaghosa's commentarial discussion of this passage will provide some clarification of the technical terminology:

> 'Physical functions' means in-breathing and out-breathing. 'Verbal functions' means reasoning and deliberation. 'Mental functions' means conceptualization and sensation. 'Scattered' means destroyed or lost. On this matter some say that the sentence: 'The mental [functions] of one who has attained cessation have ceased' means that the mind has not ceased, and that therefore this attainment

possesses mind. The proper reply to them is: [if your view is correct], the sentence: 'The verbal functions' of one [who has attained cessation] have ceased' would mean that such a person's speech had not ceased, with the result that one who had attained cessation would be able to sit down to discuss doctrine and perform recitation. Further, the sentence: 'the mental functions of one who has died and passed away have ceased' would [on this view] mean that [such a person's] mind had not ceased, with the result that he would, when already dead, be able to perform actions bringing immediate retribution by killing parents or enlightened beings.[12] [Rejecting these absurd arguments] the meaning [of these sentences] should be ascertained by relying on the reasoning of teachers and not by becoming attached to words in this way. For meaning is the point of reference, not words.[13]

'Sense organs are purified' means that when actions are being performed the sense organs are, as it were, wearied, hindered and soiled in regard to those things with which they come into contact,[14] and in regard to the clarity[15] [with which they perceive] external objects. It is just as with a mirror set up at a crossroads, [which is soiled] by the dust stirred up by the wind and so forth. Just as, indeed, a mirror put into a bag and placed in a box or something similar shines brilliantly there, so also the five [sensory] clarities of the monk who has attained cessation shine with great brilliance in cessation. Therefore it is said: 'sense organs are purified'.[16]

Buddhaghosa tells us here that the term 'physical functions' refers to breathing in and breathing out, the process of respiration; 'verbal functions' to reasoning and deliberation; and 'mental functions' to sensation and conceptualization.[17] All these functions, it is agreed, no longer occur for both a dead man and one who has entered the attainment of cessation. The debate that he describes, however, between different understandings of what the cessation of physical, verbal and mental functioning might mean, gives us our first real insight into the central problems connected with the attainment of cessation.

In standard Indian fashion, Buddhaghosa begins by presenting the view with which he disagrees; also in standard Indian fashion he does not name the opponent, using the anonymous formula 'some say . . .' The point at issue is the meaning of the statement that physical, verbal and mental functions cease for both a dead man and one in the attainment of cessation. The opponent takes it to mean that, although mental activity may have ceased, this doesn't necessarily mean that the mind *simpliciter* has ceased. On such a view the terms 'mental functions' and 'mind' are not synonymous, and it is therefore possible for the opponent to suggest the preservation of some continuing mental element even for one who has entered the attainment of cessation. The opponent's conclusion is that the attainment of cessation 'possesses mind'. This, as we shall see, is to be one of the major issues in the discussion of the attainment of cessation in all the Indian schools: if this altered state is really mindless, the philosophical problems involved in accounting for the process of both entering and leaving it become acute.

Buddhaghosa, however, rejects the view that anything mental endures in the attainment of cessation on two grounds. The first is logical, an example of *reductio ad absurdum.* If, as the canonical texts state and as both Buddhaghosa and his opponent therefore perforce agree, a dead man and one who has entered the attainment of cessation are alike in their loss of physical, verbal and mental functions, then the opponent's view that the loss of mental functioning can still permit the retention of mind must apply not just to the possessor of the attainment of cessation but also to the dead man. And this, as Buddhaghosa points out, leads to absurd consequences. It would, for example, mean that a dead man, since he still possesses mind, would be able to perform heinous crimes such as the killing of parents and enlightened beings.[18] Or that a dead man, still possessing the faculty of speech, would be able to engage in discussions of doctrine and similar activities.

Buddhaghosa's second ground for the rejection of the opponent's view is hermeneutical: he judges that the attempt to preserve mind in the attainment of cessation is based on a verbal quibble rather than on an attempt to understand the intentions of the canonical text and is therefore inadmissible. He implicitly suggests—and it is hard to disagree—that the intentions of the canonical text's description of the attainment of cessation are clearly to state that nothing mental exists in this condition, and that the use of the term 'mental functions' is therefore meant to exclude not only mental activity but also mind itself, if indeed this is to be considered as something other than its activities.

The implications and ramifications of this debate will be taken up again at a later stage of this investigation. For the moment I shall concentrate on arriving at a more precise assessment of the nature of the attainment of cessation. So far, it has become clear that the attainment of cessation is (following for the moment Buddhaghosa's interpretation) completely without physical functions (which means that the process of respiration, taken as the paradigm case of physical function, has ceased); completely without verbal functions (which means that the processes of intellection and ratiocination—and therefore by extension also the activity of speech—have ceased) and completely without mental functions (which means that consciousness does not exist and that the processes of sensation and conceptualization have come to a complete halt). What then remains? According to the canonical text only two things: vitality and heat. Neither of these terms is given an explicit gloss in Buddhaghosa's commentary; they are, however, explained at some length in the immediately preceding passage of the same canonical text which provided the original discussion, translated earlier, of the difference between a dead man and one in the attainment of cessation. The passage on vitality and heat reads thus:

> Reverend, what does vitality depend upon?
>
> Vitality depends on heat.
>
> Reverend, what does heat depend on?
>
> Heat depends on vitality.
>
> Reverend, now we understand what Sāriputta has said in this way: vitality depends on heat and heat depends on vitality; but how is the meaning of these words to be understood? Reverend, I shall make a simile for you, since by means of a simile some of the intelligent men here understand the meaning of what has been said. It is just as with an oil lamp: the light is seen because of the flame and the flame because of the light. In just the same way vitality depends on heat and heat on vitality.
>
> Further, Reverend, are the vital functions states to be experienced or other than states to be experienced?
>
> Reverend, the vital functions are not states to be experienced; for if they were states to be experienced it would not be possible to demonstrate emergence [from the attainment of cessation] for a monk who has obtained the cessation of sensation and conceptualization. But since, Reverend, the vital functions are other than states to be experienced, emergence [from the attainment of cessation] for a monk who has obtained the cessation of sensation and conceptualization is demonstrated.[19]

The interdependence of vitality and heat is clearly stated here,[20] and it is further said that the 'vital functions' are not things which can be directly experienced by the subject. The text says, somewhat obscurely, that this is because emergence from the attainment of cessation would not be possible if it were the case that the vital functions are directly experienceable events. Buddhaghosa explains this by using the analogy of fire-making: when one wants to extinguish a fire with the thought that at a later period one might want to restart it, one might sprinkle it with water and cover the embers with ash. Later, in order to rekindle the flames, one might remove the covering of ash, stir up the (still glowing) embers, add fresh fuel and blow or fan the embers into new life.[21] The case is similar, Buddhaghosa suggests, with emergence from the attainment of cessation; the embers covered with ash are likened to the corporeal life-faculty,[22] and the removing of the ash-covering at the time when rekindling of the fire is desired is likened to the expiration of the time-period during which it is possible to remain in the attainment of cessation.[23] Although Buddhaghosa does not explicitly say so, it seems fair to draw the conclusion that vitality and heat cannot be said to be experienceable in the attainment of cessation, since, if they were, experiences would occur (which is contrary to the very definition of the condition), and the analogy of the invisibly glowing embers (to which the vitality and heat of the practitioner in the attainment of cessation are compared) would not hold.

This image illuminates strikingly the meaning of 'vitality' and 'heat' in the translated passage. It suggests that an individual in the attainment of cessation is conceived of as being without all but the most basic autonomic physical functions. Respiration has ceased completely, and it is likely (though not explicity stated by these texts) that heartbeat, blood pressure, body temperature and metabolic levels in general have fallen to a very low level. All that remains is a certain minimal level of bodily heat coupled with a dormant, but still present, 'life-principle'—which seems to mean little more than that the practitioner has the possibility of leaving this condition and restarting normal physical activities, just as a charcoal fire, carefully banked and covered with ash, may appear to be dead but can in reality be rekindled without too much difficulty. The physical condition of a practitioner in the attainment of cessation, then, is like nothing more than that of a mammal in the deepest stages of hibernation; there also the physical functions slow to an almost imperceptible minimum, and it is possible for the untrained observer to judge the creature dead rather than in hibernation. It is on this model that the physical condition of one who has attained cessation should be understood.

So much for the physical aspects of the attainment of cessation. What about the mental and experiential aspects? Buddhaghosa, as we have seen, makes his views on this unambiguously clear; the practitioner in the attainment of cessation is without mental functions of any kind; the condition is 'mindless' and it is explicitly stated that the ordinary mental functions of sensation, perception and concept-formation do not occur in this condition. Furthermore, all types of ratiocination—which are a necessary condition for the occurrence of verbal behaviour—have ceased to occur. Perhaps the closest analogy in Western psychological parlance to this condition would be some kind of profound cataleptic trance, the kind of condition manifested by some psychotic patients and by long-term coma patients. In these cases also no responses to stimuli occur, and it seems reasonable to assume that sensation and perception are not occurring; certainly, in the more extreme examples of catalepsy, speech does not occur and there is no initiation of any kind of action, no volition. On these levels, then, cataleptic trance bears some analogy to the Buddhist condition of cessation. However, it seems that the attainment of cessation is even more radical in its rejection of mental activity than are the dominant Western models for the understanding of catalepsy. For the Buddhist the attainment of cessation suggests not only that there is no reaction to stimuli and no initiation of action, but also that there is no internal mental life of any kind. This is not so clear in the Western understanding of catalepsy; the possibility of the existence of a complex inner fantasy life which has no outer behavioural manifestations remains open—certainly in some forms of psychosis, where this may even be the explanation for the lack of behavioural response to stimuli and initiation of activity.

There is one more point in the canonical description of the attainment of cessation translated above which needs some elucidation: this is the condition of the sense-organs, which are described as 'purified'. Buddhaghosa, as I have shown, explains this with another analogy, this time of a mirror wrapped in a bag and placed in a box. Such a mirror, he says, even though not actually reflecting anything, shines with unpolluted radiance in its wrappings. The point is that since there is nothing around in such an environment to dim its brightness it will naturally shine with full brilliance; the contrast Buddhaghosa draws is with a mirror set up at a public crossroad, which will always be polluted and dimmed by the dust stirred by the wind. The case is similar with the sense-organs; when they are in use for perceiving external objects, their natural clarity is soiled and dimmed by the inevitable distractions and passions belonging to their user. But when their user has entered the attainment of cessation no such distractions occur, and the natural clarity of the sense-organs is unimpaired. This does not, of course, mean that the practitioner in the attainment of cessation is actually perceiving anything; merely that his sense-organs, like a mirror carefully wrapped in a velvet bag, are ready to perform their functions when (as emergence from cessation takes place) they are called upon to do so. It should be remembered that, according to the psychological theory of almost all Indian Buddhist schools, sense-perception takes place partly in virtue of a natural radiance or clarity possessed by the sense-organs.

Indeed, the standard view is that the sense-organs (those of sight, taste, smell, hearing and touch) consist in a peculiar kind of physical form possessing an innate radiance, and that it is this innate quality which differentiates them from other kinds of physical form and makes it possible for them to come into contact with external objects and thus for sense-perception to occur.

To conclude this attempt to gain an understanding of exactly how the attainment of cessation is presented in the texts of the Theravāda tradition, a look at Buddhaghosa's schematic definition of that condition in the *Path to Purity* will prove useful. In the 23rd and final chapter of that work he says:

> What is the attainment of cessation? It is the non-occurrence of mind and mental concomitants as a result of their successive cessation.[24]

Dhammapāla comments on this passage:

> 'As a result of their successive cessation' means as a result of the successive cessation of the three kinds of activity [viz: physical, verbal and mental]. This occurs by way of the cessation of obstacles to this [condition] and by way of the obtaining of the eight attainments accompanied by insight. The meaning is that the attainment of cessation is the non-occurrence of mind and mental concomitants for as long as they are cut off.[25]

The same themes are stressed once again. Physical, verbal and mental activities have ceased in the attainment of cessation and there is a complete absence of mental events. Buddhaghosa provides some entertaining stories intended to illustrate the profundity of the attainment of cessation and the degree to which it prevents the practitioner from reacting to stimuli in his immediate environment. One of these stories, which makes concrete and immediate the rather abstract descriptions discussed so far, concerns the elder Mahānāga, a monk who entered the attainment of cessation in the meditation-hall of his mother's village. While he was in cessation, the meditation-hall caught fire and all the monks except Mahānāga fled; he, being in the attainment of cessation, was not aware of the fire encircling him and remained in trance while the villagers brought water, put out the fire, removed ashes, undertook repairs and scattered flowers around him.[26] Mahānāga did not emerge from the attainment of cessation until the predetermined time: external events, no matter how dramatic, could have no effect upon him.

On the basis of the selectively chosen but representative material we now have a reasonably accurate idea of the way in which the attainment of cessation was understood by the canonical and commentarial works of Theravāda Buddhism. It is, in brief, a condition in which no mental events of any kind occur, a condition distinguishable from death only by a certain residual warmth and vitality in the unconscious practitioner's body.

1.3 METHODS OF REACHING THE ATTAINMENT OF CESSATION

In the preceding section I have shown how the attainment of cessation is described in some significant texts of the Theravāda tradition and made an attempt to interpret that description. I now want to turn to a consideration of how the altered state of consciousness in question is attained, and in order to properly understand that it will be necessary to make some preliminary general remarks about Theravāda Buddhist soteriological theory.

1.3.1 Soteriological Methods and Soteriological Goals

The canonical and commentarial texts of Theravāda Buddhism describe a number of different types of soteriological method. A full analysis of the range of methods described together with their concomitant soteriological goals cannot be given in this study; I can only note the commonplace fact—commonplace both to the Theravāda tradition itself and to non-Theravādin scholars studying that tradition from without—that the soteriological methods witnessed and recommended by the tradition resolve themselves phenomenologically into two main types, which I shall call the analytic and the enstatic.[27]

The standard Pali terms for the two types are: 'the cultivation of insight' *(vipassanā-bhāvanā)* and 'the cultivation of tranquility' *(samatha-bhāvanā)*. Stated very briefly, the former is concerned with repeated meditations upon standard items of Buddhist doctrine—the four truths, the 12-fold chain of dependent origination and so forth —until these are completely internalized by practitioners and their cognitive and perceptual systems operate only in terms of them. Such analytical meditations are designed, then, to remove standard cognitive and perceptual habit-patterns and to replace them with new ones. Furthermore, these techniques are designed to teach the practitioner something new about the way things are, to inculcate in his consciousness a whole series of knowledges that such-and-such is the case. In contrast, the enstatic meditations are designed to reduce the contents of consciousness, to focus awareness upon a single point and ultimately to bring all mental activity to a halt.

It should be obvious that there is a *prima facie* tension between the two types of technique and so, necessarily, between the soteriological goals at which they are aimed. The thesis that there is some tension between these two types of technique is of course nothing new, either to the tradition or to Western scholars studying the tradition; as long ago as 1937 Louis de La Vallée Poussin stated it very clearly, and it has been explored since then by a number of Western scholars.[28] Unfortunately, it is not possible to discuss this creative tension at any length here; almost all of the material that I want to study falls firmly within the sphere of the 'cultivation of tranquillity', and the details of the scholastic attempts to combine and reconcile the two methods fall very largely outside my scope. However, a brief summary of the problem is in order, simply because there are a number of points in the Theravādin treatment of the attainment of cessation which only make sense in the light of this basic tension.

In outline, then, the tension between those techniques which are aimed at the cultivation of tranquillity and those aimed at the cultivation of insight is closely related to different views of both the root cause of the unsatisfactoriness[29] of human existence and the proper means of going beyond it. Those who follow and advocate the analytic techniques tend to perceive the basic human problem as one of ignorance, an inaccurate understanding of the way things are and a deeply rooted tendency to consistently misinterpret and misunderstand human experience and the nature of the world within which it occurs. The result of a consistent and determined effort to internalize the categories of Buddhist thought by way of the practice of analytic meditations is, it is said, identical with the removal of ignorance, the attainment of knowledge, and the development of the ability to perceive things as they really are. When this accurate knowledge and clear perception is continuously possessed by the practitioner, the root cause of bondage is removed and salvation attained. In drastic contrast, the practitioners of the enstatic techniques aimed at tranquillity tend to perceive the basic human error as one of attitude rather than cognition; the key Buddhist term here is 'thirst' *(taṇhā)*, a term that denotes all types of passionate desire and attachment. To be subject to desire of this kind is to be subject to a profound attachment to the world, an attachment which is not justified, according to Buddhist theory, either by the nature of the world or by the nature of the person showing attachment to it. A method of overcoming this profound attachment to the world—perhaps the most thoroughgoing imaginable—is the practice of those enstatic techniques which culminate in the attainment of cessation, a condition in which, as has already been suggested, no experience of any kind is able to occur, much less experience of a kind which encourages passionate attachments.

Put very crudely, the cultivation of tranquillity centres upon manipulation of the practitioner's emotional attitudes and the cultivation of insight centres upon manipulation of the practitioner's cognitive skills. The adherent of the former destroys passions by withdrawing from all contact with the external universe, whereas the practitioner of the latter asserts control over the universe by learning to know it as it is. This polarity may be expressed in different ways and is related to a similar contrast which is visible throughout the history of Indian thought on soteriological method.[30]

One side of this dichotomy consists in the identification of salvation with knowledge and with what is taken to be the inevitable effect of knowledge, control. On the view, an individual's subjection to suffering and the endless round of rebirth and redeath is explained by the fact that the person does not properly understand the mechanics of the process and is thus at its mercy; control over a process presupposes understanding of it, and it is understanding and power which, on this view, are the ultimate soteriological goals. The significance of knowledge as a soteriological tool can be traced to a very early period in Indian thought; it is stressed even in some of the Vedic hymns[31] and is, of course, central to many of the *Upaniṣads*. According to such texts, a gnostic penetration to the nature of things issues in a kind of magical immortality, a transcendence of the cycle of redeath the existence of which posed the basic soteriological problem for Indian thought. This view is very clearly expressed in some of the *Upaniṣadic* texts, especially in the famous description, found in the *Taittirīya Upaniṣad* of the liberated person as one who knows and one whose knowledge gives immortality and the ability to use all of the universe as food, the means of sustaining immortality. The lyrical hymn to this knowledge-based food-sustained power-imbued magical immortality is worth quoting:

I am food! I am food! I am food!
I am the eater of food! I am the eater of food! I am the eater of food!
I am a verse-maker! I am a verse-maker! I am a verse-maker!
I am the first-born of the cosmic order,
Earlier than the Gods in the navel of immortality!
Who gives me away has indeed aided me!
I, who am food, eat the eater of food!
I have overcome the whole world![32]

This view of salvation is paradigmatically ecstatic: the gnostic's knowledge reaches beyond self and gives power to manipulate the universe, to metaphorically consume it. A similar kind of knowledge and power is sought by the Buddhist who practices the analytic meditations with the hope of gaining true insight into the nature of the universe: Nirvana, understood on this model, becomes an ecstatic magical immortality, bestowing limitless power upon its possessor.[33]

The alternative to seeking immortality by way of knowledge and power is the central concern of this study. It centres upon the practice of enstatic technique, withdrawal from contact with the outside world, suppression of emotional and intellectual activity and is to be identified with what, in Buddhist terms, is called 'the cultivation of tranquillity'. Here the problem of bondage to the cycle of rebirth and redeath is solved by attempting to attain complete affective disentanglement from the universe, to excrete the cosmos instead of eating it, to die without returning rather than to gain a magical immortality. It is at this goal that the enstatic techniques briefly set forth already are aimed, and it is with this goal that the attainment of cessation is to be paradigmatically identified. The root error here is passionate involvement with the world, and, as should become clearer in the course of this study, involvement of any kind is quite impossible for an individual in the attainment of cessation.

With this important typological distinction in mind, the following discussion of the traditions about methods of obtaining the attainment of cessation should become clearer. One basic point to bear in mind is that most of the oddities and tensions found in Buddhist analyses of the attainment of cessation arise from attempts to introduce elements from one system of views about salvation into another. Throughout Buddhist history, intellectuals have attempted to reconcile thought-systems which are on the face of it, irreconcilable, systems which have different ideas of what salvation is and concomitantly different ideas of the methods which are appropriate for its attainment. Thus, I suggest, Buddhist intellectuals have frequently attempted to assimilate the soteriological goal of the attainment of cessation—which is essentially part of the enstasy/withdrawal/isolation complex of thought—to that of Nirvana conceived as a dispassionate intellectual comprehension of the way things are—which is part of the knowledge/power/immortality complex of thought. It should not be hard to see that problems will inevitably arise from any such attempt.

1.3.2 Obtaining Cessation: The Basic Unit of Tradition

The attainment of cessation is usually presented in Theravāda texts as the culminating point in an ascending fivefold series of altered states of consciousness. This fivefold series in turn occurs as an element in various other sets of hierarchically organized altered states of consciousness. Before offering a brief survey of the variety of contexts within which the fivefold series is found, I shall translate and discuss the basic fivefold series by itself. The unit of tradition used to preserve the standard fivefold series runs thus:

> (i) By the transcendence of all conceptualizations of form, by the disappearance of conceptualizations based upon sense-data, by paying no attention to conceptualizations of manifoldness, having attained to the sphere of infinite space [the practitioner] remains therein, thinking 'space is unending'.
> (ii) By entirely transcending the sphere of infinite space, having attained to the sphere of infinite consciousness [the practitioner] remains therein, thinking 'consciousness is infinite'.
> (iii) By entirely transcending the sphere of infinite consciousness, having attained to the sphere of nothing at all, [the practitioner] remains therein, thinking 'there is nothing'.
> (iv) By entirely transcending the sphere of nothing at all, having entered the sphere of neither conceptualization nor non-conceptualization, [the practitioner] remains therein.
> (v) By entirely transcending the sphere of neither conceptualization nor non-conceptualization, having attained the cessation of sensation and conceptualization [the practitioner] remains therein.[34]

The first four of these five stages—the 'sphere of infinite space', the 'sphere of infinite consciousness', the 'sphere of nothing at all' and the 'sphere of neither conceptualization nor non-conceptualization'—are, in Buddhist thought, both cosmological spheres and altered states of consciousness. They are frequently known as the 'four formlessnesses'[35] and are conceived as cosmological realms in which it is possible to be born and live out one (or many) lives. There are thought to be classes of divine beings who inhabit these realms, all of whom are characterized chiefly by the fact that they have no physical bodies[36] since no physical form of any kind can exist in these realms. But for the purposes of this study the main importance of this series is that it is also understood as an hierarchically ordered ascending series of altered states of consciousness, states which are accessible to an inhabitant of the realms of form by the practice of certain meditative disciplines.

These meditative disciplines are only hinted at in the unit of tradition translated above; in the first case, that of transcending the conceptualizations of physical form and attaining the sphere of infinite space, the practitioner achieves his goal, it seems, by taking the sphere of infinite space as the object of contemplative exercise. It seems that the practitioner is intended to actively think—even to verbalize[37]—that space is infinite and to contemplate this idea until the possibility of cognizing physical form in any way has completely vanished. The practitioner will then be established in a condition wherein the only object of cognition that occurs to him is that of featureless, formless undifferentiated space. Much the same applies to the second and third formless spheres—those of the infinity of consciousness and of nothing at all. Here also progress is achieved by the use of active thought and verbalization—on the one hand that consciousness is infinite and on the other that nothing whatever exists.

It is evident that the content of consciousness becomes increasingly attenuated as the practitioner progresses through the stages of formlessness. By the third stage, the practitioner has developed the ability to cognize nothingness or, more precisely, to empty the content of awareness of everything except the consciousness that nothing exists. But even this is not the highest stage possible; in the third stage, the sphere of nothing at all, the ability to form concepts and the concomitant ability to verbalize them (if indeed the two can properly be distinguished) remains. In the fourth stage—that of neither conceptualization nor non-conceptualization—even this vanishes, and the ability to form concepts exists in such an attenuated form that it is neither thought proper to say that it exists or that it does not. Finally, in the attainment of cessation, otherwise called the cessation of sensation and conceptualization, even this vanishes, and the practitioner enters a cataleptic trance, the nature of which I have already outlined.

The techniques used by the practitioner when passing through these stages are, therefore, essentially enstatic. That is, they are designed initially to progressively withdraw the practitioner from all sensory contacts with the external world and then to progressively bring to a halt all inner mental activity. The process culminates in the attainment of cessation, wherein there are no mental events and no contacts with the external world. Actions are not initiated and stimuli are not responded to; the continuum of mental events which constitutes the psychological existence of the practitioner according to Buddhist theory runs out into silence. There is some evidence, as we shall see, that this kind of cessation was identified by some Buddhists at some periods with Nirvana and was thus thought of as the ultimately desirable goal for all Buddhists.

1.3.3 Contextual Analysis

The basic unit of tradition translated and discussed in the preceding section occurs frequently in the canonical texts of Theravāda Buddhism[38] but not always in the same context. The unit of tradition describing the attainment of cessation occurs linked with several other units of tradition, describing a variety of meditative methods and soteriological goals. Also, the standard description of the attainment of cessation is itself sometimes qualified by statements which attempt to reconcile it with methods and goals which do not cohere well with its essential nature, and this indicates, among other things, that this unit of tradition and the techniques and goals which it describes presented something of a problem for early Buddhist meditation-theorists. It is, I think, possible to discern within the early canonical texts of Theravāda Buddhism a number of different attempts to make sense of the attainment of cessation. Most of these try to make it cohere with standard Buddhist soteriological theories about the importance of intellectual analysis and reasoned knowledge to the attainment of enlightenment. It should be clear enough, even from the bare outline of the attainment of cessation and the techniques which lead to it given so far in this study, that there are substantial intellectual difficulties involved in reconciling and combining into a coherent soteriological system the paradigmatically enstatic techniques involved in attaining cessation and the paradigmatically ecstatic techniques involved in intellectual analysis aimed at knowledge, power and immortality. It is beyond the scope of this study to pursue all the twists and turns taken by Buddhist meditation-theorists in their attempts to produce such a coherent soteriological system; it is important, however, to take brief note of the basic contexts within which the basic unit of tradition occurs in the canonical texts, since an informed discussion of the philosophical and systematic problems occasioned by the attainment of cessation must rest upon an awareness of the steps actually taken by the tradition to deal with the issue.

First, then, the techniques aimed at the attainment of cessation are frequently found as a sequel to a preliminary set of four altered states of consciousness, usually called the 'four *jhānā* of form'. *Jhāna* (*jhānā* is the plural form) is one of the few technical terms that I shall leave untranslated throughout this study since I have been unable to find an appropriate single-word English translation that is not either positively misleading or inadequate.[39] Stated briefly, the term denotes (any one of) a series of precisely defined altered states of consciousness, altered states which are characterized by an increasing attenuation of the practitioner's emotions. Thus, in the fourth and highest *jhāna* of form, the only emotional response left to the practitioner is that of equanimity; ratiocination, pleasure, pain and indeed all intense emotional reactions have been left behind.[40] The techniques used to gain the four *jhānā* of form are also enstatic, designed to withdraw the practitioner from emotional attachments to and contacts with the external world, as well as from the tendency to rationally analyze his experience. They therefore move in the same general sphere as those techniques aimed at the attainment of cessation—the central concern of this study—and when the two sets of techniques are combined, a coherent and far-reaching set of enstatic practices is produced, comprising nine distinct altered states of consciousness. These nine altered states are not infrequently referred to as the 'nine successive attainments' or the 'nine successive abodes'.[41] The nine altered states in this series, therefore, consist of the four *jhānā* of form, combined with the four formless states (see the extract translated in Section 1.3.2), culminating in the attainment of cessation itself.

A typical example of this type of context for the attainment of cessation may be found in the *Discourse on Much to be Experienced (Bahuvedanīyasutta)* of the *Intermediate Collection*. The context is a debate on the nature and classifications of sensation and especially on the nature of pleasant sensation. The Buddha expounds the ninefold series of altered states of consciousness outlined in the previous paragraph, stating that each stage consists in a happiness 'more pleasing and more excellent' than that belonging to the stage which has gone before.[42] The conclusion of this discourse notes that there is something of a problem involved in calling the attainment of cessation pleasurable, since this state is defined as being entirely free from all sensation whatever. The commentary explains:

> [The attainment of] cessation is called pleasurable since it possesses that pleasure which consists in absence of sensation. That which is called 'pleasure that consists in sensation' occurs by way of the five qualities of sensual pleasure [i.e., ordinary sense-pleasures which occur before the practitioner has begun enstatic practice] and the eight attainments [i.e., the eight altered states of consciousness up to, but not including, the attainment of cessation]. But cessation is defined as possessing that pleasure which consists in absence of sensation. For whether we speak of pleasure that consists in

> sensation or pleasure that consists in absence of sensation there is only a single category 'pleasure' which has the meaning of pleasure that is designated the condition of the absence of suffering.[43]

The general point here is that 'pleasure' can be predicated of the attainment of cessation even though it is defined as being without any kind of sensation. This is so because 'pleasure' means the absence of suffering, and it is certainly true that suffering is not possible for one who has reached the attainment of cessation.

This glance at the *Discourse on Much to be Experienced* provides a representative instance of the use of the attainment of cessation as the culminating point of a tightly structured series of enstatic practices; in this instance there is no attempt to introduce any elements of thought or practice from the knowledge/power/immortality complex of soteriological thought. The discourse provides instead a coherent presentation of the enstatic complex of thought and practice, and moreover a presentation which appears, *prima facie,* to consider the attainment of cessation as the ultimate soteriological goal of the practicing Buddhist. The issue of the varying and often contradictory valuations placed upon the attainment of cessation in the Theravāda tradition will have to be returned to in the next section of this study; for the moment it is important to note that this context for the employment of the standard fivefold unit of tradition describing the attainment of cessation is unrelievedly enstatic in nature.

A rather different context for the standard fivefold unit of tradition is that in which it is preceded by a unit of tradition describing a threefold set of altered states of consciousness. When the fivefold unit (four formless states plus the attainment of cessation itself) is combined with this threefold unit, there emerges a complex unit of tradition describing a set of eight altered states of consciousness together with the concomitant practices leading to them. This also is essentially a unified and tightly structured set of enstatic practices, devoted to a progressive reduction of the contents of the practitioner's consciousness and aimed ultimately at the cessation of all mental events whatsoever. It differs from the context described in the preceding paragraph simply in that the preliminary practices and altered states are different: in the former case (that of the four *jhānā* of form), the tradition presents the process leading to the attainment of cessation as beginning with a fourfold set of enstatic practices aimed at reducing the affective content of the practitioner's consciousness and the range of emotional response available, and then follows this with the fivefold set that has already been discussed (in Section 1.3.2). In the latter case, the process begins with a threefold set of what are essentially visualization exercises and passes from there to the fivefold set of practices already examined. The eightfold set thus produced is usually called the 'eight liberations' *(vimokkha),* and while there are many problems connected with this particular set of soteriological practices,[44] problems which for the most part lie outside the purview of this study, the important thing about it for my purposes is that here too, as with the ninefold set, the context for the attainment of cessation is unrelievedly enstatic. There is no attempt to bring in techniques from the ecstatic/analytic tradition.

Along with these two essentially enstatic contexts for the unit of tradition describing the attainment of cessation, there are also some interesting contexts wherein an attempt is made to combine these enstatic practices with the analytic methods which I have suggested provide the other basic modality of soteriological practice in Theravāda Buddhism. The most common way in which this is done is by inserting, at the very end of the standard fivefold unit of tradition, a small pericope[45] describing the application of wisdom *(paññā)* to the practitioner's condition. The final part of the standard fivefold unit of tradition together with this unit of tradition reads thus:

> By entirely transcending the sphere of neither conceptualization nor non-conceptualization, having attained the cessation of sensation and conceptualization [the practitioner] remains therein. Also, upon seeing by means of wisdom, his [viz: the practitioner's] defilements are completely destroyed.[46]

Given this version of the attainment of cessation—which sees the exercise of wisdom, or conceptual/verbal analysis of the way things are, as occurring after the attainment of cessation (which has already been shown to be a condition in which no mental events are possible, much less the kind of complex intellectual analysis denoted by the term 'wisdom')—the obvious difficulty is to explain why it should be thought that the gaining of the attainment of cessation should make a favourable prelude for the exercise of intellectual analysis and the concomitant destruction of 'defilements'. On the face of it quite the opposite should be true; phenomenological analysis of the attainment of cessation suggests that intellectual activity is incompatible with such a condition and that the attainment of cessation makes sense as a soteriological goal, as I have already suggested, only when it is considered as the answer to a specific problem, that of passionate attachment. The exercise of wisdom, or reasoned analysis, on the other hand, makes sense as a soteriological goal when it is considered as the answer to the problem of ignorance. It appears, then, that we have here an excellent example of the uneasy bringing together of two radically different sets of soteriological methods and two radically different soteriological goals.[47]

A historical explanation for this particular case is not too difficult to arrive at, though it is not of paramount interest for my study. Simply and briefly put, the probable historical explanation for the last-minute injection of methods and goals appropriate to the analytical/intellectual mode into a context which is otherwise exclusively enstatic is that at a very early stage in the development of the Buddhist tradition, soteriological orthodoxy arrived at the position that proper soteriological method must necessarily involve some degree of analytical/intellectual meditation upon central items of Buddhist doctrine. Put still more simply, it quickly became orthodoxy for Indian Buddhist intellectuals that salvation must involve some degree of intellectual appropriation of doctrine, and any canonical material which appeared to present a self-consistent and coherent set of soteriological practices which involved no such intellectual activity therefore needed to be emended to accord with such orthodoxy. The details of the development of this orthodoxy are now lost; we do not know when it became firmly established, whether there were ever substantial Buddhist communities whose soteriological practices were exclusively enstatic, and why some elements of the canonical material still reflect an exclusively enstatic set of practices rather than an exclusively analytic one, (or, more commonly, a mixed set). Nevertheless, I believe that this general picture can effectively be used to account for many of the oddities encountered in the texts of the four *Collections*.[48]

The problem for Buddhist theoreticians, the scholastic thinkers who produced the great systematic works of the Indian Buddhist tradition, thus quickly became one of what to do with the elements of their tradition which clearly illustrate a very positive view of the attainment of cessation, coming close at times to considering it as an independently valid soteriological goal, identical with Nirvana. The complex historical and philosophical process by which such theoreticians did accommodate such elements of their tradition cannot even be outlined here, since my main interest is in the philosophical questions raised by the attainment of cessation and not in the development of Buddhist scholastic theory *per se*. All that I want to do here is to complement the outline picture of the varied contexts provided for the attainment of cessation in the *Collections* with a glance at the place provided for it by Buddhaghosa in the *Path to Purity* and at the comments on this by Dhammapāla in the *Casket of the Supreme Meaning*.

Buddhaghosa treats the attainment of cessation in the final chapter of the *Path to Purity* and defines it as one of the four 'benefits of cultivating wisdom'. The term translated here as 'wisdom' is *paññā,* a key term which is located firmly within the sphere of analytic understanding of the nature of things and is presented throughout the *Path to Purity*—and indeed throughout the Theravāda tradition—as resulting directly from those techniques that I have been calling analytic. Why then does Buddhaghosa define the attainment of cessation as a benefit of the cultivation of wisdom when it is difficult to see that it is even tangentially related to analytic knowledge? Why should an increase in the scope and depth of the practitioner's knowledge of the way things are lead to the attainment of cessation? Buddhaghosa's answer is that the necessary conditions for entering the attainment of cessation are the following: first, that one has reached one of the two highest stages on the Buddhist path (those of having begun one's last life before attaining enlightenment and of having already attained enlightenment);[49] the idea here is that anyone less spiritually advanced than this would be hindered by the continued existence within the mental continuum—to use for a moment non-personalistic Buddhist language—of various passions and defilements. Second, that one be fully adept at the cultivation of both insight and tranquillity, which is to say that one must be master of both the enstatic and the analytic methods of meditative practice and that one must therefore have eradicated all passion and all ignorance or intellectual misapprehension. Having stated these necessary conditions, conditions which naturally rule out the possibility of the attainment of cessation being regarded as simply and solely the result of enstatic practice, Buddhaghosa goes on to give a detailed description of the means by which the practitioner actually enters the attainment:

> How is it [viz: the attainment of cessation] attained? Such attainment belongs to one who has done the preparatory tasks and who strives with tranquillity and insight; [it occurs] as a result of [the practitioner] causing the cessation of the sphere of neither conceptualization nor non-conceptualization. [In contrast], the person who strives only with tranquillity reaches the sphere of neither conceptualization nor non-conceptualization and remains there, and the person who strives only with insight reaches the attainment of fruit and remains there. But the person who strives with both [tranquillity and insight] after doing the preparatory tasks causes the cessation of the sphere of neither conceptualization nor non-conceptualization—he attains it [viz: the attainment of cessation]. This is a brief outline. In more detail: A monk who desires to attain cessation, the duties connected with his meal

> completed and his hands and feet thoroughly washed, sits down upon a well-prepared seat in a secluded place. Crossing his legs, making his body erect and placing his attention to the front he attains the first *jhāna,* and upon emerging therefrom perceives the formations therein as impermanent, unsatisfactory and without an individuating essence . . .[50] [so also for the other *jhānā* and formless states until the practitioner] attains the sphere of neither conceptualization nor non-conceptualization. Then, after one or two turns of consciousness have passed, he becomes mindless and reaches cessation. Why is it that [moments of] consciousness do not occur [for him] after [these] two [turns of] consciousness? This is because of [the practitioner's] effort toward cessation, since this monk's ascent through the eight attainments [viz: four *jhānā* and four formless states] by yoking together the qualities of tranquillity and insight is an effort toward successive cessation [of all mental events] and not toward the attainment of the sphere of neither conceptualization nor non-conceptualization. Thus it is because of [his] effort toward cessation that no more than two [turns of] consciousness occur.[51]

Dhammapāla's comments on this passage read:

> 'With tranquillity and insight' means with those [qualities] yoked together, mutually helping one another. '. . . reaches the sphere of neither conceptualization nor non-conceptualization and remains there' is said because of the absence of insight and the presence simply of tranquillity above that [stage for such a practitioner]. 'The person who strives only with insight . . .' If a noble person has the goal of the attainment of fruit[52] [only], then having reached the attainment of fruit which is appropriate to him, he remains there. . . . 'He reaches cessation' means just that [he reaches] a mindless condition. 'Because of [the practitioner's] effort toward cessation' means: (i) because of a condition of effort [on the part of the practitioner] aimed at cessation of mind; (ii) because of the cessation of mind which is concomitant with an effort aimed at producing the two powers [viz: tranquillity and insight] and so forth. 'By yoking together the qualities of tranquillity and insight' means that endowment with the powers of tranquillity and insight and the condition of mastery over the states of knowledge and concentration are sought by the reciprocal transcendence [of tranquillity and insight]. 'An effort toward successive cessation [of all mental events]' means an effort aimed at the successive cessation and destruction of the first *jhāna* and so forth [viz: including the rest of the *jhānā* and the formless states], together with their realization.[53]

While some of the scholastic technicalities in these passages may remain unclear—and to fully analyze all of them would take many pages—the overall picture is, I think, clear enough: the practitioner performs certain physical preliminaries and then progresses through the entire hierarchy of enstatically produced altered states of consciousness regarding each in turn, as the practitioner exits from it, as possessing the three characteristics which, according to Buddhist theory, define all conditioned things: that is, the enstatically produced states of consciousness are transitory, unsatisfactory and insubstantial. Another way of saying this is that they are not soteriologically ultimate. After reaching and emerging from the eighth and highest of the attainments, immediately preceding the attainment of cessation itself, the practitioner's efforts turn consciously towards cessation and, after one or at most two further moments of consciousness ('turns' of consciousness in the extract translated above) the practitioner enters the attainment and becomes mindless.

Buddhaghosa's description of the process, together with his emphasis on the fact that the attainment of cessation can only be reached by one who already has substantial analytic achievements, shows that he was concerned to try and accommodate the attainment within a coherent and comprehensive soteriological schema and therefore to provide links between the enstatic and the analytic modes of practice. This much is clear even from his definition of the attainment as a 'benefit of cultivating wisdom', and the impression is confirmed by Dhammapāla's comments on the passage just translated. A key point is Buddhaghosa's phrase 'yoking together the qualities of tranquillity and insight', and Dhammapāla's notion of this yoking as a 'mutual helping' and a 'reciprocal transcendence', an ascent through the series of enstatically produced altered states of consciousness by an alternating use of the twin powers of tranquillity and insight, each being necessary in order for the practitioner to transcend the stage reached previously. The image is one of yoking, joint harnessing, two horses with different capacities pulling the same carriage in the same direction. The image is not, however, fully explained: just why are both tranquillity and insight necessary for a practitioner to enter the attainment of cessation? The power of insight, it appears, is used to review the characteristics of the altered states attained by way of tranquillity, and to make judgements about them; this, it would seem, is a second-order activity, one that may be useful, even essential, for the practitioner's full development of the capacity to analyze phenomena and come to an understanding of their nature, but not for the ability to simply enter the altered states in question. Similarly, in order to make correct judgements about the processes involved in running a four-minute mile I am likely to need certain analytic capacities and to be possessed of certain pieces of knowledge —such as knowledge about the physiological mechanisms by which oxygen intake is processed—but it is far from clear that I need such capacities or such knowledge in order to actually run a four-minute mile.

The analogy, like all analogies, is imperfect but suggestive. It leaves open the question of whether the influential attempt by Buddhaghosa and Dhammapāla to accommodate the traditions about the attainment of cessation, and about enstatic technique generally, into the sphere of observationally analytic technique, and thus to arrive at a unified soteriological system, can be judged a success.[54] This is not a question that can be fully explored here; I have noted it only to provide an adequate context for developing an understanding of the more purely philosophical problems surrounding the attainment of cessation.

This brief survey suggests that by the time of such systematic thinkers as Buddhaghosa and Dhammapāla the attainment of cessation was not given an especially prominent place as a soteriological goal. That this is so reflects the broad consensus on the nature of enlightenment and the methods appropriate to gaining it which had emerged in the Theravāda tradition by this period: the methods of observational and intellectual analysis and the transformation of the perceptual and cognitive skills of the practitioner which goes with them had become normative and it was therefore impossible for the paradigmatically enstatic methods connected with the attainment of cessation to be anything more than marginal. This consensus is, if anything, still more marked among the orthodox intellectuals of contemporary Theravāda Buddhism.[55] It only remains, then, before turning to the more strictly philosophical problems raised by the existence and recommendation of the attainment of cessation within the tradition, to look briefly at some explicit evaluations given to the attainment of cessation within the Theravāda tradition.

1.4 EVALUATIONS OF THE ATTAINMENT OF CESSATION

I have tried to show that the attainment of cessation has a significant place within the Theravāda tradition as an independently valid soteriological goal, and that there are important sets of meditational techniques designed to lead the practitioner to it. The question remains, precisely how is this altered state of consciousness evaluated by the tradition?

In the early texts—specifically the discourses and sermons preserved in the four *Collections*—there are extremely positive evaluations of the attainment of cessation. For example, in a discourse of the *Intermediate Collection,* a hierarchy of soteriological goals is established, beginning with leaving the householder's life and 'going forth' into the life of a religious mendicant. The next highest goal is correct ethical conduct. Then comes concentration, followed by 'knowledge and vision'—identical with what I have been calling the analytic methods—and finally, more excellent than any of these, the four *jhānā* of form, the four formless attainments and cessation itself.[56] In this discourse, then, it appears that the attainment of cessation is regarded as in some sense soteriologically superior to the intellectual and verbal knowledges gained by analytic methods. Buddhaghosa's commentary on the relevant passage of this discourse says:

> How is it that the *jhānā* [and the other enstatic states, including the attainment of cessation] are more excellent than knowledge and vision? It is because they are the basis for [attaining] cessation. Whereas the lower *jhānā* [and other enstatic states] are the basis for [realizing] insight, these [*jhānā* and enstatic states] are the basis for [attaining] cessation, and should therefore be understood as 'more excellent' [than knowledge and vision].[57]

Buddhaghosa here distinguishes two different kinds of *jhāna:* the first apparently acts as a basis for the attainment of insight and the second as a basis for the attainment of cessation, and the second is superior to the first. The clear implication is that the goal of cessation is superior to that of insight or, to put this another way, that a paradigmatically enstatic goal is superior to an analytic one.

Then, in the *Gradual Collection* the attainment of cessation is explicitly identified with Nirvana as it is experienced in the practitioner's present life, and in a discourse of the *Intermediate Collection* the attainment of cessation is described as a 'comfortable abode' than which there is nothing greater or more excellent.[58] Further, another passage of the same *Collection* states that there is no 'fetter' (a technical term in Buddhist psychology, denoting various kinds of exhaustively analyzed attachment to the things of the world, things which do not, given the Buddhist analysis, warrant any such attachment) which remains unremoved for one who has reached the attainment of cessation.[59] This also is a very positive evaluation of the attainment of cessation, since the removal of all 'fetters' is close to, if not actually identical with, Nirvana itself.

Buddhaghosa also appears to identify the attainment of cessation with Nirvana, at least insofar as this can be experienced while still alive. In answer to the question of why anyone should want to attain the cessation of sensation and conceptualization, he says:

> Why do they attain it [viz: the attainment of cessation]? Tired of the occurrence and dissolution of formations [viz: everything that is caused and so impermanent] they think: 'Let us live in happiness having become mindless here and now and having attained that cessation which is Nirvana.'[60]

There are a number of problems with this explanation of the motive for attaining cessation. The most obvious is that it is unclear how a condition in which no mental events occur can possess affective tone as appears to be suggested. Presumably it would be more accurate to describe the attainment of cessation as a condition which is free from both happiness and sadness and indeed from all affective tone whatever. Dhammapāla was clearly aware of this problem and says that 'happiness' in this passage means simply 'the absence of suffering'.[61] He thus neatly sidesteps the problem of attributing affective tone to the attainment of cessation. Naturally, if there are no mental events in the attainment of cessation, there can be no mental events involving suffering, and, according to Dhammapāla, this is simply what is meant by 'happiness'.

The second major problem with Buddhaghosa's evaluation of the attainment of cessation as Nirvana is that this seems to approach uneasily close to a standard Buddhist heresy: identifying Nirvana, the soteriological ultimate, with cessation. Such a heresy appears to be a variant of what is frequently described in the canonical Pali texts as the 'annihilation view',[62] a view which suggests that the individual is identical with the psycho-physical processes which constitute him—that there is no 'further fact' of self-identity—and that at death, when these psycho-physical processes cease, the individual also necessarily ceases. Many Buddhist texts, especially those which discuss the question of the nature of Nirvana, do in fact read as though they embrace just this 'annihilation view'. But it needs always to be borne in mind that Buddhist orthodoxy on Nirvana is that no views about it can be true and that this, together with the fact that the Buddha can by definition hold no false views, entails that the Buddha holds no view about Nirvana and thus *a fortiori* certainly not one that identifies Nirvana with annihilation. This position has its own philosophical problems which I can't explore here other than to say it appears *prima facie* incoherent: if all views about Nirvana are false, then the view 'all views about Nirvana are false' is also false.[63]

However this may be, it certainly seems as though this text of Buddhaghosa's, identifying the attainment of cessation with Nirvana, is one of those that encourages some version of the 'annihilation view'. I am encouraged in this judgement by the fact that Buddhaghosa's commentator, Dhammapāla, also appears to have been somewhat uneasy with this simple identification and qualifies it doubly. First, he glosses Buddhaghosa's simple 'Nirvana' with the more technical term 'Nirvana without remainder', a term that reflects the basic division of Nirvana into two types: that which occurs in a practitioner's individual life and yet still leaves enough of a 'remainder' (of the effects of past actions) such that the practitioner is able to continue living and acting, and that which occurs upon the enlightened practitioner's death. The paradigm case of the first kind of Nirvana, naturally, is that of the Buddha himself, who was said to have attained 'Nirvana with remainder' when he reached enlightenment by sitting in meditation under the Bo tree, but who attained 'Nirvana without remainder' only after his physical death.[64] Dhammapāla, then, wants to identify the attainment of cessation with the second type of Nirvana, that which usually follows upon physical death. He does not elaborate upon his reasons for making such an identification; I assume that he makes it because 'Nirvana with remainder' permits continued thought, action, intention and so forth, whereas the attainment of cessation clearly does not. If the attainment of cessation is to be identified with any kind of Nirvana, then it must be with 'Nirvana without remainder'. The great similarities between the attainment of cessation and death (discussed in Section 1.2) are here suggested once again.

But Dhammapāla is uneasy even about this. He adds a further explanation, saying: ' "Having attained [that cessation which is] Nirvana" means as though having attained Nirvana without remainder.'[65] Once again, he does not elaborate, though the use of the Pali particle *viya*—'as though', 'like', 'as it were'—suggests some uncertainty on Dhammapāla's part about Buddhaghosa's simple identification of cessation with Nirvana. The reason for this is that, phenomenologically speaking, the only kind of Nirvana which the attainment of cessation can possibly be like is Nirvana without remainder, and yet part of the standard definition of this kind of Nirvana is that the practitioner attains it only after (physical) death. And, since the practitioner in the attainment of cessation is clearly still alive (even if only just), Dhammapāla is forced to add his 'as though'.

By looking in some detail at the thought underlying Buddhaghosa's and Dhammapāla's evaluations of the attainment of cessation I hope to have shown once more that the existence of this altered state within their tradition provided a severe problem of classification, in several different ways, for the intellectuals and systematizers of Theravāda Buddhism. The canonical orthodoxy is that the attainment of cessation is (more or less) the same as Nirvana, and this reflects the enstatic strand of Buddhist soteriological theory. Here, the attainment of cessation is the culmination of a process of retreat from interaction with the world and is thus Nirvana-in-life. But, as soon as orthodoxy began to regard the analytic strand as paramount and to define Nirvana-in-life through the paradigm of the Buddha's post-enlightenment preaching and teaching career, such a straightforward identification became impossible. The soteriological status of the attainment of cessation had to be changed and lowered, so much so that there is an obvious tension, if not an outright contradiction, between Dhammapāla's definition of it as 'something like Nirvana without remainder' and the canonical definition, mentioned above, which approaches closely to simply identifying the attainment of cessation with Nirvana-in-life. This ambiguity persists throughout the Theravādin attempts to make sense of the attainment of cessation and is therefore reflected in its evaluations of this condition.

1.5 DEBATES ON EMERGING FROM THE ATTAINMENT OF CESSATION

So far in this chapter I have tried to show how the attainment of cessation was defined by the tradition, the kinds of practice which were thought to give rise to it and the evaluations given to it. The obvious question that remains, and the one which brings us to real philosophical meat, is: given that a mindless condition of this kind is possible—one wherein no mental events occur—how can the practitioner who attains it emerge from it?

To sharpen this question somewhat, it's important to set forth a basic metaphysical postulate of the Theravāda system, namely the universal fact of causality, the Buddha's discovery of which is usually expressed in the following terse formula:

When x exists y exists;
from the arising of x, y arises.
When x does not exist y does not exist;
from the cessation of x, y ceases.[66]

There is considerable debate as to just how this should be spelled out. The following reformulation seems adequate:

(1) For the occurrence of any given event Y, there exists a necessary and sufficient condition X

Some, at least, of the standard Theravādin glosses upon this formulation support this interpretation. They understand the first two lines of the verse ('When x exists y exists; from the arising of x, y arises.') as *parallelismus membrorum,* expressing the relationship of sufficient conditionality (simply, 'If x then y', or 'x entails y'), and the last two lines of the verse ('When x does not exist y does not exist; from the cessation of x, y ceases.') in the same manner, as expressing the relationship of necessary conditionality (simply, 'If not-x then not-y' or 'the absence of x entails the absence of y').[67] It is true that the universal application of (1) is not explicitly stated, nor perhaps even suggested, by the standard formulation translated above. It is supplied by me on the basis of other texts and is, I think, clearly what is intended.[68] Another problem with (1) is that, in the formulation I have given it, it appears to rule out:

(1′) For the occurrence of any given event Y, there may be a variety of sufficient conditions X1 . . . Xn, none of which are necessary

This is a problem because there are many canonical texts which appear to adhere to (1′) rather than (1), while it seems clear that the philosophical orthodoxy of Theravāda Buddhism wishes to assert (1). David Kalupahana, a noted scholar of Theravāda, solves this problem by suggesting that the verse translated above does indeed express Theravādin orthodoxy on the issue of causality, that (1) is an adequate reformulation of it (though he does not in fact formulate (1) quite as I have) and that the frequent uses of something very much like (1′) in the Pali canon are explicable on the grounds that: 'Buddha was reluctant to confuse the minds of the latter (viz: untrained ordinary people) speaking of highly philosophical theories . . . the Buddha spoke to an ordinary man in terms intelligible to him.'[69] While having some doubts about Kalupahana's apparent easy satisfaction with the use of falsehood as a pedagogical tool, I agree with him that (1) rather than (1′) does indeed accurately reflect Theravādin orthodoxy and shall make use of it in what follows.

Now (1), of course, is a version of the principle of sufficient reason (PSR), the view suggesting that every existent has a reason for its existence. In Leibniz's classical formulation, this principle states: '. . . that no fact can be real or existent, no statement true, unless there be a sufficient reason why it is so and not otherwise.'[70] An alternative (though not quite equivalent) way of putting this is to say that every event—or fact—has an explanation. It is notorious that there are difficulties with this principle; I think that these difficulties are especially pressing when we have to do with a strong form of PSR, as in

(1). For (1) states that X entails Y and that for any Y there is an X. But this seems to lead inevitably to the position that the series of entailments leading to (explaining) Y is infinite once it is accepted (as I think the metaphysicians of the Theravāda would) that there are no events (facts) which provide the necessary and sufficient conditions for their own existence. That is, if there are no self-explanatory events, every event must be explained by some other event. And this results in infinite regress. The Theravādin, perhaps, would not be perturbed by this, since he is likely to hold axiomatically the proposition that, as a matter of contingent fact, the occurrence of any given event Y is preceded by an infinitely long chain of preceding events. This probably does not matter as long as the major point of (1) is to state simply that it is in principle possible to specify the necessary and sufficient conditions for the occurrence of any Y at any time; the infinite regress will matter, though, if the object at hand is to specify the total explanation of any Y, since the version of PSR supported by Theravāda theorists appears to make such a total explanation in principle impossible.[71] This will provide a problem for Theravādins if, as sometimes seems to be the case, they want to suggest that the Buddha (being omniscient) can in fact provide such a total explanation of any given event. For not even an omniscient being can evade the requirements of the form of PSR enshrined in (1): that in principle no explanation of (specification of the necessary and sufficient conditions for the occurrence of) any existent's existence can be total. But the whole question of the philosophical problems surrounding Buddha's omniscience is not one that can be entered into here.[72] I wish only to note that (1), the Theravādin strong form of PSR, presupposes the Buddhist axiom that the chain of caused events which constitutes the universe is beginningless.

Applying (1) to the question of emergence from the attainment of cessation, we need to know what the necessary and sufficient conditions are for such emergence to occur. The universality of (1) rules out the possibility that emergence can occur spontaneously, in an uncaused manner: there have to be (in principle) specifiable conditions for its occurrence. One important result obtained in our descriptive analysis of the attainment of cessation is:

(2) No mental events occur in the attainment of cessation

Bearing (1) and (2) in mind for a moment, let's look at what the texts say about emergence from the attainment of cessation. An explicit statement is found in a text of the *Intermediate Collection:*

> . . . it does not occur to a monk who is emerging from the attainment of cessation 'I will emerge from the attainment of cessation' or 'I am emerging from the attainment of cessation' or 'I have emerged from the attainment of cessation'. Rather, his mind has been previously so developed that it leads him to that condition [of emerging from the attainment of cessation].[73]

Clearly, emergence from the attainment of cessation does not occur as a result of an intention formed on the part of the practitioner while in the attainment. This is so since:

(3) All intentions are mental events

and their occurrence while in the attainment of cessation would violate (2). Nevertheless, the text translated above suggests that emergence does occur as a result of something mental, that is to say the previous development of the practitioner's mind. Buddhaghosa makes this a little more explicit:

> How is it [viz: the attainment of cessation] made to last? It lasts for the time predetermined for its attainment unless interrupted by death, the waiting of the community, or the call of the Teacher.
>
> How does emergence from it come about? In two ways: either by the fruition of non-return in the case of the non-returner, or of *arhatship* in the case of the *arhat*.[74]

The phrase 'the time predetermined for its attainment' indicates clearly that Buddhaghosa thinks that emergence from the attainment of cessation is determined at least partly by the intentions of the practitioner at the time of entering the attainment. This would also be the meaning of the reference to previous development of the mind in the extract from the *Intermediate Collection* above. The references to the possible interruption of the attainment by death, the waiting of the community (to enact some communal administrative judgement which requires the presence of the monk in cessation) and the 'call of the Teacher' (which here means the summons of the Buddha himself) also highlight the importance of the practitioner's intentions upon entering cessation, since it appears that the practitioner can decide when entering cessation to emerge at the appropriate time if any of these eventualities should occur (though there are problems with this to which I shall return later).

Buddhaghosa's final words in the extract translated here, the references to the two 'fruitions', refer us to the division of the Buddhist soteriological process into four 'paths' and four 'fruits'; the two 'fruits' referred to here are the two highest resultant stages upon the

Buddhist path, the 'fruit of *arhatship*' being identical with enlightenment itself. The phraseology and intention of this last part of the passage are not entirely clear. It is possible that Buddhaghosa could mean that the occurrence of these two 'fruits' is the direct cause of emergence from the attainment of cessation; this is one understanding of his use of the instrumental case here.[75] But this would be paradoxical. The fruits are, at least in part, mental events and cannot therefore be part of the attainment of cessation. By extension of (2) above, no mental event that occurs subsequent to the time at which the practitioner enters the attainment of cessation can itself be part of that attainment. As soon as any mental event occurs the attainment has come to an end. Indeed, the occurrence of any mental event defines the end of the attainment. I think, then, that it is preferable to take Buddhaghosa's mention of the occurrence of the 'fruits' as descriptive of the first mental events that occur upon leaving the attainment of cessation and not as in any real sense a cause of such leaving.[76]

Bearing this exegesis in mind, the following possible causes for emergence from the attainment of cessation are, I think, envisaged by the texts:

(4) The necessary and sufficent cause for emergence from the attainment of cessation is the practitioner's act of intention immediately preceding entry into that state

This expresses the mainstream Theravāda view. It is consistent with both (1) and (2) since it provides a necessary and sufficient condition for emergence from the attainment and does not postulate the existence of mental events within the attainment. What are the problems involved with this view? Firstly, it requires causal efficacy at a temporal distance. That is to say, if (3) and (4) are true, and given that there is always and necessarily some temporal gap between entry into the attainment of cessation and emergence from it, it must also be true that:

(5) The necessary and sufficient cause X, for any event Y, need not be temporally contiguous with that event

In the case under consideration here, the events X and Y are mental events (the intention to emerge from the attainment of cessation and emergence from it), but, presumably, the same could be true of physical events, or, indeed, of other types of event if such are allowed into the system of classification. If (3) through (5) are true, then the scholastics of the Theravāda tradition are faced with the likelihood of contradicting another basic metaphysical tenet of their system: that of impermanence, the view that all existents are transitory, which, in its later and more developed stages, became the view that every existent is momentary, i.e., endures for the shortest possible temporal interval. This postulate may be expressed:

(6) Every existent exists only for a short space of time
(7) For any existent X, causal efficacy can be predicated of X only while X exists

This formulation of the impermanence principle could be tightened somewhat by following Buddhaghosa and the later Theravāda in adopting a strict theory of momentariness which suggests that all existents/events (either term will do here as a translation of the fundamental Pali term *dhamma*)[77] last only for just long enough to exercise the causal power which in fact defines them. On this view, an existent just is what it does, and what it does is done extremely quickly—'in a snap of the fingers, the blink of an eye' to use a favourite Buddhist image. But this view is not expressed with any degree of precision in the early texts, and I shall therefore content myself with the looser formulation of the principle of impermanence contained in (6) and (7).

Now clearly, (4) and (7) taken together entail:

(8) The practitioner's act of intention immediately preceding entry into the attainment of cessation still exists at the time of the practitioner's emergence from that attainment

which in turn probably entails the falsity of (6), a proposition fundamental to the metaphysical structure of Theravāda Buddhism. Whether the falsity of (6) is entailed or not depends on just what is meant by 'a short space of time', something about which the tradition itself—at least in the earlier stages of its development—is not clear. However, whatever exactly is meant, it seems pretty clear that since both canonical and commentarial texts often speak of the attainment of cessation as lasting seven days,[78] and that it is sometimes suggested that it can last still longer,[79] at least the spirit if not the letter of (6) is contradicted. The general point is that, on the Buddhist view, causal efficacy requires the existence of that which is causally efficacious, and given Buddhist views about impermanence it is far from clear in what sense a past mental event—such as the intentions to enter the attainment of cessation and to emerge from it after a given interval—can properly be said to still exist seven days or more after its original occurrence.

Another option would be to hold (3) through (6) and abandon or reformulate (7). But this, given certain other Buddhist views on causation, would necessitate something like:

(7′) For any existent X, causal efficacy can be predicated of X when X no longer exists if and only if there is an (in principle) specifiable causal chain connecting X to its putative effects

(8′) The practitioner's act of intention immediately preceding entry into the attainment of cessation is connected to emergence therefrom by an (in principle) specifiable causal chain

and this provides its own problems, of which the most obvious is that, given (2)—that no mental events occur in the attainment of cessation—apparently the only kind of causal chain that could be specified is a chain of physical events. And this in turn would mean that the Theravādin would be forced to accept the thesis that mental events can be caused by physical events, something that in other circumstances the tradition is not willing to do. Intentions, in Theravāda theory of mind, just are not the kinds of existent/event which can properly be said to have as their directly antecedent cause a purely physical event: mental events do not arise directly from the body, though there are, of course, manifold and complex kinds of interaction between the mental and the physical, interaction which is described most clearly in Theravādin analyses of the perceptual process.[80] The fact that there is no suggestion in Theravādin texts that the mental event of emerging from cessation can have a purely physical cause is, by itself, a good indication that Theravādins are dualists in the sense that they perceive a fundamental difference between the mental and the physical.[81] The difference is, on one level, phenomenological: mental events and physical events simply appear different from one another and have different specifiable characteristics, but it is also, I think, metaphysical.[82]

The only other significant possibility imaginable if (3) through (6) are held and (7′) and (8′) are asserted is that there might be some kind of especially subtle mental causal chain which persists throughout the attainment of cessation and which connects the practitioner's act of intention upon entering the attainment with the mental events that occur upon leaving it. To take this route would be to contradict the canonical definitions of the attainment of cessation, which, as I have suggested (in Section 1.2), make it abundantly clear that no mental events of any kind occur in the attainment of cessation. Such a price might be worth paying for the Buddhist intellectual, however, since it would allow the preservation of standard theories of causation and would account for the emergence of consciousness from the attainment of cessation. I shall show in subsequent chapters that this route was in fact taken by some Buddhist thinkers, though it does not occur clearly in the Theravāda tradition.

That this option does not occur in the Theravāda is all the more surprising when it is realized that, by the time of Buddhaghosa, the tradition had developed what appears to be an ideal concept to deal with precisely the problem that concerns us, and yet this concept was not applied in the way that might have been expected. This concept is that of the 'subliminal consciousness' *(bhavanga)*, a type of consciousness which operates without an object and which continues when all empirically observable mental events in a particular continuum have ceased to occur.[83] This concept, which is not systematically evidenced in the Theravāda tradition before Buddhaghosa,[84] appears to have been constructed to account for a number of problems which are not easy to explain on the normative canonical Theravādin view of consciousness. Very briefly, and somewhat too simply, if consciousness is identified with empirically perceptible mental events, and if all mental events must be intentional in the sense of possessing an object—which is, in essence, the canonical view—then there are clearly many states in which there are no mental events. Dreamless sleep is one; the attainment of cessation is another and the death/rebirth process is yet another. In all of these conditions, there are no empirically perceptible intentional mental events and therefore, by definition, no consciousness, no mental events of any kind. How, then, can the emergence of mental events from conditions such as dreamless sleep be explained? There are a number of facets to this problem: on one level it is a variant of a problem basic to Buddhist psychology, that of accounting for continuity of identity. If mental events simply stop in dreamless sleep or the attainment of cessation and then, by some process that cannot be easily explained, begin again, in what sense is the continuum of mental events that restarts 'the same as' that which ceased? On another level it is a problem, as I have already tried to show, in the systematic causal theory which is such an important part of Buddhism: what causal account can be given for the emergence of consciousness from mindless states?

The 'subliminal consciousness' theory, then, was constructed to deal with some of these problems. Its main use in the Theravāda was in accounting for the death/rebirth process. Buddhaghosa suggests that the subliminal consciousness of an individual at death and that of the newborn baby who is 'the same as' the dying individual are causally connected as part of the same stream, even though there may be no empirically perceptible intentional mental events at all stages of the process.[85] The theory was also used to account for the emergence of consciousness from dreamless sleep. Most interestingly for the purposes of this study, though, it does not appear to have been used to account—causally—for the emergence of consciousness from the attainment of cessation. Historically it remains very unclear why this obvious intellectual move was not made; if it had been, many of the problems analyzed here would not have arisen or would have arisen in a much less severe form. All that Buddhaghosa would have needed to do would be to assert that despite the canonical definitions of the attainment of cessation as mindless, one kind of consciousness, the subliminal consciousness, does indeed endure within that attainment, and it is this that provides the required causal connection [propositions (7′) and (8′)] between the practitioner's final intentions before entering the attainment of cessation and the mental events which constitute emergence from it. However, neither he nor his commentators appear to have made any such move.

There is one final set of possible causes for the emergence of consciousness from the attainment of cessation which does appear to be at least envisaged by the tradition. This comprises sets of events which occur altogether outside the continuum of events which defines the practitioner who has entered the attainment of cessation and thus provides a quite different perspective on the issue, though not one that is given any kind of systematic development by the tradition. I mentioned earlier (Section 1.3) that part of Buddhaghosa's description of the methods by which cessation is attained has to do with the practitioner's self-assurances that certain events will not occur during the time the practitioner plans to be in the attainment of cessation. These events included the practitioner's death, the community needing the practitioner for a communal administrative act, a summons from the Buddha and others. The interesting point about these events is that if they do occur while the practitioner is in the attainment of cessation they appear to provide a sufficient condition for consciousness to begin functioning again. Thus Buddhaghosa describes what happens to a monk who is not careful to ascertain whether he is due to die before he emerges from the attainment of cessation in these terms:

> The monk should consider very carefully the limit of his life's duration. He should attain [cessation] only after thinking: 'Will my vital functions continue for seven days [i.e., the standard length of time that a practitioner remains in the attainment of cessation] or not?' For if he attains [cessation] without thinking whether the vital

> functions will cease within seven days, then since the attainment of cessation is not able to prevent death and, because there is no death within the attainment of cessation, he then emerges from the attainment of cessation.[86]

The term 'vital functions' refers to the processes of the autonomic nervous system which necessarily endure in the attainment of cessation: they are what distinguish it from death. When these cease, life comes to an end, and it appears from this passage (and the same is true for the other passages discussing what happens if the other events outlined—the community's need, the Buddha's call and so forth—should occur) that the occurrence of death provides a sufficient condition for the emergence of consciousness from the attainment of cessation. Dhammapāla's comment makes this still clearer and in an interesting way. In explaining why death cannot occur while the practitioner remains in the attainment of cessation he brings in the idea of the 'subliminal consciousness', saying that the process of dying requires this subliminal consciousness and implying thereby that the practitioner must emerge from the attainment of cessation in order to die because there is no subliminal consciousness in the attainment.[87]

This view clearly entails that there are a variety of sufficient conditions for the emergence of consciousness from the attainment of cessation, none of which need be necessary. Thus (1) is abandoned and (1′) accepted, something which I have already suggested is contrary to Theravādin orthodoxy on the subject of causality.

Further, the view suggests, or comes close to suggesting, that the continuum of physical events which constitutes the practitioner in the attainment of cessation can act as the direct cause for the emergence of consciousness, at least in the case of death mentioned in the extract translated above. This is so because death here is defined as 'interruption of the vital functions'—a purely physical event.

Finally, and oddest of all, in the other cases in which the practitioner's consciousness can be caused to emerge from the attainment of cessation, for example by the needs of the community or the summons of the Buddha, the events which cause this have nothing whatever to do with the continuum of physical events that defines the practitioner in the attainment of cessation. The needs of the community are, presumably, collections of mental and physical events which are, in some more or less well-defined sense, external to the practitioner. Further, the practitioner cannot be aware of these events, because then some mental event would be occurring in the continuum that constitutes the practitioner. This would violate the canonical definition of the attainment of cessation. There must, therefore, be some kind of (in principle specifiable) type of causal connection between the collection of mental and physical events that constitutes the needs of the community and the continuum of physical events that constitutes the practitioner in the attainment of cessation. It is not easy to see what kind of connection this could be, given that it cannot be one of direct awareness on the part of the practitioner. And in fact the texts make no effort to develop this possibility or to specify the kind of causal connection that obtains; the questions I have been asking in the last few paragraphs are nowhere asked or answered by the texts, a fact that indicates the non-centrality of the possibilities suggested here to the tradition. Nevertheless, these possibilities are both present and articulated and thus deserve mention.

In conclusion, the Theravāda tradition does not offer a clear answer to our problem, and the answers that it does suggest are fraught with problems. Propositions (1) through (4) express the usual Theravādin view of the attainment of cessation and of the emergence of consciousness from it. The major problem with this position is that (1) through (4), taken in conjunction with their entailment (5), entail the falsity of (6) and/or (7), both fundamental postulates of Theravāda metaphysics. A different way of putting this is to say that (1) through (5), taken together with (7), entail (8), which stands in direct contradiction to (the spirit of) (6). The alternative, of accepting (1) through (6) but not (7) leads inevitably, given certain other Theravādin postulates, to something like (7′) and (8′). But this in turn requires either that the emergence of consciousness from the attainment of cessation is caused by a physical event—which stands in tension with Theravāda dualism about mental and physical events—or that some kind of mental continuum endures within the attainment of cessation—which contradicts the standard canonical definitions of that state.

The Theravāda tradition does not, therefore, succeed in resolving the dilemma, though its attempts to do so are illuminating in several ways. They highlight the Theravādin tendency towards a profound dualism in regard to mental and physical events, a dualism which perceives these as different in kind, capable of interaction of various kinds but not of acting as direct efficient causes of one another. They also bring into sharp relief the pan-Buddhist view of strict impermanence, which creates for Buddhist metaphysicians their major difficulties, those of accounting for various types of continuity. One such problem area is the questions surrounding the emergence of consciousness from the attainment of cessation; others are accounting for memory, for continuity of character traits, and for the preservation of personal identity across many lives. Radical impermanence and continuing identity make uneasy bedfellows.[88] The preceding analysis of the attainment of cessation in the Theravāda tradition gives what I believe to be a peculiarly sharp illustration of the philosophical problems that can be generated—and fudged—by a tradition that espouses doctrines of radical impermanence and universal causality and is yet forced, by philosophical pressures from without and hermeneutical pressures from within, to account for continuity in purely causal terms where no such account can easily be given. This theme will arise again in my discussions of the Vaibhāṣika and Yogācāra answers to this problem, both of which are more systematic than the Theravāda version examined in this chapter.

CHAPTER TWO

THE ATTAINMENT OF CESSATION IN THE VAIBHĀṢIKA TRADITION

2.1 THE VAIBHĀṢIKA TRADITION

Three centuries after the origin of Buddhism in India the tradition had split into a number of distinct schools. These schools appear to have been only partly defined by their differing philosophical views. It was probably at least as much the case that they came into being in virtue of their geographical separation one from another as because of intellectual disagreement,[1] and it is clear that assent to even radically opposed doctrinal positions did not, throughout much of Buddhist history of India, prevent those who held such opposed positions from inhabiting the same monastic institutions and living together in (comparative) harmony.[2] Nevertheless, the schools did come to be defined by significantly different intellectual positions, and much of the scholastic literature is occasional and polemical in the sense that it is directed against specific opposed philosophical views. So, even though the schools probably originated as a result of geographical separation rather than intellectual disagreement, and even though much of the disagreement that did develop was not necessarily reflected by concomitant institutional and practical divisions, it still makes a good deal of sense from the viewpoint of the history of ideas to regard the schools as representing contrasting intellectual positions, and this is the standpoint that will be taken here.

From this standpoint, then, the Vaibhāṣika tradition may be considered as a complex and systematic set of philosophical positions expressed in texts composed in Sanskrit from approximately the first to the fifth centuries of the Christian era.[3] These texts represent the views of an influential group of Buddhist intellectuals who worked largely in Mathura, Gandhara and Kashmir and who based themselves upon the texts regarded as canonical by the Sarvāstivādin school,[4] though they by no means limited themselves to the concepts or principles of taxonomy found in those canonical texts. For the sake of convenience the intellectual development of the tradition may be divided into four major phases, each represented by a text or group of texts, and each showing marked advances and changes over its predecessor. The brief survey of these phases offered in the following pages should be taken as no more than an outline since few of these texts are available in reliable editions and still fewer have been subjected to critical study by philosophers working from outside the traditions.

I shall call the first phase the 'unsystematic commentarial'. It is represented by what became the basic text for the Vaibhāṣikas, the work which gives the school its name, *The Great Book of Options (Mahāvibhāṣā)*.[5] This is an enormous, sprawling text, one of the three longest single texts in the entire Chinese canonical collection; it has the approximate form of a commentary on the canonical works of the Sarvāstivāda and is remarkable chiefly for its length and for its apparent attempt to say something significant about every philosophical controversy then current. It, like the other Vaibhāṣika texts, was originally composed in Sanskrit but is now extant only in Chinese translation. It has not yet been systematically worked on by Western scholarship though when this is done it promises to yield a vast treasure of information, both historical and philosophical, relating to early scholastic Buddhism. The text is frequently quoted and referred to with veneration by later Vaibhāṣika authors.[6] It may date from the first century AD.

The second phase I shall call the proto-systematic; it consists in a variety of comparatively short texts, all more or less dependent upon the *Great Book of Options* but exhibiting a greater tendency towards coherent systematization of the available range of material. These texts also are largely available only in Chinese translation, although they were originally written in Sanskrit. Two of the most important are Ghoṣaka's *Nectar of Metaphysics (Abhidharmāmṛta)* and Dharmaśrī's *Essence of Metaphysics (Abhidharmahṛdaya)*. Both of these works are available in recent translations, the former in French and the latter in both French and English. The latter's organizational structure appears to have been especially influential upon all later texts in the Vaibhāṣika tradition including the *Treasury of Metaphysics* itself.[7]

Most of the intellectual energy of the authors of these protosystematic texts went into an attempt to provide organizational schemata which could comprehensively, coherently and economically describe the way things are by providing a system of classification into which every existent, potential or actual, can be allotted its appropriate place. This, of course, is no mean intellectual ambition, and, like all such attempts at comprehensive system-building, it has certain key weak points. I do not intend, in this monograph, to offer an in-depth discussion of the nature of this systematic attempt at world-explanation, much less to analyze its failures, but it is important to say something about the nature of the enterprise in order to place the Vaibhāṣika discussion of the attainment of cessation in its proper intellectual context.

Briefly, then, the theoreticians of the Vaibhāṣika tradition were operating under two major constraints in their attempt to categorize and define every existent. The first constraint was that of the tradition itself: Indian philosophers, and in this the Vaibhāṣika thinkers are typical, do not happily abandon any significant element of their own tradition, even when they do not understand it or no longer find it persuasive and significant. The Vaibhāṣika theoretician was therefore constrained to find a place in his system for every significant element in the tradition available to him, even when such elements sat very uneasily within the context of the system being developed. Many oddities in the Vaibhāṣika system can be explained by this constraint—including, I think, the intellectual acrobatics performed by the Vaibhāṣikas in their attempts to accommodate the attainment of cessation. The second constraint was that of comprehensiveness: to create a system in the full sense of that term the Vaibhāṣikas were constrained to try and account for everything. They were engaged in trying to show that the Buddhist system of categorizing existents was indeed comprehensive in that it could satisfactorily account for all types of experience and thus for the totality of (actual and possible) existents. It was this constraint which led to the creative developments in Vaibhāṣika thought during the proto-systematic period. As the thinkers of this school became aware of possible holes in the system (eventualities which had not previously been envisaged), new and more complex organizational schemata and occasionally even new categories to fit within those schemata had to be created. This process reached a kind of culmination with the composition, in the fifth century AD, of the most influential text in the Vaibhāṣika tradition and one of the most influential in the entire Indian Buddhist tradition, the *Treasury of Metaphysics (Abhidharmakośa).*

The *Treasury* is itself to be identified with the third phase in my schematic history of the Vaibhāṣika school, simply because of its pivotal importance. I shall turn in Section 2.2 to a discussion of the senses in which it is pivotal and to a brief outline of the nature of the work itself as well as of the system to which it gives expression.

The fourth phase in the intellectual history of the Vaibhāṣika school consists in the orthodox reaction to the views expressed in the *Treasury.* Such a reaction was felt to be required by intellectuals of the tradition because many extended philosophical discussions in the *Treasury* end in rejecting Vaibhāṣika orthodoxy as this had been defined by the *Great Book of Options* and refined in the texts of the proto-systematic phase. Three texts are of special significance here: two by Saṃghabhadra, a great exponent of Vaibhāṣika orthodoxy, and one by an unknown author who frequently explicitly quotes and attempts to refute arguments found in the *Treasury,* in an interesting work called the *Lamp of Metaphysics (Abhidharmadīpa).*[8] These texts are of great importance for the later history of the Vaibhāṣika school.

The Vaibhāṣika tradition is no longer part of living Buddhism in the sense that there are no monastic communities which are identifiable as Vaibhāṣika communities. It is, rather, part of Buddhist intellectual history, but a part which was peculiarly influential in India for more than a millennium and which still has influence upon the scholastic traditions of Tibetan and Japanese Buddhism. Considerable work is needed by Western scholars before the riches of this intellectual tradition can become fully available; even the basic level of textual work—the production of reliable editions and good translations—has scarcely begun, and this monograph will make only a marginal contribution to this basic spadework.

2.2 THE SIGNIFICANCE OF THE *TREASURY OF METAPHYSICS*

The *Treasury of Metaphysics* is of pivotal importance in at least three senses, and it is largely because of the pivotal position held by the text that my exposition of the Vaibhāṣika views on the attainment of cessation will make almost exclusive use of it and its commentarial interpretations.

First, then, the *Treasury* was pivotal for the Vaibhāṣika school itself; its comprehensiveness, the precision of its definitions and the success of its systems of classification meant that in spite of the unorthodoxy of some of the viewpoints expressed by its author, Vasubandhu,[9] therein, no subsequent thinker working in this tradition could afford to ignore it. Even the 'orthodox' Vaibhāṣika reactions to it treat the *Treasury* with the sincerest form of respect: imitation. Both Saṃghabhadra, one of the leading orthodox Vaibhāṣika thinkers who reacted against the *Treasury*, and the anonymous author of the *Lamp of Metaphysics* borrow many of the verses which form the framework of the *Treasury* for use in their own works.

Second, the *Treasury* was (and is) pivotal for the Indo-Tibetan Buddhist intellectual tradition as a whole and also, to a somewhat lesser extent, for some schools of the Sino-Japanese tradition. It has been used as a basic pedagogical text in the monastic educational curricula of the Buddhist schools of Tibet and Central Asia generally until the present day,[10] and its precise definitions of central technical terms obtained virtually canonical status among the Indian Buddhist intellectuals of many schools. The *Treasury* also quickly gave rise to a vast commentarial and polemical literature, initially in India and then later also in Tibet, Mongolia, China and Japan. In this study I shall make use only of the surviving commentaries produced in India—of which there are no less than seven, all preserved in Tibetan and one preserved also in the original Sanskrit[11]—and not systematically or comprehensively even of those. The size of these texts make any attempt at a complete study of the commentarial literature to the *Treasury* quite impossible at this stage of scholarly investigation. Nevertheless, the importance of this work for later Buddhist thought, even in schools which radically disagreed with its basic presuppositions, can scarcely be overstressed. The text became a kind of Buddhist encyclopaedia and work of reference in which novice scholastics could find—and often memorize—definitions of key technical terms.

The third and final sense in which the *Treasury* is pivotal is in its significance for Western scholarship; the first two phases of the Vaibhāṣika intellectual tradition—the unsystematic commentarial and the proto-systematic—are, except for minor fragments, available to the scholarly world only in their Chinese versions, a fact which creates extreme semantic difficulties in coming to grips with these texts in the context of Indian intellectual history. Chinese and Sanskrit are, after all, very different linguistically and the translation methods adopted by those who translated these works from Sanskrit into Chinese often makes the Sanskrit original, even of specific technical terms and still more of particular sentences, difficult to get at. Then, in contrast, the post-*Treasury* commentarial and polemical literature is, for the most part, available only in its Tibetan versions,[12] a historical fact which creates similar, if slightly less extreme, linguistic difficulties. It is only the *Treasury* itself that survives complete in all three of the major Buddhist canonical languages, Sanskrit, Tibetan and Chinese, and this fact alone makes it of unparalleled significance for the scholarly study of Indian Buddhism.

Before turning to a detailed analysis of what the *Treasury* and its commentaries have to say on the problems surrounding the attainment of cessation, I want to give a brief overview of the contents and nature of the text and of some basic metaphysical views expressed therein; this will be a too brief and too superficial exposition, but something of the kind is necessary in order that the details and technicalities of the discussions of the attainment of cessation in the *Treasury* might make some sense.

First, then, a few words on metaphysics and dharma. Vasubandhu, almost at the end of the *Treasury,* defines his purpose in composing that work in these words (the translation in upper case represents the verse, the *Treasury* proper; that in lower case represents the *Commentary on the Treasury of Metaphysics):*

> I HAVE MOSTLY EXPLAINED THAT METAPHYSICAL SYSTEM WHICH IS ESTABLISHED ACCORDING TO THE INTERPRETATIONS OF THE VAIBHĀṢIKAS OF KASHMIR; I AM TO BLAME FOR WHATEVER IS MISAPPREHENDED HERE, SINCE ONLY THE SAGES ARE AUTHORITIES FOR THE INTERPRETATION OF THE TRUE DOCTRINE.
>
> For the most part I have stated the metaphysical system which is established by the interpretation of the Vaibhāṣikas of Kashmir; I am to blame for whatever I have misapprehended here, since only Buddhas and sons of Buddhas are authorities for the interpretation of the true doctrine.[13]

Here Vasubandhu states what he has tried to do in the *Treasury,* using the usual method of verse-plus-commentary which is difficult to render into English in any way that appears other than pleonastic. He has, it appears, set forth a complete metaphysical system, a metaphysical system for which the Sanskrit term is *abhidharma,* a term related semantically in a complex and interesting manner to the most fundamental category of the entire system, that of dharma itself.[14] Towards the beginning of the *Treasury,* Vasubandhu defines (true) metaphysics *(abhidharma)* as 'flawless wisdom' and notes that the term also refers to the text(s) which help in producing that wisdom.

'Flawless wisdom' here means investigation of dharmas, observational analysis of what there is in the world; and what there is in the world is just dharmas, existents that possess their own uniquely defining characteristic.[15] The fundamental soteriological importance of such observational analysis and categorization of the existents that make up the world is described thus:

> APART FROM CLOSE INVESTIGATION OF EXISTENTS THERE IS NO MEANS OF PACIFYING THE PASSIONS; AND IT IS BECAUSE OF PASSIONS THAT THE WORLD WANDERS IN THIS OCEAN OF BEING. HENCE, THEY SAY THAT THE TEACHER SPOKE THIS [TEXT].
>
> Because there is no means of pacifying the passions without close investigation of existents, and because it is the passions that cause the world to wander in this great ocean of transmigration, therefore they say that the teacher—which means the Buddha—spoke this metaphysical system aimed at the close examination of existents. For a student is not able to closely investigate existents without teaching in metaphysics.[16]

A stronger claim for the importance of philosophy could scarcely be made: correct (propositionally expressible) knowledge about the existents which comprise the universe is seen as a necessary condition for the 'pacifying of the passions' which is in turn a necessary condition for, or in some formulations identical with, the attainment of salvation itself. And the *Treasury* attempts to provide a systematic presentation of precisely this knowledge, basing itself upon the category of dharma.

In the terms of the *Treasury* itself, a dharma is that which possesses its own unique defining characteristic *(svalakṣaṇa)* and that which exists inherently *(svabhāva)*. There are, naturally, many things which exist but which do not have their own inherent existence; for Vasubandhu, examples of such existents would be tables, chairs, persons and numbers. Such things are not dharmas, though they do exist in the somewhat limited sense of being possible objects of cognition and possible referents of propositions. A dharma, therefore, is not the only kind of existent, simply one which possesses a special kind of existence, an existence which marks it off from all other possible existents (by the possession of a unique defining characteristic) and which is irreducible because inherent.

Saṃghabhadra, in his critique of the *Treasury*, made the distinction between different kinds and levels of existence very clear.[17] Dharmas exist substantially or genuinely and possess the kind of inherent irreducible existence already mentioned: they cannot be reduced by observational or logical analysis into component parts, since they possess none, and the defining characteristic of any particular dharma is not shared by any other since this defining characteristic is unique. In contrast to this substantial existence *(dravyasat)*[18]—the kind of existence properly predicated of dharmas—there is existence as a designation *(prajñaptisat),* the kind of existence belonging to things simply in virtue of there being linguistic conventions which refer to them. This secondary existence, the result of linguistic convention, belongs to complex compounded entities which are composed of those entities (dharmas) which possess primary or substantial existence. Secondary existence is conventional—though still existence—because the way in which the world is classified and labelled by language is, it is argued, largely the result of specific individual and societal needs and will thus change as these needs change. So, for example, it is said that we use person-language, a set of discourse which uses proper personal names and speaks of individuals acting, intending, living and dying, largely because there is utility in so doing; person-language is not used because there actually (ultimately, substantially) are persons to whom proper personal names refer. And in this it differs, of course, from dharma-language since there actually (ultimately, substantially) are dharmas to which such language refers.

In Vaibhāṣika theory, then, there are two types of discourse which correspond to two types of existent. To put this another way, Vaibhāṣika theory recognizes an ontological distinction between irreducibly real inherently existent uniquely definable existents (dharmas) and conventionally real existents whose (conventional) existence depends upon the dharmas which comprise them. It recognizes also a corresponding linguistic distinction—between dharma-discourse which can possess a truth-value based upon its correspondence (or lack thereof) to reality, and conventional discourse, whose truth-value is necessarily a function of the linguistic and cultural conventions which make it possible. Saṃghabhadra expresses this succinctly:

> Existents are of two sorts: those which exist substantially, inherently, and those which exist as designations. These two categories correspond, in effect, to the distinction between ultimate truth and experiential truth.[19]

Propositions about dharmas can therefore be true or false *simpliciter;* propositions about persons, tables or chairs can be true or false only in so far as: (i) they obey the conventions and rules which give them sense; and (ii) they can be translated into propositions about dharmas. On criterion (i), the truth of propositions framed in conventional discourse is simply defined by the adherence or otherwise of such propositions to the appropriate conventions. On criterion (ii), the truth of propositions framed in conventional discourse is logically dependent upon their translatability into propositions framed in dharma-discourse.

This points up another useful way of viewing the whole *abhidharma* enterprise, or at least the metaphysical enterprise of the Vaibhāṣika theoreticians: it can be viewed as an attempt at a consistent, coherent and complete translation of all conventional discourse into dharma-discourse, an attempt which involves making the claim that such a translation is possible. This is a reductionist enterprise, an enterprise that involves reducing talk of medium-sized perceptible objects to talk of dharmas—which, in the system of the *Treasury* and thus of normative Vaibhāṣika theory in general—are momentary, irreducible, inherently existent uniquely definable things. There are obvious structural affinities between the Vaibhāṣika enterprise viewed in this way and the efforts of the Vienna Circle, including especially the early Carnap, to reduce or translate all factual knowledge-claims into claims about actual or possible experience. There are also obvious differences, the most prominent of which is the fact that the empiricist tendencies of at least some among the Vienna Circle are much less apparent among the Vaibhāṣika theoreticians. But the structural similarity is clear and important, since many of the logical and practical difficulties faced by Carnap and others, difficulties which ended in the effective abandonment of the enterprise, are also faced by the Vaibhāṣika thinkers, and it is not clear that the attempts on the part of the Vaibhāṣika thinkers to deal with these problems are any more successful than those of the Vienna Circle.

But I don't intend to pursue the question of the systematic difficulties facing any such reductionist translation enterprise, other than to note that there are real problems in even formulating the method without violating its principles. For example, the proposition: 'All propositions possess truth-value just in case they are propositions possessing dharmas as referents' produces a common variety of self-referential incoherence resolvable only by assuming that its referent ('all propositions') is itself a dharma—an assumption that produces its own difficulties and tends to end in infinite regress. To pursue such systematic issues, however, would take me far from my goal here, which is simply to provide a sufficiently detailed background account of the Vaibhāṣika metaphysical enterprise to make sense of the debates in the *Treasury* and its commentaries on the attainment of cessation.

Thus far, then, I have suggested that the metaphysical system of the Vaibhāṣikas is an attempt to systematically translate conventional discourse into dharma-discourse, an attempt based upon an ontological distinction between substantially real entities and conventionally real entities. We now need to look a little more closely at the nature of the ultimately real entities, dharmas, as these are understood by the Vaibhāṣika theoreticians. I've already suggested that a dharma has (or is; the formulations in the *Treasury* are not consistently clear as to whether a dharma is anything over and above its individuating characteristic, or whether its existence is to be defined solely in terms of its causal efficacy) a uniquely individuating characteristic and that it exists inherently and irreducibly in the sense that it cannot be further reduced or analyzed into component parts.

In addition to the its uniquely individuating characteristic, each dharma also possesses four general characteristics, four qualities which belong to each and every dharma in virtue of its being a dharma.[20] These general characteristics are origination, decay, endurance and impermanence; they are meant to explain in precisely what sense each existent is impermanent and what becomes of a dharma when it makes the transition from the present to the past, that is, when it ceases to be a functioning existent located in present time and becomes a non-functioning existent located in past time. The extensive scholastic debates surrounding this question in the *Treasury* show how problematic this question was for the theorists of the Sarvāstivāda school. Their problems were largely caused by the necessity of holding together the idea that everything is impermanent with the idea that past existents must still in some sense exist in the present since they are capable of being both objects of cognition (for example, in memory) and referents of propositional truth-claims. The essentially intentional model of consciousness used by the theorists of the Sarvāstivāda requires that every object of cognition and every referent of a proposition should exist: according to this model one cannot cognize a non-existent. And since it is clearly possible to both cognize and speak about past events, there must be a sense in which past events continue to exist in the present. The attempt to provide an account of how this can be the case produces metaphysical constructions which are peculiar, among Buddhists, to the Vaibhāṣika philosophers; its details cannot be pursued here,[21] and I mention it only to point out that each uniquely individuated and substantially existing dharma also has general characteristics which it shares with every other dharma.

The most important, for the purposes of this study, of the general characteristics shared by all dharmas is that of impermanence. In the *Treasury* this is defined very strictly in the sense of momentariness. All dharmas are said to be momentary in the following sense:

> What is a moment? To predicate the term 'momentary' of something is to say that immediately it obtains existence it is destroyed[22] . . . Since every conditioned thing does not exist subsequently to obtaining existence, it is destroyed precisely where it came to be.[23]

Momentary existence, predicated of all dharmas, therefore appears to be existence for the shortest imaginable time-span. The Vaibhāṣikas come close, on occasion, to defining a moment in terms of the time it takes for a dharma to perform its required causal activities,[24] and thus to defining a dharma solely in terms of what it effects causally. But this is not a consistently held view, and there are also attempts to define a moment in more precise temporal terms. For example, there is the view that there are more than 65 moments in the time it takes for a strong man to snap his fingers.[25] But the central point is that dharmas are momentary and that a moment is intended as the shortest possible unit of time.

Vaibhāṣika metaphysics, as classically expressed in the *Treasury*, distinguishes a total of 75 dharmas and divides and classifies them in numerous ways depending upon the objects at hand. The most common classification is a fivefold one to which I shall return in a moment. It is important to realize that the scheme of 75 dharmas, defined and exhaustively discussed in the *Treasury*, which intended to provide an exhaustive account of what there is in the world, an exhaustive ontology, is not intended to claim that there are only 75 momentary, uniquely individuated existents in the world. If such were the case, presumably the world—everything that is the case—would exist for (at most) 75 moments (assuming that the 75 dharmas existed serially and not simultaneously), or, given the measure just mentioned, for only slightly longer than it takes a strong man to snap his fingers. This is clearly not what is intended by the 75-dharma scheme; rather, the 75 dharmas are meant to provide an exhaustive taxonomy, a classification of all the possible types of existent. For example, there is a dharma called 'ignorance' *(avidyā)*. There is not just one uniquely individuated momentary occurrence of ignorance. Instead, the dharma 'ignorance' refers to a theoretically infinite set of momentary events, all sharing the same uniquely individuating characteristic and all sharing the same kind of inherent existence. Dharmas are therefore uniquely individuated, marked off from all other possible events, not in the sense that there can be no other momentary event sharing the individuating characteristic of a given momentary event, but rather in the sense that each and every momentary event within a particular set of such events is marked off from each and every momentary event within every other possible set. And there are (according to the Vaibhāṣikas; other schools differ) only 75 such sets, each containing a theoretically infinite number of members. Finally, the conclusion follows that every member of a given set must be phenomenologically indistinguishable from every other member since all share the same essential existence and the same individuating characteristic. They can be distinguished one from another only in terms of their spatio-temporal locations.

Dharma-discourse is thus primarily taxonomic in intent, though, as I have suggested, it also has very definite ideas as to the ontological status of the events it classifies. My final task in this introductory section, then, is to say something of the categories defined by the *Treasury* in its attempt to provide a complete classification of all types of existent. I shall follow here the standard fivefold division without attempting to cover every one of the 75 dharmas.[26] According to this fivefold division, then, there are physical dharmas, mental dharmas, dharmas related to mind, dharmas separate from both matter and mind and unconditioned dharmas.[27] Under the heading of physical dharmas, Vasubandhu provides a list of categories designed to allot a place to all possible physical events, and this is done through the categories of sense-organ and sense-object (five of each) plus one category of 'unmanifest physical form' which has a special place in Vaibhāṣika karmic theory.[28] Such things as taste, smell and tangibility are therefore dharmas. Under the heading of mental dharmas there is a single category; that of mind itself. Under the heading of dharmas related to mind there are 46 categories, covering all types of mental event regarded as both phenomenologically and essentially distinct one from another.

The relative weighting of the dharma-lists between the mental (a total of 47) and the physical (a total of 11) shows where the major interests of the architects of this metaphysical system lay and, I think, suggests something about the historical origins of the entire system. It is arguable, though by no means certain, that the *abhidharmic* taxonomic enterprise had its origins in the practice of certain types of introspective analytical meditation which were highly valued in the early Buddhist tradition and which essentially require the practitioner to deconstruct the *gestalt* of everyday experience into its component parts and to learn to label and identify the separate and transient mental events from which Buddhist theory thinks the continuities of everyday experience are constructed.[29] Once the importance of such meditational practices was assumed by the tradition, a corresponding significance was granted to the intellectual enterprise of developing a systematic metaphysic which was adequate to the task of classifying the mental events perceived by introspection. This historical explanation goes some way towards explaining the greater interest of the systems in mental events than in the nature of the physical universe.

At this point some terminological clarification is in order, since there are a number of important Buddhist technical terms having to do with mind and the mental for which it is not easy to find precise and useful English equivalents. Briefly, 'consciousness' *(vijñāna)* refers, for the most part, to that specific kind of mental event in which an object is apprehended; the occurrence of such events is causally dependent upon interaction between sense-organs and their objects, and they are thus subdivided into six kinds in accordance with the division of sense-organs into six—the mental faculty, the olfactory, the tactile, the gustatory, the visual and the auditory. There are thus six groups or classes of mental events which are referred to in this study by the term 'consciousness'.[30] Intentionality is thus a key element of consciousness; to be conscious, on this view, is to be conscious of something. By way of contrast, 'mind' *(citta),* sometimes also translated 'mental events', is a more general term. As I have already pointed out, 'mind' is the second of the standard five divisions, and 'dharmas related to mind' is the third; between them, these two categories account for 47 of the 75 dharmas, and it is generally true to say that the 46 mind-related dharmas are, both conceptually and etymologically, parasitic upon the category of mind. 'Mind' or 'mental events' then, in this study, will refer technically to any event classified by the Vaibhāṣika theoreticians as not belonging to any of the other three divisions (those dharmas considered to be physical; those considered to be neither mental nor physical and those termed 'unconditioned'). Less technically, this means that 'mind' ('mental events') will include attitudes, emotions, the activity of category-formation and all instances of consciousness.[31] Thus when the question of how mind can emerge from a mindless condition is asked (in Section 2.3), the intention is to cover any possible mental event, and when we find debates about the possible existence of consciousness in the attainment of cessation (in Section 2.3.3), the point is to ask whether there can be any intentional mental act in that condition. This distinction should become clearer as we proceed.

Another question which has been somewhat pressing in recent Western philosophy of mind is that of whether there are any criteria which can be used to effectively demarcate mind from body, the mental from the physical. This is not a question explicitly discussed at any length in the systematic texts of the Vaibhāṣika tradition; the thinkers working within that tradition seem to have found the distinctions sufficiently obvious to be unproblematic. By using the definitions of physical form found within the key texts of the traditions and abstracting somewhat therefrom, we can arrive at the position that the key defining characteristic of the physical for this school was taken to be resistance, which requires extension and spatial location.[32] It is this, above all, which distinguishes physical dharmas from mental: the former have extension and location, the latter do not. Physical and mental dharmas also, as I shall show in more detail when discussing the debates surrounding the possible causal relations between them, have different functions, different kinds of effect. Perhaps most notable here is the connection of mind and the mental with action-theory and ethics. According to Vaibhāṣika theory (and, indeed, most Buddhist theory on such matters), only dharmas classified as mental can have morally qualified effects upon the future of the continuum in which they originally occurred. Indeed, only mental dharmas can be morally qualified.

The Vaibhāṣika dualism between mental and physical, then (it should also be remembered that there are categories of dharma which are neither mental nor physical; but to discuss them in detail here would complicate the picture needlessly), is not quite appropriately described either as a dualism of substance or a dualism of attribute. Both mental and physical dharmas are substantial in the sense already indicated, but their substantiality does not have a great deal to do with the distinction between them. It is not the case, as it was for Descartes, that there are fundamentally two substances in the universe, a *res cogitans* and a *res extensa*, and the problem is therefore not, as it was for him, to provide an account of the interactions between them. Rather, for the Vaibhāṣikas, there are 75 distinct classes of substance in the world, each class possessing an infinite number of members, and each member existing (inherently and substantially) for only an instant. It is not that each mental event (or physical event) is a property of a substance, as is the case on the usual Western dualistic models. Instead, the substantiality of each event, physical or mental, is definable in terms of its functions. What a given event is, is (usually) reducible to what it does. On this model, then, the broad overarching distinction (additional to the 75-fold classification) between physical and mental is constructed phenomenologically and refers to different kinds of function. The problem for the Vaibhāṣika theorist is to construct a theory which will specify all the possible complex kinds of causal interaction which can obtain between the (infinitely many) members of the dharma-sets designated 'physical' and 'mental'. To put this another way, the Vaibhāṣika theorist must decide how thoroughgoing the functional dualism between physical and mental actually is, and how close the causal connections between the two classes may therefore become. One aspect of this debate will become clear in my analysis of the discussions surrounding the attainment of cessation.

To return to the fivefold division of dharmas. The fourth division points to dharmas that are separate from both matter and mind. There are 14 dharmas under this heading, providing categories such as 'homogeneity of species', 'origination' and so forth. This is an extremely miscellaneous list. The only obvious common factor among the categories presented here is that none of them can easily be placed within the basic division between matter and mind and that they are all *ad hoc* creations, categories designed to deal with a specific problem internal to the system rather than categories required by the tradition. It is significant that there is no precise analogue to this set of categories in the developed metaphysics of the Theravāda tradition.

The fifth and final division is that of the 'unconditioned dharmas', comprising only three categories.[33] These are distinct from the other four groups in that there is a sense in which they do not share the basic characteristic of all the other dharmas, that of momentariness. This provides some qualification to my earlier discussion of momentariness as though it applied to all existents, but it is not one that need concern us further here, since the problems connected with this category have no relevance to the attainment of cessation.

To recapitulate, the *Treasury* distinguishes between dharma-discourse and conventional ordinary-language discourse, claiming that the latter is entirely translatable into the former and that only the former possesses truth-value. The referents of dharma-discourse, naturally enough, are dharmas, momentary uniquely individuated existents, each of which can be classified as belonging to one of 75 categories. The basic division among these categories, simplifying the fivefold division discussed above, is that between physical dharmas, mental dharmas and those which are neither physical nor mental but which are, by and large, *ad hoc* categories designed to deal with specific problems. The attainment of cessation, my major concern in this study, is itself a dharma-category and is one of those 14 dharmas which are neither physical nor mental. It shares, of course, all the other characteristics of dharmas in general; it is momentary, possesses a uniquely individuating characteristic and exists inherently. To a more detailed presentation of the Vaibhāṣika debates surrounding it I shall now turn.

2.3 THE ATTAINMENT OF CESSATION IN THE *TREASURY OF METAPHYSICS* AND ITS COMMENTARIES

Much of the discussion in Chapter One (especially Sections 1.2 and 1.3) also applies here, since the canonical discourses from which the definitions of the attainment of cessation were drawn in the Theravāda tradition were also recognized and used by the Vaibhāṣikas. I shall not go over once again the ground covered there; what is said here will concentrate instead upon what is distinctive in the Vaibhāṣika treatment of the attainment of cessation.

The *Treasury of Metaphysics,* as already indicated, treats the attainment of cessation as a dharma and classifies it as neither physical nor mental. It is, nevertheless, a dharma, or rather a set of dharmas, a set of momentary events which exist substantially—as things—and which are marked off from the members of every other such set by their unique defining characteristic(s). The definitions given of the attainment of cessation in the *Treasury,* then, are best understood as an attempt to describe these characteristics and thus to justify the postulation of the attainment of cessation as a (set of) dharmas.

Vasubandhu begins by defining the attainment of cessation as 'the cessation of mind and mental events' and stating that it is identical in this respect to another dharma which is neither physical or mental, the attainment of unconsciousness. The place of this dharma, an altered state of consciousness phenomenologically indistinguishable from the attainment of cessation, within the Vaibhāṣika presentation of the path to salvation is presented diagramatically in Appendix A. Like those of the Theravāda, the Vaibhāṣika theoreticians preserve the structure of four *dhyānas* of form and four formless attainments, culminating in the attainment of cessation; they differ in that they include this extra altered state of (un)consciousness, phenomenologically identical with the attainment of cessation but obtainable at a lower stage of the hierarchy and by different classes and grades of practitioner. Like the attainment of cessation, the attainment of unconsciousness also permits no mental events to occur while it is in operation, and, also like the attainment of cessation, it is obtained by enstatic methods, a gradual reduction of the contents of consciousness by progressive withdrawal of the practitioner from interaction with the outside world. The reasons which prompted the Vaibhāṣika theoreticians to introduce this category into their system are complex and have to do almost exclusively with matters raised by the internal logic of the system itself; a discussion of them here would not further the investigation of the philosophical problems surrounding the attainment of cessation. In what follows I shall ignore many of the scholastic details and concentrate instead upon the philosophical issues; my treatment of Vasubandhu's text and of the commentaries upon it will therefore be extremely selective.

Having defined the attainment of cessation as cessation of mind and mental events, Vasubandhu then points out that it can be reached only by 'noble individuals', those persons who have entered upon the practice of the Buddhist path proper and are differentiated thereby from ordinary people.[34] One reason why the attainment of cessation is not regarded by the Vaibhāṣikas as open to ordinary people, non-practitioners of the noble Buddhist path, has some philosophical interest. Vasubandhu tells us that ordinary people cannot enter the attainment of cessation because they would regard it as non-existence *simpliciter* and would therefore fear it. Why then, Yaśomitra asks, do ordinary men not fear entry into the attainment of unconsciousness—which is open to them—since this also involves the complete cessation of mental events? The answer given is that ordinary men do not fear non-existence when they enter the attainment of unconsciousness because this attainment occurs in the sphere of form, and the physical body of the practitioner therefore continues to exist. There is thus some reason for an ordinary man to think that he will not completely cease to exist if he enters the attainment of unconsciousness. His body provides an anchor of sorts, and, as Yaśomitra points out, most of us are reasonably attached to our bodies and come close to identifying our continued identity with their continued identity. In contrast, the attainment of cessation occurs on the formless plane, after the mastery of the formless attainments, and thus in it even the body ceases to exist.[35]

Much of the remainder of Vasubandhu's discussion of the attainment of cessation is concerned with debates on matters such as whether, once attained, it can be lost, how it differs from the attainment of unconsciousness, whether its attainment results from effort or is spontaneous and so forth. The philosophically interesting part of his discussion begins when he asks the question: 'How can mind arise once again from a mind long since brought to cessation?'[36] Both Vasubandhu and his commentators distinguish a number of possible positions on this issue and attribute them to different schools. Yaśomitra's commentary to this section of the *Treasury* gives a useful programmatic statement of the position of the schools on the key issue of whether the attainment of cessation permits the continued existence of mind *(citta):*

> On this question the Vaibhāṣikas and others attribute mindlessness to the attainments of cessation and unconsciousness together with [the state of] unconsciousness; the Elder Vasumitra and others say that these attainments possess mind—an unmanifest thinking consciousness; the Yogācārins, among others, say that these attainments possess mind—the store-consciousness. Such is the division of the schools.

Vasubandhu's *Treasury* expounds each of these basic positions, together with a number of subsidiary positions, in some detail. I shall discuss them following the order in which they are treated in the *Treasury*.

2.3.1 The Vaibhāṣika Position

The first position distinguished by Yaśomitra, that the attainment of cessation is mindless, is attributed to the Vaibhāṣikas and is indeed, as I have already suggested, the normative Vaibhāṣika position.[37] Vasubandhu goes on to expound this position in the following terms:

> The Vaibhāṣikas claim that there is an immediately antecedent and similar condition [for the arising of mind from mindlessness] because of the [continued] existence of what is past.

To understand what this Vaibhāṣika view means, it is necessary to know something of the Buddhist theory of causation, since the Vaibhāṣikas are here claiming that a particular kind of cause—the 'immediately antecedent and similar condition' *(samanantarapratyaya)*—accounts for the emergence of mind from the attainment of cessation. For the Vaibhāṣikas, as for all representatives of scholastic Buddhism, to ask for an explanation of something is essentially to ask for an account of its cause(s). This has already been discussed in Section 1.5 in terms of the Theravāda school, but the basic principle applies equally to the Vaibhāṣika. Events do not occur spontaneously for these Buddhist theoreticians, and there is a specifiable (set of) necessary and sufficient conditions for the occurrence of every event. A large part of the *Treasury* is devoted to explaining, classifying and defining the various kinds of cause which provide connections between events in the world, and the 'immediately antecedent and similar condition' is one of these types of cause. It is explained by Vasubandhu elsewhere in the *Treasury* as a condition *(pratyaya)* which is of the same kind as *(samam)* and immediately antecedent to *(anantaram*—without interval, either temporal or spatial) its effect.[38]

According to standard Vaibhāṣika theory, almost every mental event both has and is an immediately antecedent and similar cause, that is, it has as a necessary condition for its occurrence the immediately preceding mental event in the relevant mental continuum, and itself acts as a necessary condition for the occurrence of the immediately following mental event in the same continuum. The exceptions to this rule include the last moment in the mental continuum of a practitioner of the appropriate soteriological techniques before he attains final Nirvana. This mental event possesses an immediately antecedent and similar condition but is not itself one since no mental events follow it.[39] The question then arises as to whether the last moment of consciousness preceding entry into the attainment of cessation, like the last moment of consciousness before entering Nirvana, possesses an immediately antecedent and similar condition but is not itself one. Conversely, it needs to be asked whether the first moment of consciousness occurring after emergence from the attainment of cessation should be understood as occurring without an immediately antecedent and similar condition while itself being one for the moment that follows it.

The Vaibhāṣika view previously quoted suggests, then, at least the following: first, that the initial moment of consciousness emerging from the attainment of cessation does possess an immediately antecedent and similar condition; second, that this immediately antecedent and similar condition cannot be temporally contiguous with its effect because there are no mental events within the attainment of cessation; and third, by entailment from the first and second points, that it is theoretically possible for an event, X, temporally distant from a subsequent event, Y, to act as the immediately antecedent and similar condition which is a necessary condition for the occurrence of Y. This is the meaning of the assertion that what is past continues to exist. Sthiramati's comment upon this passage draws out the implications:

> 'Because of the [continued] existence of what is past'—if something continues to exist, in what sense is it 'past'? The

> Vaibhāṣika answers: what is past does not possess function, but its essential nature is not lost [and in that sense it exists]. Therefore the Vaibhāṣikas claim that both something which ceased immediately before [what follows it] and something which ceased long before [what follows it] can be immediately antecedent and similar conditions.

It is required, then, by the standard Vaibhāṣika view of causation, that every mental event both have and be an immediately antecedent and similar condition (with the possible exception of the last moment of consciousness before the entry of a given continuum into Nirvana). The last moment of consciousness before entry into the attainment of cessation and the first moment of consciousness emerging from that attainment cannot escape this requirement. Since the Vaibhāṣika metaphysic requires that all dharmas, all members of the small number of sets of uniquely-defined events which are the only things of which existence can properly be predicated, exist trans-temporally, it is not difficult for adherents of this school to move to the position that even a long past event can act as an immediately antecedent and similar condition for a present event, since there is a sense in which that long past event still exists.[40]

The Vaibhāṣikas, then, stress that the 'immediately antecedent and similar condition' for any given mental event must be 'similar' in the sense that it must also be a mental event. But they are more willing to stretch the meaning of the 'immediately antecedent' requirement and to allow a temporal distance between cause and effect. The *Treasury* in fact openly asks whether a dharma which possesses a mental event as its immediately antecedent and similar condition (and all mental events must fulfil this requirement) must thereby necessarily follow without temporal interval upon the mental event which acts as its immediately antecedent and similar condition. That absence of temporal interval between cause and effect is not an entailment of possessing an immediately antecedent and similar condition is shown (to the satisfaction of Vaibhāṣika theoreticians at least) by means of the standard Buddhist logical device of the tetralemma *(catuṣkoṭi)*. This device takes two characteristics, X and Y (in the case under consideration here, X is 'possessing a mental event as immediately antecedent and similar condition' and Y is 'following without temporal interval upon that mental event'), and attempts to provide instances of an existent characterized by X but not Y, an existent characterized by Y but not X, an existent characterized by both X and Y and an existent characterized by neither X nor Y. If instances can be given in all four categories, clearly the relationship between X and

Y is contingent. Possession of X does not entail possession of Y and possession of Y does not entail possession of X. Neither are the two mutually exclusive. The Vaibhāṣikas think that they can provide instances of each of the four possibilities, and while the details of their demonstration of this fall outside the scope of this study,[41] it is worth noting that the first moment of consciousness to occur after emerging from the attainment of cessation is seen by them as an example of an existent which possesses a mental event as its immediately antecedent and similar condition and yet which occurs after a substantial time has elapsed between that condition and itself, i.e., of an existent which possesses X and not Y in the terms of the tetralemma outlined.

The upshot of this discussion is that the Vaibhāṣikas assert (i) there are no mental events in the attainment of cessation, (ii) the emergence of consciousness from the attainment of cessation must have an immediately antecedent and similar condition, (iii) the immediately antecedent and similar condition of any event may be temporally separated from that event and finally (iv) the immediately antecedent and similar condition for the emergence of consciousness from the attainment of cessation is the last moment of consciousness to occur before entering that attainment. Conclusion (iv) is stated explicitly both in the *Treasury*[42] and in another work by Vasubandhu in which the same issue is given some discussion:

> [When the stream of mental events has been interrupted for a long time in the attainment of cessation] how may it begin again? It begins again because it has as its immediately antecedent and similar condition that moment of consciousness wherein [the practitioner] entered the attainment [in question].[43]

I shall show in what follows that the other possible positions outlined in the *Treasury* on the issue of the emergence of consciousness from the attainment of cessation take issue with the Vaibhāṣikas in a variety of ways on all four conclusions outlined.

2.3.2 The Sautrāntika Position

The Sautrāntika theorists disagree with the basic metaphysical postulate that makes the Vaibhāṣika solution to the problem of the attainment of cessation possible; they reject the idea that it is in any sense meaningful to talk of the continued existence of a past object. They therefore also reject the third Vaibhāṣika conclusion discussed in Section 2.3.1: that the immediately antecedent and similar condition of any event may be temporally separated from that event. Yaśomitra, writing from an avowedly Sautrāntika perspective, says this quite explicitly and uses the image of a balance-beam to illustrate the causal relations between past and present events: what is past conditions what is present in the same way that the descent of one end of a balance-beam conditions the rise of the other.[44] No temporal gap is possible. The disagreement between the Sautrāntikas and the Vaibhāṣikas, then, centres upon the issue of whether causation at a temporal distance is possible. Because the Vaibhāṣikas think it is, they are able to suggest that the immediately antecedent and similar condition of the consciousness which emerges from the attainment of cessation is the last moment of consciousness before entry into that condition. This option is not open to the Sautrāntika theorist, who is therefore forced to look for another way of dealing with the issue. The Sautrāntika position is described in the *Treasury* thus:

> But other former teachers ask how it is that physical form arises again for those, born in the formless realms, whose physical form has long since ceased. Their answer is that in such a case physical form arises only from mind and not from physical form; similarly, mind [for one in the attainment of cessation] arises only from the body with its senses and not from mind. For the mind and the body with its senses mutually seed one another.

Vasubandhu does not, in the *Treasury*, explicitly attribute this view to the Sautrāntikas, but both Yaśomitra and Sthiramati do so in their commentaries, and it is clear from other texts that this is the standard Sautrāntika view.[45] The view amounts to this. The consciousness that emerges from the attainment of cessation has as its immediately antecedent and similar condition the physical body of the practitioner in the attainment of cessation. This is possible because, according to the Sautrāntika theoreticians, mind and body, the physical and the mental, 'mutually seed one another'—that is, each is capable of planting seeds in the other, seeds which may lie dormant until the proper time for their maturation occurs. This is an image, a metaphor, rather than a systematized view. It strongly suggests that the Sautrāntikas agree with the Vaibhāṣikas that the attainment of cessation permits no mental events to occur, since there exist only the seeds of mental events planted in the physical continuum. What happens, then, on this view appears to be that the last moments of consciousness before entry into the attainment of cessation plant seeds in the continuing stream of physical events—'the body with its senses'—and that in due time these seeds ripen and produce their fruit, the emergence of consciousness from the attainment of cessation. The analogy mentioned in the extract from the *Treasury* translated above is that of the emergence of physical events—the coming into being of a new body—for those who have for a time entered the formless realms where no bodies exist. For those in the formless realms only mental events occur, and yet it is generally accepted by all Buddhist schools that it is perfectly possible, and indeed common, for practitioners to frequently go back and forth between the realms of form and formlessness, and that when they do so new bodies come into being for them with mental events as their immediately antecedent and similar conditions. Why not then, say the Sautrāntikas, allow that the same can happen in reverse?

I suggested in Section 2.3.1 that the Vaibhāṣikas wanted to preserve the idea that the consciousness emerging from the attainment of cessation does in fact have an immediately antecedent and similar condition, but that in allotting this function to the temporally distant last moment of consciousness before entering the attainment they were prepared to loosen the stringency of the 'immediately antecedent' part of the definition. The Sautrāntikas also wish to preserve the necessity of an immediately antecedent and similar condition for the emergent consciousness, but by allotting that function to the 'seeded' physical body they are forced to loosen, almost to the point of disregarding, the requirement that the relevant condition be 'similar'. For it is difficult to see even a 'seeded' physical body, a continuum of physical events, as being generically the same kind of thing as a continuum of mental events. And it is precisely on this ground that Sthiramati, in his commentary to the *Treasury,* offers criticism of the Sautrāntika view. It should be remembered, when reading what follows, that Sthiramati is writing essentially from the Yogācārin viewpoint. Sthiramati's comment reads thus:

> If [as the Sautrāntikas claim] consciousness can arise from the body with its senses without reference to the cause which assures homogeneity of species, then, when there exists both basis and object, consciousness would occur simultaneously everywhere. But if, on the other hand [as the Vaibhāṣikas claim], mind arises subsequently by way of connection to that state of mind which existed prior [to it], then, since there is no immediately antecedent and similar condition for the second [i.e., subsequent] state of mind the conclusion is that, even when basis and object exist, there could be no simultaneous arising [of the relevant consciousness]. And if it is asked how, in the absence of mind, [mind] can arise from a seed by means of the mindless body with its senses, [the answer is] that this is not possible because there is no distinct cause [for such a thing to occur].

Sthiramati here makes three separate points. First, he suggests that the Sautrāntika view must be wrong because it ignores the necessity to take into account the 'cause which ensures homogeneity of species' *(nikāyasabhāgahetu)*, a cause which ensures that an effect is in some significant way like its cause. This causal principle, for example, is the one which ensures that the sexual intercourse of two human beings always produces other human beings as its result and not, say, elephants.[46] To assert that the mind can arise with the body and its senses as cause, thinks Sthiramati, is to assert that it can arise from something different in kind from itself. The result is that the kind of consciousness which occurs at any given moment need not be causally dependent upon the combination of sense-organ (described by Sthiramati in the translated extract as 'basis'—*āśraya*, a standard term for the sense-organs) and sense-object. For example, when the eye (visual sense-organ) and a visual sense-object come into contact, the function of the 'cause which ensures homogeneity of species' is (among other things) to guarantee that visual consciousness results rather than, say, auditory or olfactory consciousness. Thus Sthiramati suggests that if the cause which ensures homogeneity of species is ignored—as the Sautrāntikas appear to do with their theory of mind originating from body (or, more precisely, from mental 'seeds' in a physical continuum)—then any kind of consciousness whatever could result, or many types at once. Sthiramati's first point, then, amounts to the view that to allow that something physical may be the primary cause of a (series of) mental events is to create a totally arbitrary causal system. Restrictions on what can cause what would no longer apply.

Sthiramati's second major point is directed more towards the Vaibhāṣika position expounded in Section 2.3.1. If every mental event requires a previous mental event as its immediately antecedent and similar condition, and if—as this position entails—the body cannot be the immediately antecedent and similar condition of any mental event, then there can be no such condition for that mental event which consists in emergence from the attainment of cessation, not even when sense-organs come into contact with appropriate sense-object (usually a sufficient condition for the occurrence of a particular type of consciousness).

Sthiramati's third point is a criticism of the Sautrāntika image of seed. From Sthiramati's point of view, in order that mental events may begin again after entry into the attainment of cessation a distinct and specific cause is required—an immediately antecedent and similar condition. The general fact of the continued existence of the 'seeded body' in the attainment of cessation will not suffice. What mechanism accounts for the ripening of the seeds of consciousness at a given time? How, exactly, can seeds (which are mental insofar as they are 'planted' by mental acts, intentions, and insofar as they can be a direct cause for the reemergence of mental events from a condition of cessation) subsist in a physical continuum? I shall return to these problems later in Section 2.4.

In sum, the Sautrāntika position—if indeed it can be formalized sufficiently to dignify it with the name—amounts to the following: (i) there are no mental events in the attainment of cessation (this in agreement with the Vaibhāṣikas, with the caveat that the 'seeds' with which the physical continuum in the attainment of cessation is endowed may mature into mental events); (ii) the emergence of consciousness from the attainment of cessation must have an immediately antecedent and similar condition (implied but not stated explicitly; again, this is in agreement with the Vaibhāṣikas); (iii) the immediately antecedent and similar condition of any event may not be temporally separated from that event (again, I draw this conclusion from what is suggested by the material surveyed above. This is contra the Vaibhāṣika position) and (iv) the immediately antecedent and similar condition for the emergence of consciousness from the attainment of cessation is the continuing physical continuum (the body) with its senses and its 'seeds' of future mental events. Once again, a clear statement of this position is found in another work of Vasubandhu's, the *Treatise Establishing Karma (Karmasiddhiprakaraṇa):*

> Others say that [the consciousness which emerges from cessation] comes from the seeds of [the consciousness which entered cessation], based upon the body with its senses.[47]

This position involves some complications not yet mentioned; to expound those it is necessary to turn to the debate between Vasumitra and Ghoṣaka on this question outlined in the immediately following section of the *Treasury.*

2.3.3 The Debate between Vasumitra and Ghoṣaka

Following his statement of the Vaibhāṣika and Sautrāntika positions, Vasubandhu gives some details of a debate on whether mental events actually can occur in the attainment of cessation. He begins by stating the views of Vasumitra:

> The Bhadanta Vasumitra, on the other hand, says in the *Paripṛcchā:* 'This [i.e., the question of how mind arises from mindlessness] is a problem for one who thinks that the attainment of cessation is mindless; in my view, though, this attainment possesses mind [so there is no problem].'

Vasumitra, then, sidesteps the question of how mind can re-emerge from a mindless condition by denying that the condition in question —the attainment of cessation— is really mindless. As shown by the commentators quoted and discussed in the translation of this passage in Appendix B, the kind of mental events which Vasumitra thinks continue to exist in the attainment of cessation are described by the phrase 'unmanifest thinking consciousness' *(aparisphuṭamanovijñāna).* In Vasubandhu's *Treatise Establishing Karma,* it is made a little clearer what this is supposed to be:

> There are two kinds of mind: one that accumulates many 'seeds'; another that is multiple in virtue of its varieties of different objects and modes [of functioning]. [The attainment of cessation] is called 'mindless' because it does not possess the second, just as a seat with only one leg is said to be without legs.[48]

The 'unmanifest thinking consciousness', then, appears to be a kind of receptacle for the 'seeds' (already discussed in my analysis of the Sautrāntika position). It is, in essence, a consciousness with no intentional object, a consciousness that does nothing but provide a continuing mental 'something' which ultimately will act as cause for the re-emergence of mental events (active consciousness, consciousnesses with intentional objects) from the attainment of cessation. There is an obvious objection to the postulation of this kind of consciousness, raised at once by Ghoṣaka, Vasumitra's opponent in the debate recorded by Vasubandhu in the *Treasury:*

> The Bhadanta Ghoṣaka says that this is incorrect, since the Lord has said: 'Where consciousness exists there is contact, which is the conjunction of the three. Further, sensation, conceptualization and volition are conditioned by contact.' Hence, [if consciousness does exist in the attainment of cessation as Vasumitra suggests] sensation and conceptualization could not cease therein.

This is somewhat telegrammatic as it stands. Sthiramati's commentary makes clear exactly what Ghoṣaka's position amounts to. He thinks that the existence of consciousness entails also the existence of sense-organ and sense-object, and that the existence of these three together is both a necessary and sufficient condition for the existence of 'contact' *(sparśa).* 'Contact' is in fact defined in the extract translated here as the 'conjunction of the three', the three being sense-organ, sense-object and sensory consciousness. The occurrence of contact, understood in this sense, is, on Ghoṣaka's view, a sufficient condition for the occurrence of sensation, conceptualization and so forth. His conclusion is that if any kind of consciousness whatever is allowed to exist in the attainment of cessation—and this, as I have shown, is what Vasumitra wishes to suggest—there can be no possibility of sensation and conceptualization ceasing as they are supposed to do in this trance state.

Ghoṣaka is here expounding the standard Vaibhāṣika view of the nature of consciousness and the mechanisms by which it arises;[49] according to this model, consciousness is always intentional in something approaching Brentano's sense of the term. Every instance of consciousness possesses an intentional object and is the direct result of the interaction of certain classes of mental and physical events: this is the meaning of the definition of 'contact' given by Ghoṣaka, and if this model is followed, the conclusion must be that to be conscious is always to be conscious of something. Vasumitra's response to this objection is:

> It may be suggested that [contact] could occur [without sensation and conceptualization following]. [This might be suggested because], just as desire is described as conditioned by sensation, and yet it does not arise for an *arhat* when sensation arises for him, so also, when contact occurs, sensation and so forth may not necessarily follow.

Ghoṣaka, as I have just shown, asserted that the occurrence of any consciousness requires contact, which is in turn a sufficient condition for the occurrence of sensation and conceptualization. Vasumitra replies by disputing this interpretation of the Sanskrit term translated here as 'condition' *(pratyaya)*. To say that X acts as a condition for Y does not, on Vasumitra's interpretation, mean that the occurrence of X entails the occurrence of Y, and he illustrates his point by making an analogy. It is a commonplace in Buddhist thought that sensation acts as a condition for the occurrence of desire. If Ghoṣaka's interpretation of conditionality is correct, we would expect that sensation is a sufficient condition for the occurrence of desire. But Vasumitra points out that it is equally commonplace in Buddhist thought to say that sensation can occur without giving rise to desire: the paradigm case here is that of the *arhat*, the 'worthy one' who has eradicated all passions but who is still capable of having sensations. Vasumitra thus provides a counterexample to Ghoṣaka's interpretation of conditionality and suggests that the interpretation supported by this counterexample is the correct one to apply in the case of the relationship between contact and sensation-conceptualization. But Ghoṣaka has a reply:

> But this case is different because of the specification of that [sensation which conditions desire]: desire is described as occurring in dependence upon sensation which results from contact with ignorance. But there is no such specification of contact with regard to the arising of sensation.

Ghoṣaka denies the validity of Vasumitra's counterexample. In that proposed counterexample, he says, it is not said that any and every type of sensation acts as a condition for the occurrence of desire. It is only said that 'sensation which results from contact with ignorance' so acts—a very particular kind of sensation. That is to say, a distinction or specification is made among different types of sensation with regard to their ability to produce desire, but no such differentiation is made with regard to contact as condition for the arising of sensation and so forth. In the latter case, Ghoṣaka suggests, there is a straightforward relationship of sufficient conditionality; in Vasumitra's proposed counterexample, there is also such a relationship once the kind of sensation being referred to has been specified with enough precision.

The debate between Ghoṣaka and Vasumitra centers, then, upon one substantive issue: is it permissible to allow the continuance of any mental events in the attainment of cessation? Vasumitra wishes to do so in an attempt to avoid the problems involved in accounting for the re-emergence of mind from a mindless condition and describes the mental events that so exist as being constituted by an 'unmanifest thinking consciousness'. Ghoṣaka will not accept this possibility because he uses the standard Vaibhāṣika definition of consciousness as intentional and thus cannot conceive of a kind of consciousness which could be 'unmanifest' in the sense of operating only as a receptacle for mental 'seeds'. I shall return to the philosophical implications of this debate in Section 2.4 and in my discussion of the Yogācārin attempt to develop Vasumitra's view in Chapter Three.

2.4 CRITIQUE OF THE POSITIONS

Thus far I have presented an outline account of the major positions on the question of the emergence of mind from the attainment of cessation as these are stated in the *Treasury* and its commentaries. I shall now undertake a more formal restatement of these positions together with some critical assessment of them.

First, consider the major presuppositions. I suggested in my discussion of the Theravāda position (Section 1.5) that some version of the principle of sufficient reason (PSR) was held by that school, and I formulated it there in fairly broad terms:

(1) For the occurrence of any given event, Y, there exists a necessary and sufficient condition, X

The discussions of the 'immediately antecedent and similar condition' *(samanantarapratyaya)* outlined in Section 2.3 require, I think, a rather different formulation for the scholastic positions outlined in the *Treasury*. The adherents of all those positions agree that:

(2) For the occurrence of any given event, Y, there exists a necessary condition, X, which is temporally contiguous with, and phenomenologically similar to, Y

To this may be added:

(3) There are two kinds of event: mental and physical

This, as I have suggested (in Section 2.2), is something of an oversimplication, since there are events which do not belong to either of these classes. But since the existence and status of such events is a matter for intense and complex debate between the schools, and since the details of that debate are beyond the scope of this study, the oversimplification expressed by (3) will suffice. Consider now:

(4) Every event is located in a continuum; every continuum can be (theoretically) individuated from every other continuum

This (4) expresses (part of) the Vaibhāṣika (and largely pan-Buddhist) view of personal identity: a person simply is a continuum *(saṃtāna)* of events—where an event is a dharma and every dharma is a uniquely individuated momentary existent—connected by (theoretically) specifiable causal connections and capable of individuation from other such continuua by (largely) empirical criteria. This is too complex an issue to pursue here, other than to note that the major problem with such a view is to specify the criteria which individuate one continuum from another without at the same time postulating an entity which is something other than a momentary existent, a constituent of one continuum. The whole issue of the coherence and explanatory power of Buddhist views of the self deserves much more space than I can give it here; I note (4) only as an important presupposition shared by all the schools discussed in the *Treasury*. To (4) should be added:

(5) It is possible that, in a given continuum, C, at a given time, T, there be a complete absence of mental events while physical events continue
(6) It is possible that, in C at T-plus-n, mental events may begin again

These two, (5) and (6), express the canonical definition of the attainment of cessation which occasioned the discussions outlined in Sections 2.1–2.3. If all of (2)–(6) are assented to, there appears to be no way in which some degree of inconsistency can be avoided. Briefly, from (5) and (6) in conjunction with (2) it follows that the first mental event in a continuum wherein for a time there have been none must have a necessary condition which is temporally contiguous to it and phenomenologically similar to it. Presupposition (3) suggests that the only kinds of event which could be phenomenologically similar to the first mental event in a purely physical continuum —(6)—are those which belong to the class of mental events. Then, from (5) and (6) we learn that no member of that class can be temporally contiguous to the mental event described in (6), since there is, of necessity, a period of time (T to T-plus-n) during which no mental events occur in the continuum in question. The only remaining possibility which meets the criteria set forth in (2), (3), (5) and (6) seems to be that the mental event referred to in (6)—the re-emergence of mind from the attainment of cessation—might be caused by an event from a continuum other than C: only thus could it be caused by an event phenomenologically similar to it (and thus mental) and temporally contiguous with it. But this possibility is meant to be ruled out by (4); an entailment of the fact that any given continuum can be individuated from any other is (at least for Vaibhāṣika theorists) that mental events in one continuum cannot act as necessary conditions—in the sense intended by (2)—for mental events in another. The upshot is that the re-emergence of mind referred to in (6) can be accounted for only by modifying one or more of the conditions outlined here. This provides the dynamic tension underlying the debates outlined in Sections 2.1–2.3.

The debates in the *Treasury* suggested several possible ways of modifying the requirements set out in (2)–(6). The Vaibhāṣika position (Section 2.3.1) modified (2) by allowing that, although any given event required for its occurrence an event of the same type, this event need not be temporally contiguous with its result. Thus, for the Vaibhāṣika, the last mental event before entry into the attainment of cessation could properly be described as the necessary condition for the re-emergence of mental events (perhaps after a substantial temporal gap) in that same continuum. The central difficulty with this solution to the problem, as I have already suggested, is the entailment that non-existent events—in this case the long past final mental event before entry into the attainment of cessation—can have causal efficacy. This is intuitively a little odd; it is difficult to see how something which doesn't exist can bring anything about unless there are specifiable causal intermediaries between it and its postulated effect. The Vaibhāṣika theorists themselves were well aware of this and even stated it explicitly and precisely themselves (though in a rather different context): 'A non-existent can effect nothing.'[50] They are therefore forced to bring into play at this point their celebrated thesis that 'everything exists', which means simply that (temporally) past events still exist just insofar as they are able to be objects of cognition and referents of linguistic formulations of various kinds. An extension of this thesis, required by problems such as that under discussion here, is that past events are also, in special cases, able to exert causal influence. Vaibhāṣika theorists, though, were never able to give an account which proved satisfactory to the remainder of the Buddhist intellectual world, of just how this could work—why, for example, does a long past event exert causal efficacy at one particular later time rather than another?—or of how it could be reconciled with another fundamental pan-Buddhist thesis which states that all existents are momentary.

A contrast to the Vaibhāṣika position is that held by Sautrāntika theorists (Section 2.3.2). The Sautrāntikas also feel that they must modify (2), though they do so by adjusting the requirement that the necessary condition for the occurrence of any event must be phenomenologically similar to it. They suggest, in effect, that the necessary condition for the occurrence of the first mental event in a continuum which has until that point been without mental events for a while can be a physical event, or at least a somewhat peculiar mixture of physical events and mental potentialities. The Sautrāntikas call this, as I have shown, the physical body 'seeded' with mental events. This, as other Buddhist critics have pointed out, is a metaphor rather than an argument. If pushed it reduces either to the position that: (i) there really are mental events in the attainment of cessation—and thus (5) is rejected; or (ii) the re-emergence of mind referred to in (6) is actually caused by purely physical events—and thus (2) is modified. The Sautrāntika tends, I think, more towards (i) than (ii); the dualism between mental events and physical events which has been perceptible in virtually all the Buddhist theorists discussed so far runs deep enough that it cannot easily be forfeited. The one thing that Buddhists are almost universally reluctant to do is to allow that an event of either class, mental or physical, can act as a sufficient condition for the occurrence of an event belonging to the other. This is not to say that there can, from the various Buddhist perspectives on the relations between the physical and the mental, be no causal relations between mental and physical events. The discussions of sensory consciousness and 'contact' in the debate between Vasumitra and Ghoṣaka (Section 2.3.3) show that some forms of causal interaction are required; Buddhists are not adherents of Leibnizian parallelism. However, they also will not allow that, in the complete absence of mental events, any given physical event can bear a relationship of sufficient conditionality to any given mental event; at most it can be an adjunct necessary condition. I suggest, then, that the Sautrāntika metaphor of 'seed', in this instance at least, tends to reduce to position (ii), and to suggest that there really are mental events in the attainment of cessation, even if they are mental events which are, in some undefined sense, inactive or unmanifest.

This is clearly also Vasumitra's view (Section 2.3.3) with his postulation of an 'unmanifest thinking consciousness' in the attainment of cessation. He wishes to escape the dilemma by rejecting (5) and allowing as the cause for the mental event described in (6) other mental events which are directly temporally contiguous with it. The lengthy debate between Vasumitra and Ghoṣaka on the logical implications of suggesting that consciousness of some kind endures in the attainment of cessation is important because it illustrates effectively the essentially intentional model of consciousness with which the Vaibhāṣikas were working. For them, any moment of consciousness always has an intentional object, and Ghoṣaka concludes from this that the presence of an intentional object entails the occurrence of sensation and of all the other mental events which go with it. Put differently, adherence to the intentional model of consciousness entails that there can be no 'unmanifest' consciousness—no consciousness without an object—as Vasumitra wishes to suggest. Vasumitra seems to have no effective answer to Ghoṣaka's criticisms, since such an answer would require the development of a model of consciousness different from that standardly held by the Vaibhāṣikas, and Vasumitra appears not to have taken that step.

None of the alternatives discussed by Vasubandhu in the *Treasury*, then, appears to be entirely satisfactory, even in terms of the intellectual system within which it operates. The requirements of that system, with its rigid separation between mental and physical events and its equally tight and specific causal requirements, mean that there is no way of adequately accounting for the attainment of cessation as this was canonically defined. Many philosophical problems outlined in this chapter have their parallels to those discussed in the first chapter on the Theravādin attempts to deal with this issue; the major difference lies in the greater rigour with which the Vaibhāṣika theorists state the problem, and in the realization, explicitly stated in the debate between Vasumitra and Ghoṣaka that a full and consistent answer to the difficulty would require the construction of a different model of consciousness to the intentional one espoused by both Theravādins and Vaibhāṣikas. This, in essence, is what the Yogācārin theorists attempted, and the third chapter of this study will deal in outline with their use of the attainment of cessation to demonstrate the existence of a different kind of consciousness.

CHAPTER THREE

THE ATTAINMENT OF CESSATION IN THE YOGĀCĀRA TRADITION

3.1 THE YOGĀCĀRA TRADITION: HISTORY AND TEXTS

The origins of the Yogācāra tradition in India are largely lost to us. The few available pieces of evidence are sufficiently problematic that it is difficult to draw any definite historical conclusions. We simply do not know exactly when, where or, in any detail, why Indian Buddhist thinkers began to develop those philosophical views which have come to be judged by Buddhist historians and Western scholars as especially characteristic of the Yogācāra.[1]

The most that can be said with anything approaching certainty is that there begins to become apparent, in some Indian Buddhist texts composed after the second century AD or thereabouts, an increasing stress on the philosophical importance of considering and analyzing the nature of consciousness and the cognitive process. Such questions had, naturally, been of significance for Buddhist thinkers long before the second century AD, but both the ways in which they are discussed by adherents of the Yogācāra after this period and, in many cases, the philosophical conclusions drawn by such thinkers, are new. This novelty was in large part prompted by an increasing awareness on the part of Buddhist systematic thinkers that there are problems inherent in the largely intentional model of consciousness which had, until the development of the Yogācāra, been standard. Among these are the fact that it is very difficult to give a coherent account of the attainment of cessation.[2] An outline account of these new emphases will be given in Section 3.2 and related to the attainment of cessation in Sections 3.3 and 3.4; at this point, I want simply to give a historical overview of the development of the Yogācāra. In order to do this I shall designate four major phases of the Yogācāra tradition and will outline the major textual resources available for the study of each.

The first phase can be called the pre-systematic and includes the scattered mentions of key Yogācāra themes in sacred texts—texts known as *sūtras,* purporting to contain the words of the Buddha but clearly in these cases, composed long after the time of the Buddha—which span a period from the second to the fourth centuries AD. The key phrase here is one which suggests (although its interpretation is not without problems) that the universe *in toto* is a mental phenomenon, that the only thing which actually exists is mind.[3] This is a key Yogācārin emphasis. The earliest surviving version of this phrase occurs in a sacred text originally composed in Sanskrit but now extant only in Chinese translation; the Chinese translation can be dated fairly precisely to 179 AD, which means that the Sanskrit original must have been composed before that date. Thereafter, the assertion that everything is mind occurs not infrequently in sacred texts, until the famous and explicit uses of it in the *Sacred Text Which Reveals What is Hidden (Saṃdhinirmocanasūtra)* from (perhaps) the fourth century AD.[4] These increasingly explicit statements of the idea that the cosmos is simply a mental phenomenon are in no sense philosophically systematic, largely because of the genre of the material in which they appear. Texts of this kind do not provide analytical philosophical discussion since they are intended to present the word of the Buddha to his faithful hearers; for such analytical discussion we must turn to the texts of the next major phase of the Yogācāra tradition.

This phase may be called the early systematic and is preserved for us in the text called *Stages of Spiritual Practice (Yogācārabhūmi)* and in what have come to be known, following the Tibetan tradition, as the 'five books of Maitreya'. The historical and critical problems surrounding these works are enormous; most of them centre upon questions of date and authorship, issues which fortunately are of only marginal relevance for this study. Here I shall do no more than note the textual resources available for the study of this phase of the Indian Yogācāra tradition and provide some pointers towards the major historical controversies currently under debate by scholars working in this field. Representing the early systematic phase of Indian Yogācāra, then, we have four works of major importance: *The Stages of Spiritual Practice (Yogācārabhūmi), The Ornament of the Sacred Texts of the Great Vehicle (Mahāyānasūtrālaṃkāra), The Discrimination Between Middle and Extremes (Madhyāntavibhāga)* and *The Discrimination Between Things and Reality (Dharmadharmatāvibhāga).*[5]

The first, *Stages of Spiritual Practice,* has already been mentioned. This is an enormous work, partially extant in Sanskrit and entirely extant in both Tibetan and Chinese;[6] it is attributed, almost unanimously by both the Buddhist traditions and by much contemporary Western scholarship, to Asanga, perhaps the most famous and influential of the Indian Yogācāra theorists, a philosopher who probably lived at the end of the fourth and the beginning of the fifth century AD.[7] This attribution is in fact not unproblematic; it is more probable that the *Stages* is, as Lambert Schmithausen has suggested, a scholastic compilation rather than the work of a single author, since it seems to show internal evidence of growth and change.[8] This hypothesis does not, of course, exclude the possibility that Asanga had a hand in at least some parts of the text as it now stands. The *Stages,* then, is an invaluable and encyclopaedic source for the early systematic phase of the Yogācāra tradition. It evidences many characteristically Yogācārin emphases but does not develop them to the full and systematic extent visible in the later phases of the Yogācāra.

The last three works mentioned differ from the *Stages* in that they all consist of verses together with a prose commentary or commentaries. The verses alone, in all three cases, are attributed by the Tibetan tradition to the semi-mythical celestial figure of Maitreya,[9] and, whether or not this attribution is regarded as historically meaningful or acceptable, it is certainly the case that the verse-texts alone are sufficiently terse to make developing a philosophical analysis based only upon them problematic in the extreme. They were not in fact read this way within the Indian traditions; there are major prose commentaries to each of them produced by later (or in some cases almost contemporaneous) Indian Buddhist thinkers, and it is through the medium of such later commentaries that these texts are best approached. When they are so approached—as they invariably will be when they are used in this study—the result is that we gain access not to what I am calling the early systematic phase of Indian Yogācāra, but rather to some later phase represented by the commentator(s).[10] Thus no more need be said about these early systematic verse-texts here, important though they are for a full historical understanding of the tradition.

The third stage in the development of the Indian Yogācāra, and for the purposes of this study by far the most important, is what I shall call the 'classical' stage. This is associated above all with works by Asanga and Vasubandhu, the two greatest scholastic thinkers of middle-period Indian Buddhism. Something has already been said about Vasubandhu and his relationship to the Vaibhāṣika tradition in Sections 2.1 and 2.2, and a fairly detailed discussion of the historical problems surrounding any attempt to date Vasubandhu will be found in the notes to those sections. I shall adopt the position that Asanga was a somewhat earlier contemporary of Vasubandhu, that their joint period of intellectual activity occurred probably towards the end of the fourth and the beginning of the fifth centuries AD, and that together they laid the systematic foundations for all later Yogācāra thought in China and Tibet as well as India.

The textual resources for the study of this classical period are substantial: from Asanga's hand we have the *Compendium of the Great Vehicle (Mahāyānasaṃgraha)* and the *Summary of Metaphysics (Abhidharmasamuccaya),* as well as whichever parts of the *Stages of Spiritual Practice* can properly be attributed to him.[11] Both the *Compendium* and the *Summary* will be used extensively in the discussion that follows. From Vasubandhu we have commentaries upon two texts from the 'early systematic' period, a commentary to Asanga's *Compendium,* and three important short works—*The Twenty Verses, The Thirty Verses* and the *Treatise on the Three Aspects.*[12] These works also will be of importance for the discussion that follows.

The fourth and final stage in the development of Indian Yogācāra consists in the commentarial stage. All texts mentioned thus far attracted the attention of later commentators, some of whom, notably Dharmapāla, Sthiramati and Asvabhāva, developed the ideas contained therein and added interesting new philosophical emphases. The extent of this literature is enormous, and since I shall make only occasional and partial use of it in what follows (notably of Sthiramati's commentaries to Asanga's *Summary of Abhidharma* and Vasubandhu's *Thirty Verses* and of Asvabhāva's commentaries to the *The Ornament of the Sacred Texts of the Great Vehicle* and to Asanga's *Compendium of the Great Vehicle*[13]), it requires no more than a mention here.

The production of texts in this tradition naturally continued outside India, especially in China and Japan and to a lesser extent in Tibet. The major centre today for the study of the Yogācāra in all its historical and cultural forms is Japan: the almost unbelievable quantity of first-rate scholarship on the history and philosophy of Buddhism currently being produced in Japan can be seen at its best in the area of Yogācāra studies, and it is also in this area that the contrast with Western scholarship is most striking. Yogācāra thought, whether in its Indian, Tibetan, Chinese or Japanese forms, has been and remains neglected by most Western scholars studying Buddhism. There are signs that this is changing, but it will be a long time before Western scholarship can approach the achievements of Japanese scholars in this area, if indeed it ever happens. My own debts to Japanese scholarship in what follow are substantial.

In summary, then, the Yogācāra tradition as discussed in this study should be understood as a clearly enunciated set of philosophical positions, expressed classically in Sanskrit texts by Asanga and Vasubandhu dating from the fourth and fifth centuries AD.

3.2 THE YOGĀCĀRA TRADITION: KEY PHILOSOPHICAL IDEAS

3.2.1 Ontology: Representation and Mind

The basic ontological question—what is there in the world?—is answered unambiguously by the Indian Yogācāra theorists of the classical period: they say that there is nothing but mind *(cittamātra)*. Many ways of making this assertion are found in the texts, and there are many synonyms used for the basic term 'mind', but the central point is always the same. Vasubandhu makes a classical and clear statement of this position at the beginning of his *Twenty Verses*.[14] There he says that the entire cosmos—standardly divided into three 'realms' by Buddhist cosmologists[15]—is nothing but 'representation' *(vijñapti)*. This is a technical term which, in contexts such as this, refers to all mental events with intentional objects, all mental events wherein something is 'represented' or communicated to the experiencer. This means that, for example, all instances of sense-perception are necessarily also instances of 'representation'. If, as we have seen was the case for the Vaibhāṣika theoreticians, consciousness is conceived exclusively on an intentional model, involving the idea that to be conscious is always to be conscious of something, it would seem that all mental events without remainder will have to be understood as instances of 'representation' since all of them have intentional objects and all of them thus 'represent' something to the experiencer. This, I think, is what Vasubandhu intends in the *Twenty Verses*. For him, the class of 'representations' is co-extensive with the class of mental events in its entirety. This is suggested by his explicit identification of the term 'representation' with 'mind' *(citta)*—the most general of the many Buddhist terms denoting the mental.

This idea that all mental events are instances of representation is not surprising given what has been said in the preceding chapter about the significance of the intentional model of consciousness. There is, however, an exception for the classical Yogācāra theorists (including Vasubandhu in his Yogācārin phases) to this general rule that every act of consciousness must be intentional, an exception which, though rarely stated unambiguously, seems to allow for a class of mental events which are not intentional. This class is to be identified with the 'store-consciousness'. The importance of this exception for an understanding of the Yogācārin treatment of the attainment of cessation will become clear later in this chapter; that there is an exception to the general rule of the intentionality of consciousness does not affect the central ontological point being made, which is that all instances of experience which appear to be experiences of objects other than themselves are actually nothing but representation, nothing but mind.

The cosmos, then, is straightforwardly said to be nothing more than mental events, and, as Vasubandhu points out, mental representations do not necessarily (perhaps necessarily do not, though this interpretation is questionable) possess, or have as their intentional objects, physical objects external to the mind. Vasubandhu's illustration of this point in the first verse of the *Twenty Verses* is illuminating: the cosmos, he says, is a series of representations of non-existent objects in just the same way that a man with faulty vision (the Sanskrit term used here, *timira,* can mean partial blindness or some eye-defect which results in double vision) sees things which really aren't there, things which look like hairs but are really only imperfections in the eye, or an image which appears to be of two moons when there is really only one. In such cases, Vasubandhu suggests, there is no external object corresponding to the mental representation, and he wishes to extend this analogy to all of the objects in the three-realmed cosmos.

It might appear that these two examples—seeing what seems to be a hair but is really a defect in the retina and seeing two moons where there is really only one—have differing philosophical import. The first might be taken to be an example not of seeming to see something which is really nonexistent, but rather of misinterpreting one's perception of something that actually does exist. In contrast, the second (two moons) example seems unambiguously to be an instance of seeing something which actually isn't there. Despite this apparent ambiguity I think Vasubandhu's central point is clear: he means to speak only of seeing objects which actually do not exist; it is these to which the (apparent) objects in the three-realmed cosmos are compared.[16]

There is clearly a radical difference between the ontology of the Yogācārin theorists and that of the Vaibhāṣikas expounded in the preceding chapter. There we saw a realistic and pluralistic substance-based ontology; here we find an idealistic-sounding firmly anti-substance ontology whose interest is centred almost exclusively upon the workings of consciousness. The question of how and why the Yogācārin theorists developed this new ontology is largely a historical issue and thus not strictly relevant to the purposes of this study. All that need be said about it here is that the idealism of the classical Indian Yogācāra was slow to develop (it is not clearly expressed, for example, in most of the *Stages of Spiritual Practice,* one of the earliest systematic texts of the Yogācāra tradition), and that it appears to have arisen out of an attempt to make ontological generalizations from experiences produced by meditative practices. Buddhist meditational practice has, since the earliest times, included visualization techniques which, among other things, are designed to 'deconstruct' the meditator's everyday experience of enduring medium-sized perceptual objects and to replace it with images over which the meditator has complete control.[17] Such techniques, when taken as relevant to and even necessary for the attainment of Nirvana, salvation, tend to encourage practitioners in the belief that the way things appear as a result of these techniques is likely to be closer to the way they actually are than is the everyday subject-object structure of experience. The important step from the epistemological and psychological point that one can learn to control to a very large extent—perhaps even completely—the nature of one's experience, to the metaphysical and ontological point that all experience represents only itself appears not to have been a difficult one for the Yogācāra theorists to take.[18]

More important than the purely historical issue, though, is the systematic one of exactly how the Yogācārin ontological position as stated so far should be understood. There has been substantial disagreement among scholars, both Western and Japanese, as to whether the Yogācārin ontology should properly be called idealistic.[19] There is disagreement, for example, on the question of whether Asanga and Vasubandhu in the key classical texts already mentioned, are putting forward a primarily epistemological point (that all we have access to is mental representation) or a primarily ontological one (that mental representation is all there actually is). Stated briefly, the position taken in this study is that the ontology of the classical Indian Yogācāra is strictly idealist in the sense that: (i) it explicitly denies that there are any extra-mental entities, and (ii) its whole philosophical interest is centred upon an examination of the workings of consciousness. I find it impossible to understand the *Twenty Verses*, the *Thirty Verses* and the *Treatise on Three Aspects* in any other way.

Support for this view of the classical Indian Yogācāra may be found by looking at the kinds of objection raised against it by Indian philosophers. Vasubandhu outlines some of these objections in his prose commentary to the second verse of the *Twenty Verses*, and it is clear that they are just the kinds of question which have been asked of idealists in the West. They amount to this: if all there is in the world is mental events how can one explain the (apparent) spatio-temporal location of such events? How is it that these events are intersubjective, that they are apparently perceived and experienced simultaneously by a large number of different experiencers? And finally, how is it that mental representations, which have no corresponding external object, can do the kinds of things which (real) external objects can do? One's empty stomach is, after all, not satisfied by food eaten in a dream, and the sword-cuts suffered in a dream-fight are not usually fatal.

I don't wish to pursue in detail Vasubandhu's answers to these questions, given in the remainder of the *Twenty Verses* and, from a rather different perspective, in the *Thirty Verses*. It must suffice to say that he uses examples of dream and collective hallucination to try and show that limitation in time and place, intersubjectivity and causal efficacy can all be explained on the 'nothing but representation' model. There are, as might be expected, severe philosophical problems with this attempt, but they are not directly relevant to the purposes of this study. I shall simply note, therefore, that Vasubandhu asserts unambiguously that only mental events exist, whether designated as 'representations', 'consciousness', 'mind' or 'the thinking consciousness', and that, given this presupposition, his major attempt at explaining the intersubjective and collective nature of our experience centres upon the image of the dream or the collective hallucination. Thus, in the seventeenth verse of the *Twenty Verses* (upper case) and in his prose commentary thereto (lower case) Vasubandhu says:

> ONE WHO HAS NOT WOKEN UP DOES NOT UNDERSTAND THAT THE THINGS HE SEES IN A DREAM DO NOT EXIST (17cd)
>
> In this way the world sleeps, its sleep impregnated with the habit-patterns of false mental construction, seeing unreal objects as

> though in a dream; not being awake one does not properly understand that these [objects] do not exist. But when one awakes, obtaining that transcendent knowledge which makes no false constructions and which acts as an antidote to that [false construction], then, as a result of being face-to-face with a subsequently attained pure mundane knowledge, one properly understands that the objects of sense-perception do not exist. The principle is the same [in the case of awakening from a dream as in the case of realizing that the objects of sense-perception do not exist].[20]

Buddhas, enlightened beings, are of course those who are fully awake (this is one of the meanings of the verbal root from which the term 'Buddha' is derived), and Vasubandhu here suggests that when one is fully awake one will realize that external objects do not exist and that the only thing which does exist is 'mind' or 'representation'. And it is precisely upon the nature of the mental, the operations of consciousness in constructing a world of experience, that all the attention of the Yogācāra theorists is focussed; it was primarily to explain its operations that they developed the theory of the 'three aspects' *(trisvabhāva)* under which experience—which, it must be remembered, is all that there is—functions. To this theory I now turn.

3.2.2 The Functioning of Mind

The idea that experience has three aspects[21] is fundamental to Yogācārin soteriology and epistemology. The notion is a complex one and will not be given a systematic and complete exposition in what follows; I shall concentrate upon those elements of the theory which will be of most relevance for understanding the Yogācārin treatment of the attainment of cessation.

At the beginning of a work devoted exclusively to discussing the three aspects, Vasubandhu defines them thus:

> The three aspects are the imagined, the relative, and the perfected. This is said to be the profound thing which wise men know.
>
> That which appears is the relative because it occurs in dependence upon conditions. The way in which it appears is the imagined because it is simply imagination.
>
> The eternal non-existence of the mode of appearance of what appears should be understood as the perfected aspect; this is because it does not change.[22]

The three aspects, then, are the 'imagined' *(parikalpita),* the 'relative' *(paratantra)* and the 'perfected' *(parinispanna).* These are not ontologically distinct; I have already suggested that for Vasubandhu the only thing which actually exists is mind or representation. Thus the three-aspect theory simply describes different ways in which mind can function, different modes under which experience can appear to the experiencer.

The centrepiece of the theory is the relative aspect of experience. This is simply identified with mind,[23] mind undertood as experience *in toto.* It is called 'relative' because, as Vasubandhu says in the extract quoted, it is 'dependent upon causes and conditions'. Asanga, in his *Compendium of the Great Vehicle,* makes this a little more specific:

> If the relative aspect [of experience] is simply representation, the basis for the appearance of external objects, in what sense is it 'relative' and why is it called 'relative'? [It is 'relative'] because it issues from the seeds which are its own tendencies, and is thus dependent upon conditions other [than itself]. It is called 'relative' because as soon as it has arisen it is incapable of enduring by itself for even a moment.[24]

This extract introduces some more technical terms which need explanation. Asanga tells us that the relative aspect of experience is relative because it is causally dependent upon 'the seeds which are its own tendencies'. Both 'seed' *(bīja)* and 'tendency' *(vāsanā)* are extensively discussed by Asanga in the first chapter of his *Compendium;* there he tells us that tendencies to do this or that—to be passionate, to be hateful, to be greedy—are the result of seeds planted by previous actions. This point is illustrated with the exremely common image of the sesame seed. The sesame seed, itself 'perfumed' by the plant which bore it with the 'tendency' to produce plants which are similarly perfumed, produces the 'tendency' in the flowering plant which grows from it to have a certain perfume, even though the seed itself no longer exists; in just the same way, actions of any kind produce (sow) seeds which in turn issue in 'tendencies' or 'capacities' which will have their effects upon the future actions of the original agent.[25]

The developed form of the seed-tendency theory, found in the classical texts of the Yogācāra, is essentially an attempt to formulate a theory according to which it is possible to combine talk of tendencies or capacities on the part of persons with a metaphysic which denies (i) that there are enduring individuals, and (ii) that there are enduring events. This is one of the basic problems of Buddhist metaphysics, and the peculiar Yogācārin answer to it involves the construction of a theory of mind which goes a long way towards providing a theory which can coherently allow for talk of capacities and tendencies belonging to persons. The cost, of course, is that the theory stands in some tension with earlier Buddhist theories of the person, theories which stress radical impermanence and are thus hard put to it to account for enduring character traits.

However, in the extract from the *Compendium* quoted above the seed-tendency theory is used only to explain what the 'relative' aspect of experience is relative to. It explains that the causes and conditions which govern the ways in which mind functions—the kinds of experience which occur—are essentially the tendencies or habit-patterns produced in the mental life of that particular experiencer by his past actions and intentions. This suggests that the relative aspect of experience, which consists simply in mental representations, mental events of all kinds, is all that there is, but that these mental events can operate in different ways, appear under different aspects, according to the 'seeds' and 'tendencies' of the continuum of mental events in which they occur. And this brings us to a consideration of the other two aspects under which experience can occur: the imagined and the perfected.

Vasubandhu has already told us that the imagined is 'simply imagination' and that it consists in the way in which things appear, the way in which experience constructs a world for itself, in contrast to the fact of its functioning which he identified with the relative aspect of experience. Later in the same text he specifies exactly what this means: the way in which experience functions (for all but enlightened beings) is as duality, in terms of the relationship between subject and object. The imagined aspect of experience consists essentially in dualism, a subject-object structure which does not reflect the way things (according to this theory) actually are. It should be remembered that there is no radical ontological distinction between the relative and the imagined aspects of experience: the latter is simply a mode of the former, a way in which the former sometimes functions or appears. This intimate link between the relative and the imagined is illustrated by the fact that the important technical term 'imagination of the unreal' *(abhūtaparikalpa)*, while used normally of the relative aspect, is also sometimes applied to the imagined aspect. The identification of the imagined aspect of experience with a dualistic subject-object structure is made especially clear in Vasubandhu's commentary to the *Discrimination Between Middle and Extremes* and in

Sthiramati's sub-commentary to that work. Vasubandhu begins in that text by defining the dual structure which is essential to the imagined aspect of experience: he says that it consists simply in the imaginative construction of a dichotomy between subject and object. It is precisely this, he says, which is the 'imagination' of the 'unreal'. Sthiramati goes on to say:

> The term 'imagination of the unreal' means either that in which the duality [of subject-object] is imagined, or, alternatively, that by which such a duality is imagined. The use of the word 'unreal' indicates that one imaginatively constructs this [world] through the categories of subject and object, when [in fact] it does not exist [according to those categories]. The use of the word 'imagination' indicates that external objects do not exist in the way that they are imagined. In this way it had been made clear that the defining characteristic of this [imagination of the unreal] is completely free from [the duality of] subject and object.[26]

Here Sthiramati explains that the imagination of the unreal, which links the first (relative) aspect of experience to the second (imagined) aspect of experience, is characterized by duality, the duality of subject and object, and that in actuality there are neither subjects nor objects. He continues:

> What then is this [imagination of the unreal]? Broadly speaking, the imagination of the unreal is the [totality of] mind and mental phenomena which relate to past, present and future, which consist in causes and effects, which belong to the three-realmed cosmos, which have no beginning, which issue in Nirvana and which conform to Samsara. Specifically, though, it is the imagination of subject and object. Here, 'imagination of object' means consciousness appearing as living beings and inanimate objects; and 'imagination of subject' means [consciousness] appearing as that representation which is the 'self'.[27]

Here it becomes especially clear that the distinction between the imagined and relative aspects of experience is phenomenological rather than substantive. Sthiramati makes it clear that the 'imagination of the unreal' is simply everything there is, every kind of mental phenomenon; the list of 'mind and mental phenomena' in the extract translated above is meant simply as a series of different ways of saying 'all mental phenomena'—those which occur in any time, which are caused or have effects, which issue in salvation or which belong to the world of rebirth and suffering. There is no remainder. This inclusive definition, it will be remembered, is also the definition of the first aspect of experience, the relative. That too is the same as mind or mental representation, which in turn is simply, according to classical Indian Yogācāra, what there is in the world. Thus there is a sense in which the first aspect of experience and the second are identical; the difference between them is one of mode or phenomenological flavour. Vasubandhu says in the *Treatise on the Three Aspects,* as I have already noted, that the relative aspect of experience is simply experience as it appears; the imagined aspect of experience is that same experience (which is all there is) appearing in the mode of a subject—a person—cognizing objects. Both of these are called 'imagination of the unreal' because, ontologically speaking, there are neither persons nor objects; there is only experience.

There is a similar identity-in-difference between the relative and perfected aspects of experience. The perfected is tersely defined by Vasubandhu in the *Treatise on the Three Aspects* as the absence of duality[28] and more extensively by Asanga in the *Compendium* as the complete absence of the imagined aspect of experience.[29] The major point is that the perfected aspect of experience is that wherein experience just occurs, no longer characterized by the (imagined) duality of subject and object. This perfected aspect of experience, then, is also not ontologically distinct from the relative aspect (or the imagined aspect), since the relative is all there is. It is simply the relative aspect of experience occurring without (erroneously) constructive mental activity. It is also, of course, the kind of experience possessed by Buddhas.

It should have become clear in the course of the preceding brief and somewhat abstract account of the three-aspect theory of experience developed by the classical Yogācāra that what we are dealing with here is essentially a theory of the ways in which consciousness operates, the ways in which mental activity occurs. It's true that this theory is apparently based upon an ontological postulate, that only mental events exist (Section 3.2.1), but it is equally true that this ontological postulate is not, for the most part, where the central interest of the Yogācāra theorists lay. They were concerned primarily with describing the operations of consciousness and suggesting how they might be modified with the soteriological goal of producing the experience of Buddhas, a ceaseless stream of 'perfected experience'. To this end they developed a theory of mind substantially different from those already surveyed in Chapters One and Two of this study, and to this, most especially to the idea of the 'store-consciousness' *(ālaya-vijñāna),* I shall turn in Section 3.2.3. Before doing so, though, all that has been said in the preceding pages about the ontological importance of mental representations and the complex relationships among the three aspects of experience needs to be drawn together;

that can hardly be done better than by using one of the many similes used by the Yogācāra theorists to explain their position. I shall use the simile of the magically produced elephant,[30] given in many Yogācāra texts[31] but stated concisely and clearly in the *Treatise on the Three Aspects*. There Vasubandhu says:

> It [viz: the three aspects of experience considered collectively] is just like something which, being made by magic using incantations, appears as an elephant. In such a case there is nothing but an appearance; there is no elephant at all.(27)
>
> The elephant is the imagined aspect [of experience] and its appearance is the relative; the non-existence of the elephant in such a case is considered to be the perfected [aspect of experience].(28)
>
> Thus the imagination of what does not exist appears, based upon the underlying consciousness, as duality [of subject and object]. But duality is completely non-existent; there is nothing but appearance in such a case.(29)
>
> The underlying consciousness is like the magical spell; reality is considered to be like the wooden object [from which the magician constructed his elephant-illusion]; imagination should be undertood as like the appearance of the elephant; duality is like the elephant.(30)[32]

The analogy used here presents the following picture: we have a magician using spells to construct, for some onlookers, the illusion of an elephant. The raw material used for this illusion—the magician's props—are some pieces of wood. The process begins with the use of a *mantra* or magical spell; this is the efficient cause for the appearance of the illusion in question. This, Vasubandhu tells us, corresponds to the 'underlying consciousness', a synonym for the already mentioned 'store-consciousness', to be discussed further in Section 3.2.3. It is by the constructive operations of the mind, here corresponding to the magical power used by the magician, that the illusory elephant is created, and it is the 'appearance' or representation of this elephant in the mind which Vasubandhu identifies with the relative aspect of experience. This identification points up the fact that what the classical Indian Yogācāra means by the relative aspect of experience is simply the totality of (intentional) mental events, all the mental images that actually occur. In the case of the illusory elephant, the mental image or representation that actually occurs is simply one that can appropriately be labelled 'elephant'—without, of course, such occurrence and such labelling entailing or even suggesting anything about the ontological status of the elephant in question.

The imagined aspect of experience, then, continuing to interpret the analogy already set forth, is the way in which the experience of the elephant occurs; not merely the occurrence of the experience, but also the occurrence of the experience in subject-object mode, expressible in the proposition 'I am now seeing an elephant'. This proposition, according to classical Yogācāra theory, erroneously hypostasizes two entities: the subject doing the perceiving and the object being perceived. Neither has any real existence on this theory, and to think that they do—or rather, for experience to occur within these categories—is precisely to be subject to the imagined aspect of experience and thus to hold as true a whole series of propositions which, on this theory, are manifestly false.

At this point it might appropriately be asked what it might be like to experience an elephant, magically created or otherwise, without doing so through the medium of subject-object categories. While no explicit answer is given to this, the classical Yogācāra theorists are quite clear that to experience things without such experience being filtered through subject-object categories is precisely to experience them in the perfected mode. The interpretation given by Vasubandhu of the perfected aspect of experience in the case of the magically created elephant stresses that it involves (at least) the realization of the truth of the propositions 'no elephant exists' and (remembering that the magician in the example used pieces of wood as the material basis for the magical creation) 'what actually exists is the wood from which the magician created the elephant in question'. It does not seem that, by identifying the pefected aspect of experience with 'reality'[33] (in verse 30 of the extract quoted earlier) and by correlating this 'reality' with the pieces of wood used by the magician, Vasubandhu intends to suggest that there actually is some material sub-stratum from which the magical illusion of the cosmos is created. In fact, the treatment of the same simile in another Yogācāra text extends the analogy and makes clear what is meant: it is said that just as the pieces of wood used by the magician are the material cause for the perception of an illusory elephant, so the imagination of the unreal (identified here with the relative aspect of experience) is the material cause of the judgement 'I am perceiving an elephant'. Experience in its perfected aspect simply sees (in the former case) that what there is is not an elephant but some pieces of wood and, in the latter case, that what there is is not a subject perceiving an object but simply the (erroneously) constructive functioning of the 'imagination of the unreal'.[34]

To summarize, the three-aspect theory of experience developed by the classical Indian Yogācāra was intended primarily as a descriptive analysis of how consciousness actually functions. It suggests that consciousness is usually intentional, which means that, phenomenologically speaking, it usually operates dualistically. And this is the imagined aspect of experience. Further, it suggested that the nature of those representations or mental images which make up the flow of everyday consciousness is dependent upon causes and conditions; this is the characteristically Yogācārin way of expressing the pan-Buddhist assumption that everything is caused (for a discussion of which view in its Theravāda form see Section 1.5). And this aspect of experience is called the relative. Finally, the three-aspect theory suggests that it is possible for experience to function nondualistically: this is the perfected experience of enlightened beings, the phenomenological nature of which is sometimes said by the texts to be strictly ineffable, but which clearly involves at least a realization (and an expressible realization) that everything is just mind or just representation. It is with this realization that the connection between the three-aspect theory and the ontological points made in Section 3.2.1 becomes apparent: while the three-aspect theory may be intended primarily as a descriptive analysis of experience, it makes sense only within the context of the (ontological) theory that what there is is just mind. But there is more to the Yogācāra theory of consciousness even than this. The term 'store-consciousness' has already been introduced, and since the elaboration of this concept, involving as it does an important move away from the intentional model of consciousness used by the Vaibhāṣikas and largely presupposed by the three-aspect theory, is of central and direct relevance to the Yogācārin treatment of the attainment of cessation, I shall now briefly describe it.

3.2.3 The Store-Consciousness

The 'store-consciousness' theory, perhaps the most prominent defining characteristic of the philosophical systems developed by the theoreticians of classical Indian Yogācāra, is best understood as an attempt to systematize an image. The image, already pointed to, is that of seed and growth; its philosophical purpose is to provide a picture by means of which Buddhist thinkers could try to make sense of the experienced facts of the continuity of personal identity, such things as memory, continuity of character traits, the continuing sense that each person has of himself as identifiably an individual, identifiably different from other individuals and identifiably the same person as he was in the past. Accounting for such experienced facts (the existence of which, interestingly, no Buddhist thinker makes any serious attempt to deny) becomes a problem, as I have already suggested, when thinking philosophically within the constraints of a system which holds it to be axiomatic that there are no enduring substances, and, *ex hypothesi*, that there are no enduring substances to which personal proper names refer. Without such enduring substances, it is unclear how the experienced facts of personal continuity can be explained, and the problem is made significantly more pressing when the axiom that there are no enduring substances to which personal proper names refer is held together with other, almost equally basic, axioms about the efficacy of action, which is to say of karma.

Briefly, the point is this: Buddhist theoreticians have consistently held as true both the axiom that there are no persons (if persons are understood as enduring substances) and the axiom that every morally qualified volitional action has morally qualified volitional effects upon its agent in the future. The second axiom—which encapsulates in over-simplified form the essentials of Buddhist theories about karma, about action and its effects—seems to require a degree of continuity between the agent of an action and the experiencer of its result which is *prima facie* somewhat difficult to reconcile with the first axiom. It seems to require that, in some more-or-less strong sense, the person performing an action at time T be 'the same' as the person experiencing the results of that action at (say) T-plus-100. We have here, then, two logically separable but historically closely related issues. The first is a problem of explanation: how is it that the experienced facts of personal continuity (including, of course, the issue of rebirth, of multiple lives experienced by 'the same' individual) can be explained while still holding to the truth of the no-self axiom? The second is a problem of internal consistency: how can the axioms dealing with the efficacy of action and its 'location' in persons be coherently combined with the axioms which deny the continued existence of such persons?

The history of Buddhist attempts to deal with these issues is a long and complex one; its details are far beyond the scope of this study.[35] I mention it here only to point to the rationale underlying the development of theories about the store-consciousness. I have already said that the store-consciousness may best be understood as an attempt to systematize an image; the image in question, that of seed and growth, was used by Buddhist thinkers long before the period of the classical Yogācāra and was particularly prominent in the works of the Sautrāntika theorists.[36] In its unsystematized form the image merely says that each action deposits 'seeds' in the continuum of caused momentary events which comprises the 'person' who performed the action, and that these seeds may have no immediate effects upon that continuum. Only later will they 'mature' and bear fruit, which means that only later will they have specifiable effects upon the future of that continuum wherein they were originally planted.

The use of such an image immediately raises questions: where, for example, are the seeds located while they are ripening? Real seeds require a locus, a basis, some earth in which to grow. Can the seed-image be extended in this way, and if it can what sort of locus or basis is intended? The Sautrāntika theorists, who first made extensive use of the seed-image, did not provide a systematic answer to this question. The systematic answer provided by the Yogācārin theorists was simply that there is such an enduring locus or basis and that it is called the store-consciousness. Indeed, one of the major descriptive epithets applied to the store-consciousness is 'that which possesses all seeds'. Asanga, in the first chapter of his *Compendium of The Great Vehicle,* describes the store-consciousness in such terms, and the same epithet is used in almost all Indian Yogācāra texts of the classical period.[37]

The essential point is that the store-consciousness is a philosophical construct designed to account conceptually for the kinds of continuity issue mentioned above, and that the major way in which it does this is through what I have been calling the seed-tendency theory. Briefly stated, this theory suggests that an agent's actions sow seeds in that agent's store-consciousness; these seeds in turn produce—or, perhaps more accurately, simply are—tendencies, character traits, future possibilities of action. They are located in the store-consciousness and will mature and have their effects upon the functions and activities of the agent in the future.

That the store-consciousness is an *ad hoc* category, designed to deal with philosophical problems which could not, on the prevailing Vaibhāṣika and Sautrāntika models of consciousness, effectively be explained, is shown strikingly by the ways in which the existence of such a consciousness is argued for by the theorists of classical Yogācāra. Such arguments (to be treated in more detail in Section 3.3) are almost always of two kinds. The first is scriptural and hermeneutical—to the effect that the historical Buddha really intended to speak of the store-consciousness, even though the record of his pronouncements is scarcely explicit as to his having done so;[38] these scriptural arguments, while vital for the tradition itself and fascinating for the historian of Buddhism, are not of primary interest for the historian of ideas. Members of the second class of arguments usually have the form of negative counterfactuals: without X, Y would not have occurred. Or, without X, Y cannot be explained. And since Y (here standing for such phenomena as the experienced facts of the continuity of personal identity, the enjoyment of karmic effect by 'the same person' as the agent of the original action and trans-life continuity of personal identity) does occur and requires explanation, X (here representing the store-consciousness) must necessarily exist. Such argument-forms are scattered throughout the texts of classical Indian Yogācāra; I shall point to just a few examples.

First, arguments of this form link the store-consciousness with the process of rebirth. The store-consciousness 'grasps' or 'appropriates' a new physical body after the death of the old, and thus the store-consciousness provides the required trans-life principle of continuity.[39] Second, arguments of this type are used to explain how the processes of defilement by passion and purification from passion—key soteriological ideas, of course for all of Buddhism—are possible. The theorists of the classical Yogācāra suggest that these processes, which require that there be cumulative effects of good or bad actions upon an agent, cannot properly be explained without postulating an enduring locus for the karmic seed-tendencies of the purifying or defiling actions in question.[40]

The major functions of the store-consciousness considered as a category in classical Yogācāra theory, then, are explanatory. It should be clear even at this point, to anticipate the argument somewhat, that one of the phenomena which the store-consciousness might be used to explain—which, in fact, it appears to have been in part designed to explain—is that of the attainment of cessation. I shall show in what follows that the classical eightfold proof of the existence of the store-consciousness developed by Yogācāra thinkers stresses this explanatory function of the store-consciousness, and that the attainment of cessation plays an important part therein. It should not pass unremarked that the store-consciousness was thought of even by those who defended it as an innovative and controversial idea; this is sufficiently demonstrated by the fact that it was thought to need proof. Uncontroversial ideas, in Buddhism or anywhere else, rarely need proof. But before doing so, something more needs to be said about the ontological status of the store-consciousness and its relationship to the three-aspect theory of experience, since an understanding of these questions will be important for a proper understanding of the Yogācāra treatment of the attainment of cessation.

First, then, the question of ontological status: if the store-consciousness was constructed as an *ad hoc* explanatory category, and if the kinds of problem it was designed to answer were essentially those connected with continuity, is it regarded by classical Yogācāra thinkers as possessing 'permanence', and if this does turn out to be the case how is the inevitable tension with the earlier and theoretically binding Buddhist stress on radical impermanence dealt with? The Yogācāra theorists were, of course, aware of this problem, since they were not infrequently accused by non-Buddhist (and even some Buddhist) opponents of re-introducing a permanent self, a permanent locus for the continuity of personal identity, into Buddhist theory.[41] The standard reply to this accusation is simply that the store-consciousness too is impermanent, that the seeds and tendencies of which it consists are transitory existents defined solely in terms of their causal efficacy, and that the postulation of the store-consciousness does not, therefore, offend against the Buddhist axiom of impermanence.[42] The issue of whether this answer is philosophically satisfactory cannot be pursued here other than to note that it sounds suspiciously like an instance of special pleading. No Indian Buddhist philosopher, simply in virtue of being such, could happily assent to the proposition that any element of his system is permanent; but there is no doubt that, considering the purposes for which the category of the store-consciousness was developed and the ways in which it is often discussed by Yogācāra theorists, it approaches more closely to permanence than any earlier Buddhist mode of discussing personal identity. Nevertheless, the standard definitions assert simply that the store-consciousness is itself composed of a series of momentary (though self-reproducing) seed-tendencies.

The store-consciousness is clearly also related intimately to the three-aspect theory of experience outlined in Section 3.2.2. Essentially it is the cause of the relative aspect of experience, since it is only in virtue of the seeds and tendencies accumulated in the store-consciousness that conscious experience can occur at all.[43] It is thus, by extension, also the cause of the imagined and perfected aspects of experience, since, as I have suggested, these differ one from another only in the mode under which they operate.

However, the store-consciousness is not strictly identical with any of the three modes of experience since—and this distinction will be very important in what follows—those things in which it consists (seeds and tendencies) do not produce experience while they remain in the store-consciousness. Experience, understood in the sense of conscious intentional mental events, happens only outside the store-consciousness, when the seeds and tendencies therein 'mature' to bring it about. This suggests an important conclusion: the store-consciousness, even though it is in an instance of 'consciousness' *(vijñāna)* and thus should follow the standard Buddhist definitions of consciousness as something which cognizes, something which has an intentional object,[44] does not in fact consist of intentional mental events. The classical Yogācāra texts, in fact, are somewhat equivocal about this; they show a marked disinclination for a straightforward assertion that the store-consciousness simply consists of mental events without objects though this is clearly the direction in which the logic of their thought pushes them. Instead we find them saying that the 'objects' of the store-consciousness are not such that an agent can be consciously aware of them, that they are extremely subtle and that conscious experience does not therefore occur in the store-consciousness.[45] This represents a substantial change in the use of the Sanskrit term I am translating as 'consciousness' and it was essentially this change which made the distinctive Yogācāra treatment of the attainment of cessation a possibility.[46]

In summary, then, the store-consciousness of the classical Yogācāra theorists in India will be treated in this study as an *ad hoc* intellectual construct designed to account for problems of continuity in Buddhist theories of personal identity. It is, of course, much more than this. It has substantial and interesting effects upon the soteriology of the Yogācāra theorists, but these effects—and indeed Yogācārin soteriology as a whole—will have to remain almost entirely outside the purview of this study.

3.3 THE EIGHTFOLD PROOF OF THE STORE-CONSCIOUSNESS

From an early stage in the development of Yogācāra thought, the theorists of that tradition felt it necessary to demonstrate that their key concept, that of the store-consciousness, played an essential explanatory function. Without it, they argue, it becomes impossible to explain, among other things, the processes of death and rebirth, the interrelationships among the six sense-consciousnesses, and individual's gradual purification through appropriate soteriological practice, and his final attainment of Nirvana, and—most significant for the purposes of this study—both the fact of entering into and the possibility of exiting from the attainment of cessation.

To formalize and systematize this demonstration, the Indian Yogācāra thinkers of the classical and commentarial period developed an eightfold proof. This proof is found, enshrined in a brief mnemonic verse coupled with detailed prose exegesis, in substantially identical form in both Asanga's *Stages of Spiritual Practice* and in Sthiramati's commentary to Asanga's *Summary of Metaphysics*.[47] My exposition will be based upon this version of the proof of the existence of the store-consciousness, though it is by no means the only one available.[48] Each argument has the form of a negative conditional: without the store-consciousness certain phenomena cannot be explained or cannot occur, phenomena which do occur and which thus require an explanation.

3.3.1 The Impossibility of Appropriating a New Body

The first argument has to do with the 'appropriation' or taking on of a physical body and with the need to postulate the store-consciousness, or some functional equivalent, in order to explain this process. According to standard pan-Buddhist (and indeed pan-Indian) theories about death and rebirth, every individual undergoes more than one life and thus possesses more than one physical body over time. Put differently, the individual does not cease to exist when a particular physical body dies. This position is somewhat modified in Buddhism because of idiosyncratic non-substantialist theories about what an individual is. But in spite of such difficulties it is still necessary for Buddhist theorists to provide some account of how new bodies are 'appropriated' at the beginning of new lives, and the first argument suggests that no such account can be given unless the existence of the store-consciousness is agreed to.

The first argument turns upon some important presuppositions, the most significant of which are the definition of the six 'functioning consciousness' *(pravṛtti-vijñāna)* and certain ideas about karma, action and its effects. The 'functioning consciousnesses' are the standard six sense-consciousnesses (the familiar five plus the mental consciousness—the organ of thought is, for Buddhists as for most Indian theoreticians, just as much a sense as the eye or the ear). Each of the six senses has a consciousness belonging to it; this means simply that all intentional mental events may be divided into six categories depending upon which sense-organ they are primarily related to. Thus we have 'visual-consciousness-events', mental events which have as their object something cognized by the eye, and similar classes of event belonging to the other sense-organs. Further, the occurrence of any specific mental event in any one of these categories can be completely explained (that is, an exhaustive categorization of its causes can be given) by listing certain events that are either contemporaneous with or immediately preceding it. As our text puts it:

> The functioning consciousnesses—for example the visual consciousness—are caused by present conditions. In more detail [this means that] the functioning of the six sense-consciousnesses has been described as occurring on the basis of sense-organ, sense-object, and attention [which are present conditions].

To rephrase this, the necessary and sufficient conditions for the occurrence of any mental event which has an intentional object are that there be present, at time T, the appropriate sense-organ, a possible object and attention to the object on the part of the experiencing subject. Yet if this is true, and if a complete account of conscious experience (the 'functioning consciousnesses') can be given without reference to past events, then no place is allowed for the causal efficacy of karma, of actions performed in the past. And this in turn would mean that no account could be given of why a particular individual 'appropriates' or takes on a particular body, rather than some other, when reborn, since the event of being reborn cannot involve any of the six functioning consciousnesses and thus has to be explained by the causal efficacy of past actions. And it is here that the store-consciousness comes in as an explanatory category, for it is the store-consciousness, caused as our text says by 'prior karmic formations', which can provide a locus for karmic effect and thus an explanation of how the rebirth process occurs. The store-consciousness can function in this way because, unlike the six sense-consciousnesses, a complete causal account of its operations in terms of present events cannot be given. Above all else, the store-consciousness provides a locus, a basis, a principle of continuity; in it karmic effect can be located—largely through the image of seed and growth—and thus by it the present causal efficacy of long past events can be explained.

There are other ramifications to this somewhat complex first argument which I shall not enter into in any detail. Most of them can be understood under the general rubric of the necessity for providing continuity within the continuum of events that constitutes an individual, together with the need for providing an account of the way in which past actions can have effect in the present. The structure of the argument is the usual one of negative conditional: without the store-consciousness there's no way to provide continuity or account for the causal efficacy of past action since the only other possible candidates—the six sense-consciousnesses—function only in terms of present causes and conditions. Further details will be found in the translation of the entire text in Appendix C.

3.3.2 The Impossibility of Origination and Simultaneous Functioning of the Sense-Consciousnesses

The second of the eight arguments runs thus: suppose that at time T a person P desires to perceive with the senses a particular object O. If the only kinds of consciousness which exist are the six transitory sense-consciousnesses which, according to some Buddhist theories, can function only one at a time, then: (1) Simultaneous cognition of O with more than one sense-organ at T would be impossible; (2) The initial moment of consciousness—either in a new life or with regard to the perception of a particular object—could not be causally explained. The store-consciousness allows for both (1), the simultaneous functioning of more than one sense-organ, and (2), the initial moment of consciousness. This argument stresses that without the store-consciousness or something similar no explanation for (1) and (2) can be given.

This argument also rests upon specific and somewhat technical Buddhist ideas about causation already discussed in Chapter Two. To briefly recapitulate, the theory says that for each and every moment of consciousness there must be an immediately (temporally) preceding and (qualitatively) similar condition for its occurrence. The radically discontinuous model of the functioning of consciousness provided, for example, by the Vaibhāṣika theoreticians required that for each moment of, say, visual consciousness there be an immediately preceding moment of visual consciousness, and so for all the other kinds of sense-consciousness. This model, according to the Yogācārins, will not explain the first moment of a particular kind of sense-consciousness in a particular continuum: where is the immediately preceding and similar condition for the occurrence of visual consciousness in the mind of a man whose eyes have been closed for hours? Neither, they say, will it explain the simultaneous functioning of several different sense-consciousnesses, as when we see, hear, touch and smell an object all at the same time. In contrast, the store-consciousness, say the Yogācārins, will provide such an explanation since it can act as the immediately preceding and similar condition for every moment of consciousness. This is the point of the common image of waves and water used (though not explicitly as part of the eightfold argument) to explain the relationship between the store-consciousness and the six sense-consciousnesses. In his *Commentary to the Thirty Verses* Sthiramati says (quoting another unnamed text):

> . . . when there is a condition for the arising of a single wave in a great flood of water only a single wave occurs; and when there is a

> condition for the occurrence of two or three or many waves, then just so many occur. [In such a case] it is not that the great flood of water streaming along ceases to exist; it is simply that there is no sense in designating it as such. Similarly, when there is a condition for the occurrence of a single [sense]-consciousness based upon and located in the store-consciousness—which is like a flood of water—then only the visual consciousness functions [for example]. But if there is a condition for the arising of two or three [sense]-consciousnesses, then as many as five may function at the same time.[49]

We find here, then, another example of the store-consciousness being used as a principle of continuity, an explanatory category to account for phenomena difficult to explain on the model of radical impermanence and discontinuity evidenced by both Theravāda and Vaibhāṣika theoreticians.

3.3.3 The Impossibility of Clear Mental Consciousness

The third argument approaches the problem of the simultaneous functioning of different consciousnesses from a different angle, concentrating this time upon the operations of the mental consciousness *(manovijñāna)*. Once again, according to standard Buddhist theory of mind, the intentional objects of instants of mental consciousness must themselves be mental events, which means that they must be moments of cognition produced by the other five sense-consciousnesses. If, as the opponents of the store-consciousness theory suggest, different sense-consciousnesses cannot function simultaneously, then by the time the mental consciousness gets around to considering those moments of cognition produced by other sense-consciousnesses they have receded into the past and what we have is an instance not of sensory cognition (which must be of a present object) but of memory. And memory-events, for Buddhists, are phenomenologically distinct from sensory cognitions; the former are indistinct or unclear whereas the latter are distinct or clear. Thus our text says:

> . . . at just the moment when one remembers an object experienced in the past, mental consciousness functions in an unclear manner. But the manner in which the mental [consciousness] functions when its object is present is not unclear in this way. . . .

And, continues the argument, since mental consciousness as a matter of fact does operate in a clear and distinct manner, its object must be present. And this means that it must function simultaneously with those other sense-consciousnesses whose cognitions provide its objects, and this in turn, as our text has already argued, can only be the case if the existence of the store-consciousness is agreed to.

3.3.4 The Impossibility of Mutual Seeding

This argument begins from the observed fact that qualitatively different mental events—those that have mutually incompatible qualities or belong to mutually incompatible psycho-cosmic realms[50]—succeed one another very rapidly in most mental continuua. Thus, for example, one can pass from a mental event which is unambiguously ethically good, such as the impulse to donate food or land to the monastic order, to one which is equally unambiguous in its ethical negativity, such as sexual desire for one of the monks (or nuns) to whom one was just about to donate. Given the following presuppositions: (1) that all mental events are caused by an immediately preceding mental event, (2) that no two qualitatively incompatible mental events can co-exist in a single continuum at the same time, and (3) that no mental event can have as its cause a qualitatively different mental event, it becomes somewhat difficult to provide a causal explanation for the observed fact with which the argument begins. This, so the Yogācārins would have us believe, is the position that we are left with by the metaphysical presuppositions of either the Vaibhāṣikas or the Sautrāntikas. The answer to the problem is the store-consciousness, which can act as a locus within which mutually incompatible 'seeds' can exist and have their respective effects.

The point of mentioning 'mutual seeding' as the summary title of this argument is to criticize Sautrāntika ideas about seed and growth: that idea suggested that the sense-consciousnesses can mutually 'seed' (have direct causal effects upon) one another, and, by extension, that mental events with mutually incompatible qualities can act as sufficient conditions for one another's occurrence. For the Yogācārins, by contrast, this is not possible. What is needed is a locus within which seeds of qualitatively mutually incompatible mental events can reside and from which they can mature. This is the understanding of the seed and growth metaphor defended by the theorists of the classical Yogācāra in India, and, of course, the required locus is identified with the store-consciousness.

3.3.5 The Impossibility of Action

The term translated here as 'action' *(karma)* actually has a somewhat wider connotation in this context. It refers to the structures of experience in general or, perhaps more precisely, to mental action which, given the ontological presuppositions of the Yogācāra, is the only kind of action there is in any case. It is explained in our text by the term 'representation' *(vijñapti),* a key Yogācārin technical term, explained and discussed previously in Section 3.2.1 above. This, it will be remembered, is an umbrella term used to refer to the processes of the mental life in their entirety. What there is in the world, on this theory, is consciousness representing itself to itself; the various ways in which these representations appear (as subject, as object and so forth) account for the fact that we ordinarily think of ourselves as perceiving subjects seeing objects external to us. This subject-object structure is fundamental to everyday experience and is further subdivided in this argument into four aspects, i.e., the inanimate universe, the animate universe (selves and other minds), the experience of self as subject and the operations of cognition. The first two subdivisions are equivalent to the object aspect of the standard subject/object division of experience, and the latter two are equivalent to the subject aspect.

The essential point made in this fifth argument is that this fourfold structure of experience is continually present; it makes no sense to split it up and attribute it separately to each sense-consciousness, as would have to be done if the store-consciousness is denied and it is asserted that the sense-consciousnesses cannot operate simultaneously. The only way, argue the Yogācārin theorists, in which this continuing fourfold structure of all experience can adequately be explained is to say that it is located in the store-consciousness. Once again we can see the importance of the store-consciousness as a category designed to explain continuity—in this case the continuing structures of experience.

3.3.6 The Impossibility of Physical Experience

Here the argument begins from the perceived fact that at any given time physical experience for a given individual is variegated. The argument is reminiscent of the fourth argument, which began from the observed fact of the rapid succession of qualitatively different mental events in a single continuum. Here, the argument centres upon the physical, stressing that if it is true that there is non-uniform physical experience for a particular individual at a particular time, and if it is also true that non-uniform experience requires non-uniform causes for its occurrence, then it would seem that it is difficult to explain where these non-uniform causes are to come from if the Vaibhāṣika/Sautrāntika model of one-[state of] consciousness-at-a-time is held to. So our text says:

> Why can there be no bodily experience if there is no store-consciousness? This is so because, for one who is thinking or pondering correctly; for one who is thinking or pondering incorrectly; for one whose mind is concentrated; or for one whose mind is unconcentrated—[for all these] those bodily experiences which occur would neither be nor be experienced as manifold and variegated [as in fact they are]. Thus there is a store-consciousness.

The point is that the uniformity of an individual's conscious state of mind at any given time (concentrated, pondering and so forth) cannot by itself explain the variegated nature of the physical experience undergone by that same individual. The store-consciousness is postulated for that purpose, since only the store-consciousness can hold 'seeds' of various and mutually incompatible qualities at one and the same time. The argument by now should be a familiar one.

3.3.7 The Impossibility of Mindless Attainments

This seventh argument is the most important for our purposes. The Yogācārin theorists clearly opt here for a redefinition of the attainment of cessation, a redefinition which is prepared to allow that this altered state of consciousness is mindless *(acitta* or *acittaka),* but not that it is without consciousness *(vijñāna).* Yet they clearly recognize that the attainment of cessation must be without consciousness if what is meant by 'consciousness' is intentional consciousness, consciousness of something by one or more of the sense-organs. For the canonical definitions of the attainment of cessation, as we have seen, leave no doubt on this matter: there are no intentional mental events in this condition. But to be without consciousness *simpliciter* would be, for the purposes of this argument, to be dead. And this also is something which would go against the canonical definitions of the attainment of cessation. Therefore, the argument goes, there must be consciousness of a sort in this condition, and the only option remaining is that this consciousness be the store-consciousness:

> Why, if there is no store-consciousness, can the mindless attainments not occur? This is because [in the absence of the store-consciousness] the consciousness of one who has attained either unconsciousness or cessation would have issued forth from that person's body. And if [such a person's consciousness] does issue forth [from the body in that way] then he would simply die.

> For the Lord has said: 'Consciousness does not issue forth from his body [i.e., the body of one who has attained unconsciousness or cessation].'

I shall return to a more detailed consideration of this argument in the next section.

3.3.8 The Impossibility of Death

Death is in part defined by our text as the separation of consciousness from the body. The question is asked: which consciousness is separated from the body at death? The answer given is that it cannot be one of the intentional sense-consciousnesses, since these always have a particular object and at death, when consciousness departs from the body, there are no objects because there is no conscious experience. Thus the only kind of consciousness which can properly be said to depart from the body at death would be the store-consciousness since this can operate without objects (this is not stated but implied) and thus without necessitating the occurrence of conscious experience. The store-consciousness is also, of course, as we have already seen, that which appropriates a new body at the moment of rebirth; it therefore makes sense that it should be the consciousness which departs from the old body at death.

3.4 CRITIQUE OF THE YOGĀCĀRA POSITION

The Yogācāra position on the emergence of consciousness from the attainment of cessation should now be clear, at least in outline. Bearing in mind my earlier discussions of the options on this question (see especially Sections 1.5, 2.3 and 2.4), the position amounts to this:

(1) For the occurrence of any given event, Y, there exists a necessary condition, X, which is immediately antecedent to and phenomenologically similar to, Y

This view was also held (with some modifications) by both the Theravādins and the Vaibhāṣikas. I showed in Section 2.4 that the problems in explaining emergence from the attainment of cessation arise if one also assents to:

(2) It is possible that, in a given continuum of events, C, at a given time, T, there be a complete absence of mental events while physical events continue
(3) It is possible that, in C at T-plus-n, mental events may begin again

for assenting to (1), (2) and (3) immediately raises the question of what the immediately antecedent and phenomenologically similar necessary condition, X, for the re-emergence of mental events after their cessation in C, could possibly be. In the debate on this matter in the *Treasury of Metaphysics,* three major positions were outlined: The first position, the Vaibhāṣika position, accepted (1)–(3) and stated that X must be the last moment of consciousness before entering the attainment of cessation. This weakens drastically the 'immediately antecedent' part of (1). The second position outlined in the *Treasury,* that of the Sautrāntikas, also seemed in principle to assent to (1)–(3) and used the metaphor of seed to suggest that X must be a (mental) seed somehow located in a continuum where [as in (2)] there are actually only physical events. This seemed problematic because the status of such seeds remained unclear: are they mental or physical? If mental, how can they be located in a purely physical continuum? If physical, then the 'phenomenologically similar' requirement contained in (1) must be weakened or removed. The third position extensively discussed in the *Treasury* was that of Vasumitra, who boldly rejected (2) and thus identified X with an 'unmanifest thinking consciousness'. The problem here was that, if the only model of consciousness available is an intentional one, then any and every instance of consciousness must have an object and must, as we saw that Ghoṣaka insisted, entail the occurrence of all kinds of mental events which the canonical definitions of the attainment of cessation rule out as impossible.

The Yogācāra contribution solves many of these questions by making two moves: the first is to develop a new model of consciousness, to suggest that not all consciousness need be intentional in the way that the six sense-consciousnesses are and thus to avoid Ghoṣaka's criticisms of Vasumitra's position. The second is to develop and systematize the Sautrāntika image of seed by specifying a (mental) locus within which (mental) seeds can subsist as part of a continuum which is largely physical (as in the attainment of cessation). The device used to achieve both these ends is, of course, the store-consciousness. The store-consciousness is an instance of consciousness *(vijñāna),* and yet it is one that does not allow for the occurrence of any conscious experience. The store-consciousness is not conscious of anything; one cannot experience anything with it. This, in a sense, is just the point of postulating its existence, since it is required to function in conditions (the attainment of cessation, the transition from death to rebirth and so forth) in which there can be no conscious experience. The store-consciousness is thus not intentional in the sense in which the other six sense-consciousnesses are: it has no object and directly produces no experience (though it does, of course, bear the seeds from which various kinds of experience are produced indirectly through the medium of the sense-consciousnesses). It can thus do the job of Vasumitra's 'unmanifest thinking consciousness' without being open to the same criticisms that were brought against that idea in the *Treasury* and its commentaries. Historically it seems clear that one of the main reasons which prompted the Yogācārin theorists to devote so much intellectual energy to the question of the store-consciousness was just this need to account for entrance into and emergence from the attainment of cessation. And, in order to give such an account, they had to synthesize the suggestions of the Sautrāntikas—about seeds—and that of Vasumitra—about an 'unmanifest' (non-intentional) consciousness.

It should be stressed once again that the Yogācārin theorists are, when thinking ontologically, idealists. That is, if asked what there is in the world they will answer 'only mind' or 'only representation'. The problem for the Yogācārin theorists is, therefore, not to show how mental events can re-emerge within a continuum in which there are only physical events (for since there are no physical events any continuum which consisted only of physical events would simply be one in which there were no events at all, a non-existent continuum; this is part of the point of the seventh argument outlined in the preceding section), but rather to show *what kind* of mental events can continue in the attainment of cessation. It was for this purpose that the category of the store-consciousness was created and elaborated.

In sum, the theorists of the classical and commentarial period of Yogācāra thought in India dealt with the dilemma of the attainment of cessation by assenting to (1), rejecting (2) and by entailment (3) and explaining the attainment of cessation as a condition in which there is a cessation only of intentional mental events, not of all mental events. That which remains is the store-consciousness, a non-intentional objectless mental entity which acts as the receptacle or locus for the (mental) seeds from which the intentional sense-consciousnesses re-emerge. Thus the store-consciousness is also the immediately antecedent and phenomenologically similar condition for the re-emergence of consciousness from the attainment of cessation. It can be immediately antecedent because it is present during every moment of the practitioner's existence in the attainment of cessation; and it can be phenomenologically similar because it, like the re-emerging consciousness of which it is the necessary condition, is a mental phenomenon.

CHAPTER FOUR

THE ATTAINMENT OF CESSATION AND THE MIND-BODY PROBLEM

In this study I have examined a set of debates about a particular altered state of consciousness, a state produced by specified meditational techniques in which, as the canonical texts of the Indian Buddhist tradition tell us, there are no mental events whatever. I have shown that certain propositions relating to the question of the physical and the mental and the relationships between them were held and argued for by all the Buddhist schools whose views on this matter have been looked at in this study, and that these propositions underlie the debates surrounding the attainment of cessation. These propositions were also, I think, held by almost all intellectual representatives of Indian Buddhism; they are, with only minor reservations, pan-Buddhist. It may therefore be useful to set them out here as fully and formally as possible. Almost all of them have come up for discussion in various earlier parts of this study; the evidence for them is given in the appropriate sections. In this concluding chapter I shall simply present them as philosophical theses and offer a few comments about their relevance to the question of the relationship between the mental and the physical. First, then:

(1) For any X, if X exists X is a transitory event or can be analyzed into such

Proposition (1) entails many other interesting propositions, most of which lie outside the purview of this study. Significant for our purposes, though, is:

(2) There are no substances

where 'substance' is understood to mean something like 'enduring, independent, uncaused, individuated existent which possesses qualities'. Proposition (2) is entailed by (1), and it is important to stress it at the outset because it makes clear that Buddhist intellectuals were not, when discussing the mind-body problem, considering the possible relations between qualitatively different substances—as, for instance, was Descartes. They were instead considering the kinds of causal relations which might obtain between sets of transitory events, and this makes an enormous difference to the shape of the debate.

Two more key propositions assented to and argued for in various ways by the intellectuals of all three schools looked at in this study are:

(3) Personal proper names refer only to causally connected continuua of transitory events
(4) The transitory events of which such causally connected continuua are comprised are of two basic types: mental and physical

If it is accepted that personal proper names refer to anything (or indeed that any nouns do so), then clearly (1) entails (3): if the only things which exist are transitory events, then those must be what personal proper names refer to. Proposition (4) then simply states in a somewhat simplified form a basic point about pan-Buddhist theories of personal identity. Given that (3) is true, it's pertinent to ask what kinds of event go to make up the continuua to which personal proper names are affixed, and there are fully detailed and highly complicated answers given to this question by all Buddhist schools. The most basic answer, that found in all Buddhist theory on the matter from the very earliest period, is put in terms of the five 'aggregates' *(skandha)*, a listing of which is said to provide an exhaustive account of what it is that personal proper names refer to. Briefly, these five are physical form *(rūpa)*, sensation *(vedanā)*, conceptualization *(saṃjñā)*, dispositions (a free translation of the important and effectively untranslatable term *saṃskāra)*, and consciousness *(vijñāna)*. Some of these terms have arisen earlier in this study and have been discussed in their appropriate places; I do not wish to repeat those discussions here, or to enter upon new, and necessarily highly technical, discussions of each of them. An enormous technical literature, both Asian and Western, has grown up around each of them, and they are understood somewhat differently by the theoreticians of each Buddhist school with which this study has been concerned. I wish here to make only the very basic point that, apart from the first of these five 'aggregates', physical form, all terms which refer to the constituent parts of the individual have to do with mental events. This division between the mental and the physical is reflected by a still more basic and simple division made much use of in early Buddhist texts: that between 'name' *(nāma)* and 'form' *(rūpa)*, where 'name' covers pretty much what is intended by the last four of the five aggregates. It is this basic division between the mental and the physical which (4) is intended to reflect.

Given (3) and (4) two further questions immediately arise. First, what are the significant differences between these two kinds of event, the mental and the physical? Second, what kinds of causal connection can properly hold between members of each of these two classes? This, in a nutshell, is the Indian Buddhist version of the mind-body problem.

To take the first question first: what are the significant differences between physical events and mental events? The basic distinction between the mental and the physical has to do with intentionality: transitory events categorized as belonging to the set of physical events can be the objects of transitory events categorized as belonging to the set of mental events in various ways, but not vice-versa. More generally still, Indian Buddhist intellectuals would probably hold that the distinguishing characteristic of the mental is intentionality (with the appropriate exception made for the non- or only marginally intentional store-consciousness); this is not a characteristic which can be attributed to members of the class of physical events. Furthermore, in the case of persons (who are, remember, causally connected continuua of transitory events), physical form consists only in the body, whereas the other four aggregates account for everything else: the affective emotional life, concept- and category-formation, intentions, dispositions, volitions and cognitive acts—the entire spectrum of the mental life. Significant also is the fact that, with some minor qualifications, it seems to be the case that only mental events can be ethically qualified (that is, either good or bad) and therefore only mental events can be productive of karmic effect. Finally, I also sense in the detailed analyses of the five aggregates found in the scholastic texts of all schools, a fundamental awareness that mental events are simply phenomenologically different from physical events, though the exact way in which this is the case is not usually spelled out as clearly as one might wish. In sum, the answers given by Indian Buddhist theoreticians to the first question—what are the significant differences between the mental and the physical? —are not very different from those given to the same question by Western dualists of various kinds. Even for the Yogācāra, that school which rejects any ontological distinction between the mental and the physical, the phenomenological distinction is maintained: mental events simply have a different flavour than do physical events.

The question of the difference between the mental and the physical is naturally answered rather differently by the Yogācāra, since for them there is no ontological distinction between the two in any case. Everything is mind. This ontological difference between the Yogācāra and the other Indian Buddhist schools makes surprisingly little difference to the way in which the philosophers of the former school discussed the problem. They preserve the fundamental phenomenological difference between the mental and the (quasi) physical and are thus still under obligation to provide a causal account of the relations between members of the two sets.

What kinds of causal connection, then, can properly hold between members of each of these classes? This, as for all dualists, even for non-substantivist dualists like the Buddhists, is the most difficult philosophical question in theory of mind. For if the reductionist step of identifying one class of events with another (as, for example, by mind-brain identity theorists or by some epiphenomenalists) is refused, and if a strong sense of difference between the two sets is maintained, the philosophical issue of how to relate members of the two classes becomes pressing.

The question of the attainment of cessation, an altered state in which no mental events occur, was chosen for this study in part because it illustrates, in a dramatic and pointed way, the range of Buddhist responses to the question of the causal relations between mind and body, the mental and the physical. This is true because the canonical descriptions of the attainment of cessation require that in it there be, for a given period of time, no mental events, and also that mental events can, after the appropriate time-period has passed, re-emerge. What, in such a case, are the causal determinants which explain such re-emergence? This takes us at once into the realms of Buddhist causal theory. I have shown that such theory requires assent to at least the following:

(5) Every event has, as a necessary condition for its occurrence, a cause which is (temporally) immediately antecedent and (phenomenologically) of the same kind

Proposition (5) is understood rather differently by different schools. I showed that the Theravāda theorists seem at times to espouse a stronger form of (5) which approaches a version of the principle of sufficient reason. But, even though there is disagreement about whether (5) should be reformulated to read:

(5′) Every event has, as a necessary and sufficient condition for its occurrence, a cause which is (temporally) immediately antecedent and (phenomenologically) of the same kind

it seems that all schools would assent to (5). Now (5), when taken in conjunction with (4), suggests that, in regard to those continuua to which we affix personal proper names,

(6) In a continuum wherein there are no mental events at time T, there can be no mental events at time T-plus-one; and in a continuum wherein there are no physical events at time T, there can be no physical events at time T-plus-one

This is not to say that there can be no cases in which an event of one class can act as the necessary condition for the occurrence of an event of another class, much less that there can be no causal interactions of any kind between members of the class of physical events and members of the class of mental events. Counterexamples to such generalizations are frequent in Buddhist texts; paradigmatic is the usual account of visual perception (any instance of which is a member of the set of mental events), in which a necessary condition for the occurrence of visual perception is the existence of an external material object (any instance of which is a member of the set of mental events). The occurrence of any given mental event, then, is usually seen as the product of a collocation of necessary conditions, of which some may be physical and some mental; the important point is that at least one of these necessary conditions must itself be a mental event (or, *mutatis mutandis,* a physical event for a physical event). And this explains (6): in a continuum wherein there is a complete absence of events of one kind or another, no such necessary condition can exist for the future occurrence of events of that kind. Such is the dilemma posed by the attainment of cessation.

The detailed answers to this dilemma given by the Buddhist schools have been dealt with in this study; I shall not recapitulate them here. The important point to notice is just how radical a dualism this is. Physicalism in any form (identity theory, epiphenomenalism and so forth) is not an option: none of the schools is prepared to assert that physical events may, in and of themselves, act as the necessary condition for the re-emergence of consciousness from the attainment of cessation. All of them, in various ways, try to show either that there are in fact mental events of some kind still occurring in the attainment of cessation, or that the appropriate kind of causal connection can operate at a temporal distance. The most radical answer, that of the Yogācārin theorists, is to suggest that in fact there are only mental events, that what appear to be physical events are in fact simply a phenomenologically distinct sub-set of the set of mental events and that the idea of a continuum in which there are no mental events is simply the idea of a continuum in which there are no events at all—a non-existent continuum.

It seems, then, that in looking at the Indian Buddhist debates surrounding the attainment of cessation the following conclusions can be drawn about the basic Buddhist view of the relations between the mental and the physical. First, the mental and the physical are categories of event which are phenomenologically irreducibly different. Second, these events are not attributes or properties of any substance; to give an account of their causal functions and interrelations is to give an exhaustive account of what there is in the world. Third, certain kinds of causal interaction between the mental and the physical are envisaged, but no event of one class may ever come into existence solely as the result of the occurrence of an event of another class. In sum, we have a non-substantivist event-based interactionist psycho-physical dualism.

This theory of the relations between mind and body, the mental and the physical, seems internally coherent, consistent with the axioms (ontological and causal) which underlie it. Its major problems have to do not with internal consistency (though that does become a problem, as we have seen, when Buddhist theorists try to explain limiting cases such as the attainment of cessation) but with difficulties in explaining certain observable phenomena. If (5) is true then it seems exceedingly difficult to explain the beginnings of various kinds of mental phenomena: how is it that visual consciousness can begin for a man born blind who regains his sight after many years of blindness? How is it that mental events can begin in a continuum in which, for one reason or another, they are absent? How is it that affective reactions can begin for an autistic child for whom there have previously been none? These are precisely the kinds of questions raised by the Yogācārin theorists against the Vaibhāṣikas and Sautrāntikas, and it was largely in order to deal with them that the category of the store-consciousness was developed. Another way of putting questions such as these would be to ask whether, without a substance-based ontology, without postulating an entity of which the mental and physical events described by Buddhist theorists can be predicated, it is possible to make sense of the observed facts of continuity of identity, of memory, of character traits and of beginnings and ends? More simply, is a non-substance-based ontology explanatorily adequate to its task? This is the fundamental question facing Buddhist theorists, and while I do not wish to propose an answer to it—to do so would require an extended discussion of theories of personal identity and of the important Buddhist critique of substance—I do wish to suggest that it is indicative of a significant intellectual weakness within the tradition that the tradition itself perceived the necessity for construction of a (mental) category which is very much like a substance: the store-consciousness. Causally connected continuua of events seem to have been found, by the Buddhist intellectual tradition in India, inadequate to perform the explanatory tasks required of them. It is more difficult than it seems to dispose of mental substances, and the debates among the Indian Buddhist schools concerning the attainment of cessation make this especially clear.

GLOSSARY

This glossary contains the more important technical terms discussed in the main part of this study. They are listed by English alphabetical order in the left-hand column. The translation used in this work is given in the right-hand column together with, where relevant, brief expository comments. I have given the technical terms in the language(s) in which they occurred most frequently in this work: (S) indicates Sanskrit and (P) indicates Pali.

abhidharma (S), abhidhamma (P)	metaphysics
abhūtaparikalpa (S)	imagination of the unreal
ākāśānantyāyatana (S)	sphere of infinite space, first formless attainment
ākiṃcanyāyatana (S)	sphere of nothing at all, third formless attainment
ālayavijñāna (S)	store-consciousness
aparisphuṭamanovijñāna (S)	unmanifest thinking consciousness
arhat (S/P)	left untranslated. Literal meaning probably 'worthy one'. Refers to one who has attained enlightenment
asaṃjñisamāpatti (S)	attainment of unconsciousness
āśraya (S)	basis
avidyā (S)	ignorance
āyu (S/P)	vitality
āyusankhārā (P)	vital functions
bīja (S)	seed
catuṣkoṭi (S)	tetralemma
citta (S/P)	mind
cittamātra (S)	mind-only
cittasankhārā (P)	mental functions

dharma (S), dhamma (P)	left untranslated, can mean generally 'doctrine', the truth, duty, the way things are, a category which abolishes the fact-value distinction; more specifically, a uniquely individuated transitory existent
dhyāna (S), jhāna (P)	left untranslated, a term designating a series of altered states of consciousness, usually a fourfold series; sometimes translated 'meditation' in other studies
duḥkha (S), dukkha (P)	unsatisfactoriness, generally translated 'suffering'
karma (S), kamma (P)	action
kāyasankhārā (P)	physical functions
manas (S)	thought
manovỳñāna (S)	mental consciousness
mantra (S)	magical spell
naivasaṃjñānāsaṃjñāyatana (S)	sphere of neither cognition nor non-cognition, fourth formless attainment
nikāyasabhāgahetu (S)	cause which ensures homogeneity of species
nirodhasamāpatti (S/P)	attainment of cessation
paratantra (S)	relative
parikalpita (S)	imagined
parinișpanna (S)	perfected
prajñā (S), paññā (P)	wisdom
prajñaptisat (S)	existence as a designation
pratyaya (S)	condition
pravṛttivijñāna (S)	functioning consciousness
rūpa (S/P)	physical form
samanantarapratyaya (S)	immediately antecedent and similar condition
samathabhāvanā (P)	cultivation of tranquillity
saṃjñā (S)	conceptualization
saṃjñāvedayitanirodha (S)	cessation of sensation and conceptualization, equivalent to 'attainment of cessation'

saṃtāna (S)	(mental) continuum
skandha (S)	aggregate
sparśa (S)	contact
svabhāva (S)	inherent existence, literally 'own-being'
svalakṣaṇa (S)	uniquely defining characteristic
tṛṣṇā (S), taṇhā (P)	thirst
timira (S)	partial blindness, possibly cataracts or double vision
trisvabhāva (S)	three aspects (of experience)
usmā (P)	heat
vacīsankhārā (P)	verbal functions
vāsana (S)	tendency
vedanā (S/P)	sensation
vijñāna (S), viññāṇa (P)	consciousness
vijñānānantyāyatana (S)	sphere of infinite consciousness, second formless attainment
vijñapti (S)	representation
vimokṣa (S), vimokkha (P)	liberation, a series of eight altered states of consciousness
vipassanābhāvanā (P)	cultivation of insight

ABBREVIATIONS

Most of these abbreviations are for text-names. In all cases the texts were originally written in either Sanskrit or Pali. There are some instances in which the original does not survive and the title given is a reconstruction either from a Tibetan translation or transliteration or (less frequently) from a Chinese translation. Such instances are marked with an asterisk (*). For commentaries which have alternative titles—usually one is the name of the text commented on plus *bhāṣya, ṭīkā, vyākhyā* and the like, and the other is the individual title of the commentary itself—my practice has been to abbreviate the title which follows most closely the title of the text commented upon, to give that title first, and to follow it with the individual title in parentheses ().

AA	*Abhidharmāmṛta
AD	Abhidharmadīpa
ADV	Abhidharmadīpavṛtti (Vibhāṣāprabhā)
AH	*Abhidharmahṛdaya
AK	Abhidharmakośa
AKBh	Abhidharmakośabhāṣya
AKT	*Abhidharmakośabhāṣyaṭīkā (Tattvārthā)
AKSBh	*Abhidharmakośaśāstrakārikābhāṣya
AKTL	*Abhidharmakośaṭīkā (Lakṣaṇānusāriṇī)
AKTU	*Abhidharmakośaṭīkā (Upāyikā)
AKV	Abhidharmakośavyākhyā (Sphuṭārthā)
AKVr	*Abhidharmakośavṛtti (Marmapradīpa)
AN	Anguttaranikāya
AS	Abhidharmasamuccaya
AS(G)	Gokhale's [1947b] edition of the fragments of AS
AS(P)	Pradhan's [1950] edition/reconstruction of AS
ASBh	Abhidharmasamuccayabhāṣya

C	Cone xylographic edition of the Tibetan Tripiṭaka
D	Derge xylographic edition of the Tibetan Tripiṭaka
DA	Dīghanikāya-aṭṭhakathā (Sumangalavilāsinī)
Dhs	Dhammasangaṇi
DhsA	Dhammasangaṇi-aṭṭhakathā (Atthasālinī)
DN	Dīghanikāya
KN	Khuddhakanikāya
KSP	Karmasiddhiprakaraṇa
MA	Majjhimanikāya-aṭṭhakathā (Papañcasūdanī)
Miln	Milindapañha
MMK	Mūlamadhyamakakārikā
MN	Majjhimanikāya
MS	Mahāyānasaṃgraha
MSBh	Mahāyānasaṃgrahabhāṣya
MSU	Mahāyānasaṃgrahopanibandhana
MSA	Mahāyānasūtrālaṃkāra
MSABh	Mahāyānasūtrālaṃkārabhāṣya
MSAT	Mahāyānasūtrālaṃkāraṭīkā
MV	Madhyāntavibhāga
MVBh	Madhyāntavibhāgabhāṣya
MVT	Madhyāntavibhāgaṭīkā
N	Narthang xylographic edition of the Tibetan Tripiṭaka
P	Peking xylographic edition of the Tibetan Tripiṭaka
PP	Prajñāpāramitā
PTS	Pali Text Society
RGV	*Ratnagotravibhāga
SA	Samyuttanikāya-aṭṭhakathā (Sāratthappakāsinī)
SN	Samyuttanikāya
T	Triṃśikā
TBh	Triṃśikābhāṣya
Taishō	Taishō Tripiṭaka, the standard edition of the texts in the Chinese Tripiṭaka; a number is assigned to each text
Tōhoku	Tōhoku catalogue [Ui et al. 1934] of the texts in the Kanjur and Tanjur of D; a number is assigned to each text
TS	Tattvasaṃgraha
TSN	Trisvabhāvanirdeśa

V	Viṃśatikā
VM	Visuddhimagga
VMT	Visuddhimaggaṭīkā (Paramatthamañjūsā)
VV	Vigrahavyāvartanī
VVr	Viṃśatikāvṛtti
YBh	Yogācārabhūmi

APPENDIX A

THE PLACE OF THE ATTAINMENT OF CESSATION IN THE SOTERIOLOGICAL PATH OF THE ABHIDHARMAKOŚA-BHĀṢYA

The numbered stages (1–8) in the left-hand column indicate the eight meditational attainments; in the right-hand column are placed the cosmological spheres in which they occur. Under each of the four *dhyānas* of form are given the states of mind which can occur therein. The attainment of cessation is shown as the culmination of the practitioner's progress through the formless sphere; it has an analogue in the attainment of unconsciousness, which occurs after progress through the sphere of form.

This is actually only (part of) one of the many soteriological paths described in the *AKBh*. It is called the *bhāvanāmārga* or 'path of cultivation' and is concerned, as can be seen, largely with the practice of enstatic technique. There are other paths concerned much more with intellectual analysis of Buddhist doctrine; attempts to combine the two kinds of practice into a unified theory are common, though not usually entirely successful, in Buddhist texts of this kind.

THE PATH OF CULTIVATION
(bhāvanāmārga)

Altered States of Consciousness	Cosmological Realms
	Sphere of Desire (kāmadhātu)
1 First dhyāna of form (vitarka-vicāra-prīti-sukha-cittaikāgratā) 2 Second dhyāna of form (adhyātmasamprasāda-prīti-sukha-cittaikāgratā) 3 Third dhyāna of form (upekṣā-smṛti-samprajñāna-sukha-samādhi) 4 Fourth dhyāna of form (aduḥkhāsukhavedanā-upeksāpariśuddhi-smṛtipariśuddhi-samādhi) Attainment of Unconsciousness (asaṃjñisamāpatti) Unconsciousness (āsaṃjñika)	Sphere of Form (rūpadhātu)
5 Infinite Space (ākāśānantyāyatana) 6 Infinite Consciousness (vijñānāntyāyatana) 7 Nothing At All (ākiṃcanyāyatana) 8 Neither Cognition nor its Absence (naivasaṃjñānāsaṃjñāyatana) Attainment of Cessation (nirodhasamāpatti)	Sphere of Formlessness (arūpadhātu)

APPENDIX B

DEBATES ON THE RE-EMERGENCE OF CONSCIOUSNESS FROM THE ATTAINMENT OF CESSATION IN THE ABHIDHARMAKOŚA-BHĀṢYA [72.19–73.4]: SANSKRIT TEXT, ENGLISH TRANSLATION AND ANNOTATION

In this appendix I give the Sanskrit text and annotated English translation of that section of the *AKBh* dealing with the re-emergence of mind from the attainment of cessation (Pradhan [1975:72.19–73:4]).

This debate occurs in the second chapter of the *AKBh*. Selected extracts from Yaśomitra's commentary (the *AKV*, extant in Sanskrit) and from Sthiramati's commentary (the *AKT*, extant only in Tibetan) are also given. The debates presented here are extensively discussed in Section 2.3. Sectional divisions and section headings are provided by me.

<1 THE VAIBHĀṢIKA POSITION>

How can mind arise once again from a mind long since brought to cessation? The Vaibhāṣikas claim that there is an immediately antecedent and similar condition [for the arising of mind from mindlessness] because of the [continued] existence of what is past.

katham idānīṃ bahukālaṃ niruddhāc cittāt punar api cittaṃ jāyate | atītasyāpy astitvāt iṣyate vaibhāṣikaiḥ samanantara-pratyayatvam | |

(1) Yaśomitra prefaces his commentary here with a summary statement of the positions of the schools on the issue of whether mind *(citta)* exists in the *nirodhasamāpatti*: 'On this matter the Vaibhāṣikas and others attribute mindlessness to the attainments of cessation and unconsciousness, together with [the state of] unconsciousness; the elder Vasumitra and others say that these attainments possess mind—an unmanifest mental consciousness; the Yogācārins, among others, say that these attainments possess mind—the store-consciousness. Such is the division of the schools.' *(tatrācittakāny eva nirodhāsaṃjñisamāpatty āsaṃjñikānīti, vaibhāṣikādayaḥ | aparisphuṭamanovijñānasacittakānīti sthaviravasumitrādayaḥ | ālayavijñāna-sacittakānīti yogācārāḥ | iti siddhāntabhedaḥ |* [*AKV* 245.21–23].
(2) The key term *samanantarapratyaya*, translated here as 'immediately antecedent and similar condition', is standardly glossed as a *karmadhāraya: samaś cāyam anantaraś ca pratyaya iti samanantarapratyayaḥ* [*AKBh* 98.10–11]. According to Vaibhāṣika theory, every mental event both has and is a *samanantarapratyaya*, an immediately antecedent and similar condition. For discussion, see Section 2.3.
(3) Sthiramati comments: ' "Because of the continued existence of what is past"—if something continues to exist, in what sense is it past? The Vaibhāṣika answers: what is past does not possess function, but its essential nature is not lost [and in that sense it exists]. Therefore, the Vaibhāṣikas claim that both something which ceased immediately before [what follows it] and something which ceased long before can be immediately antecedent and similar conditions.' *('das pa yang yod pa'i phyir zhes bya ba 'byung ste | gal te yod na ji ltar 'das pa yin zhe na | byed pa 'gags pa'i 'das pa zhes bya ba'i rang gi ngo bo yongs su btang ba'i phyir ni ma yin no | de'i phyir 'gags*

ma thag pa lar 'gags nas yun ring du lon pa yang bye brag tu smra ba rnams mtshungs pa de ma thag pa'i rkyen nyid du 'dod do | [*AKT* TO 265b6–8]). Yaśomitra's commentary here rejects the Vaibhāṣika view that if something which has just ceased can be said to still exist, then the same must be true of something which has long ceased (*yadi samanataraniruddham astīty abhyupagatam bahukālaniruddham apy astīti kiṃ nābhyupagamyata iti vaibhāṣikaiḥ* | [*AKV* 245.25–26]), and offers the standard Sautrāntika view that nothing which has ceased (i.e., become past) may be said to exist in the present, though a past event may provide part of the causal nexus which allows an immediately following present event to occur. The standard image of the ascent and descent of a balance-beam (*tulādaṇḍa*—something like a see-saw) is used to describe the temporal relations of cause and effect. The debate between Sautrāntika and Vaibhāṣika in the *AKV* thus centres upon whether causal action at a temporal distance is possible.

<2 THE SAUTRĀNTIKA VIEW>

But other former teachers ask how it is that physical form arises again for those, born in the formless realms, whose physical form has long since ceased. Their answer is that in such a case physical form arises only from mind and not from physical form; similarly, mind [for one in the attainment of cessation] arises only from the body with its senses and not from mind. For the mind and the body with it senses mutually seed one another.

apare punar āhuḥ kathaṃ tāvad ārūpyopapannānaṃ ciraniruddhe 'pi rūpe punar api rūpaṃ jāyate | *cittād eva hi taj jāyate na rūpāt evaṃ cittam apy asmād eva sendriyāt kāyāj jāyate na cittāt* | *anyonyabījakaṃ hy etad ubhayaṃ yad uta cittaṃ ca sendriyaś ca kāya iti pūrvācāryāḥ* |

(1) Yaśomitra [*AKV* 246.15] and Sthiramati [*AKT* TO 265b8–266a1] agree that the 'former teachers' mentioned here are the Sautrāntikas. (2) It will be remembered that existence in the formless realms is, by definition, existence without physical form, existence consisting of mental events only. Since it is generally admitted that those born in the formless realms can be later reborn in the realms of form, the question here is that of what, in such a case, acts as the *samanantarapratyaya,* the immediately antecedent and similar condition, for the arising of physical form. Clearly, the question is structurally similar to the issue of what causes the re-emergence of mind from a mindless condition. The (Sautrāntika) answer given is that mind and body 'mutually seed one another' (*anyonyabījaka*), which Yaśomitra explains as meaning that there is a seed of the body with its senses in the mind and a seed of the mind in the body with its senses (*citte 'pi sendriyasya kāyasya bījam asti kāye ca sendriye*

cittasyeti [*AKV* 246.18–19]). Sthiramati offers the following comment: 'If [as the Sautrāntikas claim] consciousness can arise from the body with its senses without reference to the cause which assures homogeneity of species, then, when there exist both basis and object, consciousness would occur simultaneously everywhere. But if, on the other hand, mind arises subsequently by way of connection to that state of mind which existed prior [to it], then, since there is no immediately antecedent and similar condition for the second [i.e., subsequent state of mind] the conclusion is that, even when basis and object exist, there could be no simultaneous arising [of the relevant consciousness]. And if it is asked how, in the absence of mind, [mind] can arise from a seed by means of the mindless body with its senses, [the answer is] that this is not possible because there is no distinct cause [for such a thing to occur.' *(gal te ris mthun pa'i rgyu la ma bltos par dbang po dang bcas pa'i lus las rnam par shes pa skye ba yid yin na | rten dang dmigs pa cig car gnas pa na yul thams cad la rnam par shes pa skye bar 'gyur ro | sems snga ma gang yin pa de la rag las pas sems phyi ma skye bas na | gnyis pa la mtshungs pa de ma thag pa'i rkyen med pas rten dang dmigs pa yod kyang cig car mi skye bar thal bar 'gyur ro | gal te sems yod pa ma yin yang sems med pa'i dbang po dang bcas pa'i lus kyi sa bon las so zhe na | 'di yang mi rigs te | khyad par gyi rgyu med pa'i phyir ro |* [*AKT* TO 266a2–4]). The philosophical implications of this position are discussed in Section 2.3.

<3 THE DEBATE BETWEEN VASUMITRA AND GHOṢAKA (1)>

The Bhadanta Vasumitra, on the other hand, says in the *Paripṛcchā:* 'This [i.e., the question of how mind arises from mindlessness] is a problem for one who thinks that the attainment of cessation is mindless; in my view, though, this attainment possesses mind [so there is no problem].'

The Bhadanta Ghoṣaka says that this is incorrect since the Lord has said: 'When consciousness exists there is contact, which is the conjunction of the three. Further, sensation, conceptualization and volition are conditioned by contact.' Hence, [if consciousness does exist in the attainment of cessation as Vasumitra

bhadantavasumitras tv āha paripṛcchāyāṃ yasyācittakā nirodhasamāpattis tasyaiṣa doṣo mama tu sacittakā samāpattir iti | bhadantaghoṣaka āha tad idaṃ nopapadyate | sati hi vijñāne trayāṇāṃ saṃnipātaḥ sparśaḥ | sparśapratyayā ca vedanā saṃjñā cetanety uktaṃ bhagavatā | ataḥ saṃjñāvedanayor apy atra nirodho na syāt |

suggests] sensation and
conceptualization could not
cease therein.

(1) The identification of this Vasumitra is not entirely certain. Yaśomitra [*AKV* 246.18–19] says that this Vasumitra also wrote the *Pañcavastuka* and other works; this *Pañcavastuka* may be the work commented upon by Dharmatrāta [Taishō 1555]. There is also a Vasumitra whose opinions are frequently referred to—usually with the greatest reverence—in the *Mahāvibhāṣā*. However, both Yaśomitra [*AKV* 245.21–22] and Sthiramati [*AKT* TO 266a7–8] say that the Vasumitra referred to in the *AKBh* holds that an 'unmanifest thinking consciousness' *(aparisphuṭamanovijñāna)* endures in the attainment of cessation, and this alone is enough to make it likely that the Vasumitra under discussion here is not the one reverentially quoted so often in the *Mahāvibhāṣā,* since in that text a very different view on the *nirodhasamāpatti* is attributed to Vasumitra, one that is essentially the same as the standard Vaibhāṣika view (for some discussion of texts from the *Mahāvibhāṣā* to support this see La Vallée Poussin [1971:I.212 n.2] and Hakamaya [1975:36–37]). Both La Vallée Poussin [1971:I.xlv] and Lamotte [1970–81:273 n.77] have suggested that the Vasumitra referred to here, while not the Vasumitra of the *Mahāvibhāṣā* is probably a Sautrāntika. I can find no hard evidence to support this view, and much to suggest that it is incorrect, not least the fact that neither Yaśomitra nor Sthiramati identify this Vasumitra as a Sautrāntika and both attribute to the Sautrāntikas a view different from that expressed in this passage. The question of this Vasumitra's scholastic affiliation therefore remains open.
(2) This verse from the *Paripṛcchā* is also quoted in Vasubandhu's *KSP*. Hakamaya [1974:19 n.6] gives the Tibetan text, from which it is easy to see that, although there are minor discrepancies between the *AKBh* version and that in the *KSP,* both rest on the same Sanskrit original. The philosophical point here, discussed in more detail in Section 2.3, is that the problem of how mind re-emerges from the attainment of cessation is only a problem if mental events do indeed come to a complete halt in that state. Since Vasumitra thinks that they do not, he has no problem.
(3) Ghoṣaka is the probable author of the **Abhidharmāmṛta,* an influential pre-*AKBh* Sarvāstivādin text.
(4) The definition of 'contact' *(sparśa)* given here ('the contact of the three') occurs with variants in many Buddhist texts. The *AKBh* provides a detailed discussion at 143.2ff. See also La Vallée Poussin [1971:II.95ff]. Yaśomitra's comment makes clear that the 'three' are sense-organ, sense-object and consciousness: *trayāṇāṃ saṃnipāta iti* | *indriyaviṣayavijñānānām* | [*AKV* 246.23]). Sthiramati's comment reads: 'A detailed explanation of the words: 'Sensation and so forth are conditioned by contact . . .' has been given [in the *sūtra*]. Since the result follows automatically when an unobstructed cause exists, then in accordance with contact [which is the unobstructed cause of sensation and conceptualization] the cessation of sensation and

conceptualization cannot occur in the attainment of cessation.' *(reg pa'i rkyen gyis tshor ba dang zhes bya ba rgyas par 'byung ba la | gegs byed pa med pa'i rgyu yod na 'bras bu gdon mi za bar 'byung bas 'gog pa'i snyoms par 'jug pa'i rdzas 'di la 'du shes dang tshor ba dag kyang 'gog par mi 'gyur te |* [*AKT* TO 266b2–3]). The general philosophical point here is that since the existence of consciousness requires the existence of (at least) sensation and conceptualization, Vasumitra's view that there can be an unmanifest *(asparisphuṭa)* consciousness in the attainment of cessation requires that there also be sensation and conceptualization—and this is ruled out by the alternative name of the attainment: *saṃjñāvedayitanirodha.*

<4 THE DEBATE BETWEEN VASUMITRA AND GHOṢAKA (2)>

It may be suggested that [sensation and conceptualization] could [cease in the attainment of cessation even when consciousness exists therein]. [This might be suggested because], just as desire is described as conditioned by sensation, and yet it does not arise for an *arhat* when sensation arises for him, so also when contact occurs sensation and so forth may not necessarily follow. But this case is different because of the specification of that [sensation which conditions desire]: desire is described as occurring in dependence upon sensation which results from contact with ignorance. But there is no such specification of contact with regard to the arising of sensation.

Therefore, the Vaibhāṣika states that the attainment of cessation is mindless.

athāpi syāt yathā vedanāpratyayā tṛṣṇety uktam satyām api tu vedanāyām arhato na tṛṣṇotpattir evam saty api sparśe vedanādayo na syur iti | na | tasyā viśeṣitatvāt | (Pradhan reads. . . . *syur iti | tasyāviśeṣitatvāt |* I follow Tibetan: *khyad par du byas pa'i phyir de ni ma yin te* [P GU 88b7–8] and Chinese (Sakurabe [1969:327–8 n.7])) *avidyāsaṃsparśajaṃ hi veditaṃ pratītyotpannā tṛṣṇety uktaṃ na tu vedanotpattau sparśo viśeṣita ity asamānam etat | tasmād acittakā nirodhasamāpattir iti vaibhāṣikāḥ ||*

(1) The argument here centres upon the interpretation of the *bahuvrīhi* compound x-*pratyaya.* It may be taken to mean that whatever is qualified by this compound (in our case *tṛṣṇā)* has x as a sufficient condition. This was Ghoṣaka's interpretation: his argument suggests that an occurrence of consciousness *(vijñāna)* acts as sufficient condition for an occurrence of contact *(sparśa)* which in turn acts as sufficient condition for an occurrence of sensation *(vedanā).* A counterexample is offered here in the shape of

vedanāpratyayā tṛṣṇā: Ghoṣaka's opponent (probably still Vasumitra, though unnamed by the commentaries. See La Vallée Poussin [1971:I.213], who follows the Japanese editors of the Chinese text that he was using) argues that the relationship of sufficient conditionality as an interpretation of x-*pratyaya* does not apply here since an *arhat* may have sensation and yet not experience desire. Suppose, the opponent suggests, the relationship of sufficient conditionality also does not apply in the case of *sparśapratyayā vedanā?*

Ghoṣaka's reply (also the standard Vaibhāṣika view) suggests that the sufficient-conditional interpretation of x-*pratyaya* holds and that the counterexample is not genuine. If the x-term of the compound is made more specific—as it is here, *avidyāsaṃsparśajavedanā* instead of simply *vedanā*—then the relationship of sufficient conditionality still applies, though restricted to the more specific definition of the x-term. Finally, argues the Vaibhāṣika, in the case of the relationship of sufficient conditionality between *sparśa* and *vedanā* there is no such more precise definition of the x-term, and (Vasumitra's) counterexample does not apply.

(2) The conclusion simply restates the Vaibhāṣika position that the attainment of cessation possesses no mental events. This is not because Vasubandhu necessarily agrees with this view; indeed, to judge from his discussions of the same issue in the *KSP*, he does not agree and holds something much closer to the Sautrāntika position. But it is Vasubandhu's intention in the *AKBh* to expound the Vaibhāṣika position whether or not he happens to agree with it.

APPENDIX C

THE EIGHTFOLD PROOF OF THE STORE-CONSCIOUSNESS IN THE ABHIDHARMA-SAMUCCAYABHĀṢYA [11.18–13.20]: SANSKRIT TEXT, ENGLISH TRANSLATION AND ANNOTATION

The Sanskrit text given here is taken from Nathmial Tatia's [1976] edition of the *ASBh*. There is no doubt that this text represents also that which originally stood in that section of the *YBh* called *Viniścayasaṃgrahaṇī*, though this text is now available only in Tibetan translation. The Tibetan translations of both *ASBh* and *YBh* are close to identical and Sthiramati, the probable author of *ASBh*, explicitly refers to the *Viniścayasamgrahanī* in his text. I have profited greatly from the Tibetan texts and Japanese translation of this passage given by Hakamaya [1978].

The eightfold proof begins with a terse summary verse *(uddāna)* intended for mnemonic purposes (not included here), proceeds with a brief statement of each of the eight arguments (included here as 'introduction') and then gives a detailed presentation of each argument. In what follows I give, numbered by argument (one through eight), the Sanskrit text of each argument together with English translation. Following the text/translation of each argument I give explanatory annotations and, where relevant, references to other texts.

<INTRODUCTION>

The existence of the store-consciousness may be demonstrated in eight ways.

Namely, without the store-consciousness: (1) There is no appropriation of a [physical] basis. (2) There is no initial functioning [of consciousness]. (3) There is no manifest functioning. (4) There is no condition of being a 'seed'. (5) There is no action. (6) There is no physical experience. (7) There are no mindless meditative attainments. (8) There is no fall of consciousness.

aṣṭābhir ākārair ālayavijñānasyāstitā pratyetavyā | tadyathā 'ntareṇālayavijñānaṃ

(1) *āśrayopadānāsaṃbhavataḥ*

(2) *ādipravṛttyasaṃbhavataḥ*

(3) *spaṣṭapravṛttyasaṃbhavato*

(4) *bījatvāsaṃbhavataḥ*

(5) *karmāsaṃbhavataḥ*

(6) *kāyikānubhavāsaṃbhavato*

(7) *'cittakasamāpattyasaṃbhavato*

(8) *vijñānacyutyasaṃbhavataś ca* ||

This brief statement of the purport of each of the eight arguments will be clarified by the more detailed presentations to follow.

<1 THE IMPOSSIBILITY OF APPROPRIATING A NEW BODY>

Why can there be no appropriation of a [physical] basis? This has been said to be for five reasons, namely:

kena kāraṇenāśrayopadānaṃ na yujyate | āha pañcabhiḥ kāraṇaiḥ | tathāhi |

(i) The store-consciousness is caused by prior formations whereas the functioning consciousness—for example the visual consciousness—are caused by present conditions. In more detail, the functioning of the six

(i) *ālayavijñānaṃ pūrvasaṃskārahetukam | cakṣurādipravṛttivijñānaṃ punar vartamānapratyayahetukam | yathoktam*

indriyaviṣayamanaskāravaśād vijñānānāṃ pravṛttir bhavatīti vistareṇa | idaṃ prathamaṃ kāraṇam ||

sense-consciousnesses has been described as occurring on the basis of sense, sense-object and attention [which are present conditions]. This is the first reason.

(ii) Further, the six categories of [sense]-consciousness are experienced as good and bad. This is the second reason.

(ii) *api ca kuśalākuśalāḥ ṣaḍ vijñānakāyā upalabhyante | idaṃ dvitīyaṃ kāraṇam ||*

(iii) Also, the set of what may be comprised in the maturation of what is neutral [i.e., neither good nor bad]—this is not experienced among the six categories of [sense]-consciousness. This is the third reason.

(iii) *api ca ṣaṇṇāṃ vijñānakāyānāṃ sā jātir nopalabhyate yā 'vyākṛtavipākasaṃgṛhītā syāt | idaṃ tṛtīyam kāraṇam ||*

(iv) Also, the six categories of [sense]-consciousness function with determinate physical bases. And it is not proper to say either (a) that a particular sense-consciousness appropriates only that physical basis in virtue of which it functions and that there might be no appropriation of the remainder; or (b) that there might be appropriation in the absence of consciousness.

(iv) *api ca pratiniyatāśrayāḥ ṣaḍ vijñānakāyāḥ pravartante tatra yena yenāśrayeṇa yad vijñānaṃ pravartate tad eva tenopāttaṃ syād avaśiṣṭasyānupāttateti na yujyate upāttatāpi na yujyate vijñānavirahitatayā | idaṃ caturthaṃ kāraṇam ||*

(v) Further, the error [of postulating] the repeated appropriation of a physical basis is refuted [only if the store-consciousness is postulated]. For the visual consciousness and the rest [of the sense-consciousnesses] sometimes function and sometimes do not. This is the fifth reason.

(v) *api ca punaḥ punar āśrayasyopādānadoṣaḥ prasajyate | tathāhi cakṣurvijñānam ekadā pravartate ekadā na pravartate evam avaśiṣṭāni | idam pañcamaṃ kāraṇam |*

Thus, [appropriation of a physical basis] is not possible [without the store-consciousness] because of: (i) causation by previous actions [in the case of the store-consciousness] and by

iti pūrvakarmapravarttamāna pratyayahetuto (Tatia reads *pratyahetuto;* I follow Hakamaya [1978:8] and Tibetan) *'pi kuśalākuśalato 'pi taj jāty anupalaṃbhato 'pi*

present conditions [in the case of the sense-consciousnesses]; (ii) [the experience of the six sense-consciousnesses] as both good and bad [and that of the store-consciousness as exclusively neutral]; (iii) the non-experiencing of what belongs to the set [of the neutral by the six sense-consciousnesses]; (iv) the determinate physical bases [belonging to the six sense-consciousnesses, and the lack of such belonging to the store-consciousness]; (v) and the fault of repeated appropriation [of a physical basis by the six sense-consciousnesses unless the existence of the store-consciousness is postulated].

pratiniyatāśrayato 'pi punaḥ punar upādānadoṣato 'pi na yujyate ||

This first argument is divided into five sub-sections. Section (i) points out that an exhaustive categorization of the causes of the *pravṛttivijñānāni* can be given by listing present or immediately preceding events, and that this leaves no place for causation by long past events. It is the *ālaya* which provides the locus for, and thus accounts for, this second kind of causation. See *TBh* ad *T* XIX (Lévi [1925:37.21ff]). Sections (ii) and (iii) state a fundamental presupposition of Buddhist theories about karma and causation: that the causal principle which brings about the maturation of karmic effect is in itself neutral. Since the six 'functioning consciousnesses' are not neutral in this way but consist in experience which has both affective and moral tone, Sthiramati argues that the *ālaya* must be postulated in order to allow for the maturation of karmic effect which in itself has no moral or affective tone. See La Vallée Poussin [1928–29:152ff; 292–296]; *MV* I.10 and *MVBh* and *MVT* thereto (Pandeya [1971:26.9ff]. Sub-argument (iv) points out that the appropriation of a new physical body at the moment of a new birth would not be possible without a *vipākavijñāna,* a 'maturation consciousness' which can only be the *ālaya.* This is because the other six consciousnesses cannot appropriate the physical body as a whole since each of them has its own specific physical basis or locus (visual consciousness is located in or based on the eye and so forth). Each one of the six *pravṛttivijñānāni* therefore appropriates only its own specific physical basis. Something more is required to appropriate the whole of the physical body at once, and this, according to the argument, can only be the *ālaya.* On the meaning of 'appropriation' *(upātta)* see *AKBh* 23:13–17. Generally on the argument from rebirth see *MS* I.4–5 (Nagao [1982:10–11,83–89], Lamotte [1934:177–185], and Lamotte [1973:57–58]). *MS* I.35 (Nagao [1982:38,199–200]; Lamotte [1973:57–58]). Compare La Vallée Poussin [1928–29:193–194].

<2 THE IMPOSSIBILITY OF ORIGINATION AND SIMULTANEOUS FUNCTIONING OF THE SENSE-CONSCIOUSNESSES>

Why can there be no initial functioning [of consciousness]? Suppose someone should suggest that if there is a store-consciousness the result will be the simultaneous functioning of two consciousnesses. This is the proper reply: what you think of as an error is no error, since it is precisely the case that two consciousnesses function simultaneously. Why? Because it is incorrect to say that someone who wants simultaneously to see, hear, taste, touch, smell and think about [an object] has, from the beginning, consciousnesses which function one after the other. For in such a case attention, sense-organ and sense-object are not distinct.

kena kāraṇenādipravṛttisaṃbhavo na yujyate | sa cet kaścid vaded yady ālayavijñānam asti tena dvayoḥ vijñānayoḥ yugapat pravṛttir bhaviṣyati | sa idaṃ syād vacanīyaḥ | adoṣa eva bhavān doṣasaṃjñī | tathāhi bhavaty eva dvayor vijñānayor yugapat pravṛttiḥ | tat kasya hetoḥ | tathā hy ekatyasya yugapad draṣṭukāmasya (Tatia reads *dradṣṭukāmasya;* I follow Hakamaya [1978:10] and Tibetan) *yāvad vijñātukāmasyādita itaretaravijñānapravṛttir na yujyate | tathāhi tatra manaskāro 'pi nirviśiṣṭa indriyam api viṣayo 'pi ||*

On the general point about the simultaneous functioning of more than one sense-consciousness, see La Vallée Poussin [1928–29:411–412] and compare Lamotte [1934:239–248]. If, as standard Buddhist causal theory suggests, there can be only one *samanantarapratyaya* in any one continuum at any one time, then, without the *ālaya* there can be only one kind of consciousness in any one continuum at any one time. The *ālaya,* however, can act as *samanantarapratyaya* for all the various sense-consciousnesses at once (see *TBh* ad *T* XV, Lévi [1925:33.18–34.11], and compare La Vallée Poussin [1928–29:398–400]) and thus allow for both their simultaneous functioning in a single mind and for the first moment of a particular kind of consciousness in a given mind. The point about the non-distinctness of attention *(manaskāra),* sense-organ *(indriya)* and sense-object *(viṣaya)* merely suggests that the body of necessary and sufficient conditions for the occurrence of any instant of sense-consciousness (which is simply equivalent to attention, sense-organ and sense-object) is simultaneously present for all of the varied sense-consciousnesses. There is therefore no reason why they should not operate simultaneously (as in fact they do according to Yogācāra theory).

<3 THE IMPOSSIBILITY OF CLEAR MENTAL CONSCIOUSNESS>

Why is it that, if [different] consciousnesses do not function simultaneously, there is no clarity in that mental consciousness which follows upon the visual consciousness and so forth [i.e., the rest of the sense-consciousnesses]? The reason is that at just the moment when one remembers an object experienced in the past, mental consciousness functions in an unclear manner. But the manner in which the mental [consciousness] functions when its object is present is not unclear in this way. Therefore, either there is simultaneous functioning [of the sense-consciousnesses] or the mental consciousness is unclear.

kena kāraṇenāsatyāṃ yugapad vijñānapravṛttau manovijñānasya cakṣurādivijñānasahānucarasya spaṣṭatvaṃ na saṃbhavati | tathāhi yasmin samaye 'tītam anubhūtaṃ viṣayaṃ samanusmarati tasmin samaye 'vispaṣṭo manovijñānapracāro bhavati na tu tathā vartamānaviṣayo manaḥpracāro 'vispaṣṭo bhavati | ato 'pi yugapat pravṛttir vā yujyate 'vispaṣṭatvaṃ vā manovijñānasya ||

This argument is straightforward and has been adequately explained in Chapter Three. On the mind as a sense, see *AKBh* ad *AK* I.17 and I.23.

<4 THE IMPOSSIBILITY OF MUTUAL SEEDING>

Why do the six groups of [sense]-consciousness not mutually seed one another? What is not good arises immediately after what is good; what is good arises immediately after what is not good; what is indeterminate arises immediately after both; what belongs to an intermediate realm arises immediately after what belongs to an inferior realm; what

kena kāraṇena bījatvaṃ na saṃbhavati ṣaṇṇāṃ vijñānakāyānām anyonyam | tathāhi kuśalānantaram akuśalam utpadyate akuśalānantaraṃ kuśalam tadubhayānantaram avyākṛtam hīnadhātukānantaraṃ madhyadhātukam madhyadhātukānantaraṃ praṇītadhātukam evaṃ praṇītadhātukānantaraṃ yāvad dhīnadhātukam sāsravānantaram anāsravam anāsravānantaraṃ

belongs to a superior realm arises immediately after what belongs to an intermediate realm; what belongs to an inferior realm arises immediately after what belongs to a superior realm; the undefiled arises immediately after the defiled; the defiled arises without interval after the undefiled; the transcendent arises immediately after the mundane; the mundane arises immediately after the transcendent. It is not proper to predicate the quality of being a seed in this manner of those [six types of sense-consciousness]. Further, a mental continuum which ceased to function a long time ago functions again after a long time and it is not proper to say that it comes from that [long-ceased mental continuum].

sāsravam laukikānantaraṃ lokottaram lokottarānantaraṃ laukikam | na ca teṣāṃ tathā bījatvaṃ yujyate | dīrghakālasamucchinnāpi ca saṃtatiś cireṇa kālena pravartate tasmād api na yujyate ||

The idea that the six sense-consciousnesses can mutually 'seed' one another is a Sautrāntika view, similar to that discussed in Section 2.3.2. It is rejected here in favour of the idea that the *ālaya* acts as the receptacle for all 'seeds'—future possibilities of action and sensation—even when these seeds have mutually incompatible qualities. See La Vallée Poussin [1928–29:182–189]. Compare *MS* I.28ff.

<5 THE IMPOSSIBILITY OF ACTION>

Why, is it that if [different] sense-consciousnesses do not function simultaneously action does not occur? This is, in brief, because action is fourfold: (i) that which appears as receptacle [i.e., the material world]; (ii) that which appears as basis [i.e., the physical body of oneself and others]; (iii) that which appears as 'I'; (iv) that which appears as object [of cognition]. These [four kinds

kena kāraṇenāsatyām yugapad vijñānapravṛttau karma na saṃbhavati | tathāhi samāsatas caturvidhaṃ karma | bhājanavijñaptir āśrayavijñaptir aham iti vijñaptir viṣayavijñaptiś ceti | etā vijñaptayaḥ kṣaṇe kṣaṇe yugapat pravartamānā upalabhyante | na caikasya vijñānasyaikasmin kṣaṇe idam evaṃ rūpaṃ vyatibhinnaṃ

of] appearance are experienced as functioning conjointly in every moment: thus it is not possible that action analyzed in this [fourfold] manner should be attributed to a single [sense]-consciousness in a single moment.

This fourfold analysis of karma is paralleled in *MVBh* and *MVT* ad *MV* I.4 (Pandeya [1971:14.3ff]). There the term *pratibhāsa* is used instead of *vijñapti* and the four categories are *artha* (for *bhājana), sattva* (for *āśraya), ātma* (for *aham)* and *vijñapti* (for *viṣaya).* Despite the differences in terminology, the general point remains the same. All experience in every moment, according to the Yogācāra, has these structures. The fact that they continue in this manner can only be adequately explained if they have a continuing locus other than the transient sense-consciousnesses.

<6 THE IMPOSSIBILITY OF PHYSICAL EXPERIENCE>

Why can there be no bodily experience if there is no store-consciousness? This is so because, for one who is thinking or pondering correctly; for one who is thinking or pondering incorrectly; for one whose mind is concentrated; or for one whose mind is unconcentrated—[for all these] those bodily experiences which occur would neither be nor be experienced as manifold and variegated [as in fact they are]. Thus there is a store-consciousness.

kena kāraṇenāsaty ālayavijñāne kāyiko 'nubhavo na yujyate | tathā hy ekatyasya yoniśo vā 'yoniśo cintayato vā 'nuvitarkayato vā samāhitacetaso vā 'samāhitacetaso ye kāye kāyānubhavā utpadyante 'nekavidhā bahunānāprakārās te na bhaveyur upalabhyante ca | tasmād apy asty ālayavijñānam ||

This argument has been adequately explained in Section 3.3.6.

<7 THE IMPOSSIBILITY OF MINDLESS ATTAINMENTS>

Why, if there is no store-consciousness, can the mindless attainments not occur? This is because [in the absence of the store-consciousness] the consciousness of one who has attained either unconsciousness

kena kāraṇenāsaty ālayavijñāne 'cittā samāpattir na saṃbhavati | tathā hy asaṃjñisamāpannasya vā nirodhasamāpannasya vā vijñānam eva kāyād apakrāntaṃ syāt | nānapakrāntaṃ tataḥ kālakriyaiva bhavet | yathoktaṃ bhagavatā

or cessation would have issued forth from that person's body. And if [such a person's consciousness] does issue forth [from the body in that way] then he would simply die. For the Lord has said: 'Consciousness does not issue forth from his body [i.e., the body of one who has attained unconsciousness or cessation].'

vijñānaṃ cāsya kāyād anapakrāntaṃ bhavatīti ||

Compare with the discussion of the difference between the attainment of cessation and death from Theravāda sources set forth in Section 1.2. See also La Vallée Poussin [1928–29:204–214] and *MS* I.50–55 (Lamotte [1973:71–77]; Nagao [1982:48–50,231–246]).

<8 THE IMPOSSIBILITY OF DEATH>

Why, if there is no store-consciousness, can death not occur? This is because the consciousness of one who is dying abandons the body, growing cold [gradually] either from the top [down] or from the bottom [up]. But there is never a time when the thinking consciousness is not functioning [with an intentional object]. So it is because of the departure of the store-consciousness—which acts as appropriator of the body—that the coldness of the body and its lack of sensation are experienced. It is not [because of the departure] of the thinking consciousness. Therefore, [death] cannot occur [without the store-consciousness].

kena kāraṇenāsaty ālayavijñāne cyutir api na yujyate | tathāhi cyavamānasya vijñānam ūrdhvadehaṃ vā śītikurvan vijahāti adhodehaṃ vā | na ca manovijñānaṃ kadācin na pravartate | ato 'py ālayavijñānasyaiva dehopādānakasya vigamād dehaśītatā upalabhyate dehāpratisaṃvedanā ca | na tu manovijñānasya | ato 'pi na yujyate ||

The spatial metaphor—of the body cooling at the moment of death either from the top down or from the bottom up—relates to standard Buddhist ideas about the future destiny of the dying individual. The person will go either 'upwards', to one of the heavenly realms, or 'downwards', to one of the hells, depending on spiritual condition and the weight and flavour of his accumulated karma. In the former case, the person dies from the feet upwards as the store-consciousness ascends through the top of the head on its way to rebirth in a higher cosmic realm; in the latter, the person dies from the head downwards. This is made clear in *MS* I.42 (Lamotte [1973:62–63]; Nagao [1982:41,210–211] where this point is explicitly made. The basic point of this eighth argument—discussed in detail in La Vallée Poussin [1928–29:195–199]—is to show the following. (1) Death is defined as the departure of consciousness from the body. (2) All the possible types of consciousness with the exception of the store-consciousness are straightforwardly intentional; i.e., they have distinct objects and definite modes of functioning. (3) A full explanation of the process of death requires the postulation of a type of consciousness that is not intentional. (4) Death can only be explained by postulating the existence of the store-consciousness.

NOTES TO INTRODUCTION

[1]The phrase 'altered state of consciousness' is close to being accorded status as technical term referring to a discipline by those—largely in experimental and theoretical psychology—who are concerned to develop psycho-physiological methods to measure and assess the apparently enormous range of discrete 'states' of modes of operation of the mind. The pioneering works in this field were those of Tart [1969; 1971; 1972; 1975a; 1975b]; for a more recent review see Rawlinson [1979].

[2]La Vallée Poussin [1917:110–112].

[3]It is this view which lies behind the fairly frequent characterization of the *dhamma*—Buddhist doctrine in this context—by the term *ehipassika* literally 'come and see' [*DN* 2.217; 3.5; 3.227]. Buddhist doctrine is supposed to be verifiable by experience, although it remains unclear to what extent the Buddha actually held the strongly empiricist view suggested by this term, and it is still less clear whether such a view of Buddhist doctrine is philosophically defensible. Recent defenders of the view that 'early Buddhism' was a strict empiricism have been K. N. Jayatilleke and his pupils, notably D. J. Kalupahana and Gunapala Dharmasiri. Discussions may be found in Jayatilleke [1963]; Kalupahana [1975]; and Dharmasiri [1974]. Frank J. Hoffman [1982] has provided a recent critique of this view—which has become almost an unquestioned orthodoxy among the Sinhalese scholars of Kalupahana's generation—as also has A. D. P. Kalansuriya [1981].

[4]Jayatilleke, for example, appears to think that the (apparently) theoretical constructs of Buddhist philosophy are actually both produced and verified by experiences gained during the practice of meditation. He gives a particularly clear statement of this view in his discussion of the function of inference in Buddhism: 'Inductive inferences in Buddhism are therefore based on a theory of causation. These inferences are made on the data of perception, normal and paranormal

(by 'normal' perception Jayatilleke means sense-perception, and by 'paranormal' he means experiences produced by various meditative techniques). What are considered to constitute knowledge are direct inferences made on the basis of the data of such perceptions. All the knowledge that the Buddha and his disciples claim to have in "knowing and seeing" (v.supra, 741), except for the knowledge of Nirvana, appears to be of this nature.' [1963:457].

[5]The precise nature of the relationship between any given instance of virtuoso religious experience and the conceptual scheme or world-view within which it came to birth has been extremely well discussed by Steven Katz [1978, 1982, 1983] and Gimello [1978, 1983]. Katz comes to the following conclusion after surveying a broad range of so-called 'mystical' experiences in their cultural and intellectual contexts: '. . the experience of mystics comes into being as the kind of experience it is as a necessary consequence of the linguistic, theological and social-historical circumstances which govern the mystical ascent.' [1983:43].

[6]'Psychotropic', like 'altered state of consciousness' is a term in current usage among those who study altered states of consciousness from a psychological perspective. It is usually used as an adjective to describe any technique or method which results in the alteration of the psyche's condition, and thus can be appropriately applied to Buddhist meditation.

[7]The Pali equivalent is *saññāvedayitanirodha* and the standard Tibetan translation is *'du shes dang tshor ba 'gog pa*. The Sanskrit also occurs in the form *saṃjñāveditanirodha*. In this work I shall use the Sanskrit forms unless there is a particularly good reason for doing otherwise, as when texts which exist only in Pali or Tibetan are being discussed.

[8]Especially in the accounts of the Buddha's last moments in the *Mahaparinibbānasutta* of the *DN* and the parallel account in the *SN*. It's interesting to note that the *SN* account—in every other respect parallel to the *DN* account—omits mention of the *nirodhasamāpatti* while Buddhaghosa's commentary on the *SN* account [*SA* 1.223] treats it as though the *nirodhasamāpatti* were present. The *DN* account reads: *atha kho bhagavā paṭhamajjhānaṃ samāpajji | paṭhamajjhānā vuṭṭhahitvā dutiyajjhānaṃ samāpajji | dutiyajjhānā vuṭṭhahitvā tatiyajjhānaṃ samāpajji | tatiyajjhānā vuṭṭhahitvā catutthajjhānaṃ samāpajji | catutthajjhānā vuṭṭhahitvā ākāsānañcāyatanaṃ samāpajji | ākāsānañcāyatana-samāpattiyā vuṭṭhahitvā viññāṇañcāyatanaṃ* (One would expect *viññāṇānañcāyatanaṃ*, though the contracted form given is much more common in the *suttas;* Buddhaghosa calls this the 'customary term' *rūlhisadda* [*VM* 712.3(10.31)]; Rewatadhamma gives *rūlhī-) samāpajji | viññāṇañcāyatana-samāpattiyā vuṭṭhahitvā ākiñcaññāyatanaṃ samāpajji | ākiñcaññāyatana-samāpattiyā vuṭṭhahitvā nevasaññānāsaññāyatanaṃ samāpajji | nevasaññānāsaññā-samāpattiyā vuṭṭhahitvā saññā-vedayita-nirodhaṃ samāpajji | atha kho āyasmā ānando ayasmantaṃ anuruddhaṃ etad avoca | parinibbuto bhante anuruddha bhagavā ti | na āvuso ānando bhagavā parinibbuto saññā-vedayita-nirodhaṃ samāpanno ti |* [*DN* 2.156.4–19]. The process is then reversed, from the

attainment of cessation down to the first *jhāna* and then reversed again, from the first *jhāna* to the fourth; after entering the fourth *jhāna* the Buddha attains *parinibbāna.* The *SN* account [*SN* 1.158;.3–11] is identical except that the cessation of sensation and conceptualization is not mentioned and Ananda's question is therefore also omitted. Buddahaghosa's comment on the *SN* version, however, treats it as though the attainment of cessation is mentioned, and gives extensive discussion to Ananda's question. He explains that Anuruddha knows that the Buddha has not died but is instead in the *nirodhasamāpatti* because he has himself, on at least one occasion, accompanied the Buddha as far as the exit from the stage of neither conceptualization nor nonconceptualization *(nevasaññānāsaññāyatana)* and thus is aware of the difference between death and the cessation of sensation and conceptualization: *kathaṃ pana so aññāsi | thero kira satthārā saddhiṃ yeva taṃ taṃ samāpattiṃ samāpajjanto yāva nevasaññānāsaññāyatana-vuṭṭhānaṃ tāva gantvā idāni bhagavā nirodhaṃ samāpanno anto nirodhe ca kāla-kiriyā nāma na atthi ti aññāsi |* [*SA.* 1.223.19–23]. The textual problems involved here cannot be pursued in this study, but it's noteworthy that they occur; even in this *locus classicus,* it seems, a mention of the attainment of cessation was felt to be problematic.

[9]*yathā-bhūta-ñāṇa-dassana* (Skt. *yathā-bhūta-jñāna-darśana),* a frequently occurring compound of key importance in Buddhist soteriological theory, and more especially in those areas of such theory which prize the intellectual/analytical methods of practice. Literally, 'knowledge and vision which is in accord with what has become' (taking *ñāṇa-dassana* as a *dvanda* and the entire compund as a *kammadhāraya,* with *yathā-bhūta* qualifying *ñāṇa-dassana;* this is, I think, the most likely interpretation, though others are possible), more freely the meaning is something like knowing that things are the way they are and perceiving in accordance with that knowledge. Translating the compound in this way allows the useful philosophical gloss 'knowing that' (for *ñāṇa,* here understood as knowledge capable of propositional formulation) and 'seeing as' (for *dassana,* here understood as an active transformation of the perceptual faculties in accordance with the propositional knowledge denoted by *ñāṇa).* The frequent occurrence of this compound—and many cognates—illustrates splendidly the importance of the intellectual/cognitive/verbal modes of human existence to the analytical modes of meditational practice and the soteriological goals that go with them. The contrast with the concentrative mode could scarcely be more marked: neither *ñāṇa* nor *dassana* could possibly occur in the attainment of cessation.

[10]I take this to refer to a style of reasoning developed within the Indian Buddhist tradition and represented within the texts of that tradition from about the first century BC to the tenth century AD. It is a heavily analytic style, very precise and lucid, concerned with definitions and argument-forms. How it operates will become clear in the course of this study. It is important to notice that the phrase 'Indian scholastic Buddhism' crosses the traditional boundary between 'Hīnayāna' (lesser vehicle) and Mahāyāna Buddhism.

[11]The commentary referred to here is Dhammapāla's *Paramatthamañjūsāṭīkā (VMT).*

[12]The name of this school means 'school (or doctrine) of the elders' and it is the term applied to their own system of beliefs by the Buddhist intellectuals of South and South-East Asia, especially Burma, Thailand, and Sri Lanka. A more detailed discussion will be found in Section 1.1.

[13]The name of this school—also one of the so-called Hīnayāna schools, different from the Theravāda in that it is no longer a living tradition—is usually derived from the title of a text (or texts; there are several Indian *abhidharma* texts now extant only in Chinese translation which bear this name or a variant of it. See the brief essay under *Mahāvibhāṣā* in the Bibliography) which defined orthodoxy for the school. The Vaibhāṣikas, then, are 'the followers of the *[Great Book of] Options ([Mahā]Vibhāṣā).* A more detailed discussion of the tradition may be found in Section 2.1.

[14]Etymologically this term means 'followers of the *sūtra*' (viz: sacred texts supposed to be the words of the Buddha rather than commentarial exposition). The history of this school remains obscure, as does the issue of whether it should even be called such; there are no specifically Sautrāntika sacred texts as is the case with the Theravāda, Vaibhāṣika and Yogācāra traditions. Historically there is little doubt that, like the Vaibhāṣika, this group originated from within the Sarvāstivāda tradition. Refer to Section 2.1 for a more detailed discussion.

[15]I refer to the *Abhidharmakośabhāṣyaṭīkā* (AKT) called *Tattvārthā,* which is almost certainly a work of Sthiramati's, and to Yaśomitra's *Abhidharmakośavyākhyā (AKV)* called *Sphuṭārthā.*

[16]Literally, 'practitioners of spiritual discipline *(yoga)*'. Refer to Section 3.1 for a detailed discussion.

[17]Classically expressed by Berger and Luckmann [1966].

[18]Notably Wittgenstein [1953] and Quine [1969]; the (still continuing) industry that has grown up around the posthumous publishing of Wittgenstein's multi-coloured notebooks, while not yet fully digested by the philosophical community, adds to the development of which I speak.

[19]See, revealingly, Carrithers [1983:95] and for some subtle and nuanced discussions Geertz [1983]. Sperber [1985] provides what is, to my knowledge, the most philosophically sophisticated discussion of relativism yet produced by an anthropologist.

[20]See Kuhn [1962; 1970a; 1970b] and Feyerabend [1974].

[21]I refer here especially to the pervasive influence of Derrida on hermeneutical theory; for an application of his method to philosophical texts, see de Man [1978].

[22]Most recently see Coward [1985] and Rouner [1984]; a debate on the significance of this approach to questions of religious truth may be found in Hick [1981]; Griffiths and Lewis [1983]; and Hick [1983].

[23]See Barnes and Bloor [1982].

[24]Since the publication of Gadamer's *Truth and Method* in English in 1975 (translated from the second German edition), a reading of his hermeneutical theory has become *de rigueur* among American historians of religion and literary critics. It does not seem to me that his influence has been entirely beneficient, largely because of his muddled thinking on questions of truth and judgement.

[25]There has been, of course, an enormous amount of superficial and uncritical normative judgement passed upon foreign (to the individual undertaking the judging) conceptual systems: for example that by (some) Christian missionary intellectuals on what was taken to be truth in the religious systems adhered to by potential converts to Christianity. There has also been an enormous amount of careful scholarly work, in the exegetical mode, of the internal dynamics and structures of foreign (to the scholar doing the studying) conceptual systems: for example, most of the work undertaken by scholars from the Chicago School of the history of religions. But a meeting of careful scholarship in the exegetical mode with a critical spirit concerned to ask questions about truth, coherence and so forth, has been, in the English-speaking academies of the twentieth century, rare in the extreme. This is beginning to change, I think, only amongst those few Western philosophers who have gained some degree of familiarity with non-Western philosophical traditions, and who, having been trained in the analytical tradition take questions of coherence, interpretive adequacy and truth to be of paramount importance. See for example Yandell [1974]; Betty [1976; 1978; 1983a]; and Sharma [1984]. Compare the recent debate between Betty [1983b] and Loy [1983]. The most pressing need is for more philosophically acute minds prepared to devote serious analytical study to non-Western philosophical systems.

[26]See M. Monier-Williams [1899:xxxvi] for the basic system; modified only for the vowels ṛ and ṛi and the two sibilants ś and ṣ.

[27]Explained by Wylie [1959].

[28]See Nelson [1974].

NOTES TO CHAPTER ONE

[1]This is true, for example, of some of the texts which now form part of the *KN*. The story is a complex one. See Norman [1983:57–96] for an outline account of the problems and Aronoff [1982] for a detailed discussion of the problems surrounding the canonicity of the prose sections of the *Jātakatthavaṇṇanā*.

[2]By 'primitive' here is meant simply pre-Aśokan Buddhism, the life and thought of Buddhist communities in Northern and Central India from around 450 BC to around 250 BC. This early formative period is witnessed only by the texts under discussion here—together with their analogues preserved in other languages—and by scattered (and largely later) inscriptional and other archaeological evidence. Anything said about this period, either from the perspective of the history of ideas or from the sociological and institutional perspective, is necessarily highly speculative.

[3]It is no part of my purpose in this monograph to explain or defend this approximate dating of the material in the *Suttapiṭaka* (the Pali name for the first part of the canonical collection) of the Pali canon, or indeed of the entire canon. It is not in any case a terribly controversial matter; a full discussion of the historical issues may be found in the first two chapters of Griffiths [1983a]. Standard works with useful historical discussions of the problem of primitive Buddhism and the formation of the canonical collection are Schayer [1935]; Keith [1936]; Bareau [1955a; 1955b]; Régamey [1957]; Lamotte [1958:136–209] and Frauwallner [1956]. Frauwallner's work has been especially influential in its discussion of the date and significance of the *Skandhaka* section of the *Vinayapiṭaka* (the second section of the tripartite canonical collection) though it has not been received without criticism—see Prebish [1973]. It's significant, I think, that the heated debates on the nature of 'primitive' or 'pre-canonical' Buddhism which were such an importanat part of the Western scholarly study of the Buddhist tradition from its inception until the second world war, have almost dropped

out of sight. Here, as so often, the methods and goals of the study of Buddhism mirror those involved in the study of Christianity: when the quest of the historical Jesus was in full swing and the Protestant obsession with origins dominated historical research into the Christian tradition, much the same was true for the study of Buddhism; and when the search for origins became unpopular in the theological universe, the same happened among those professionally concerned with the study of Buddhism. Allowing for a certain time-lag, a 'new quest' for the historical Buddha can be expected at any moment—perhaps the first signs of such an enterprise are already visible in Bareau [1963; 1971].

[4]The five *Collections* or *Nikāyā* are *Dīghanikāya (DN), Majjhimanikāya (MN), Samyuttanikāya (SN), Anguttaranikāya (AN)* and *Khuddhakanikāya (KN)*. References to these texts will be to volume, page and line of the Pali Text Society editions, unless otherwise noted. Full details of these editions will be found in the Bibliography. The Pali version of these texts is only one among several surviving collections; a complete collection of substantially parallel texts survives in Chinese translation, though this is a translation based upon versions of these texts originally preserved in Indic languages other than Pali; there are some parallel texts in the Tibetan canonical collections and there are fragmentary survivals in other Indic languages. The Pali versions possess no particularly privileged historical position other than that bestowed upon them by their completeness, the fact that they form the basis of a living tradition and that they are easily accessible in the West in (moderately) well-edited versions. Complete English translations of the material in *DN, MN, SN* and *AN* are also easily available, although these vary tremendously in quality. Details are given in the Bibliography. The best recent review of the literature is Norman [1983].

[5]There are, as is almost always the case in attempting to date any historical figure in India, severe historical problems connected with the dating of Buddhaghosa, and no final agreement has been reached on the issue, though the fifth century seems the most likely date. Discussions may be found in Adikaram [1946:2–8]; Rahula [1966:xxiv–xxvi, 98]; Nyanamoli [1976:xv–xxvii]; Buddhadatta [1957:142–157] and Norman [1983:120–130].

[6]Exactly what Buddhaghosa wrote, what he redacted and what he translated remain subjects for debate. Even if there were indeed Old Sinhala versions of the standard commentaries to the *Nikāyā*, as is suggested by Buddhaghosa himself, and even if Buddhaghosa was dependent upon the material contained in those commentaries, it still remains true that the Pali commentaries which we know today must in large part be credited to him. To the works cited in the previous note compare Geiger [1956]; Law [1974] and Norman [1983:118–120].

[7]The problem of Dhammapāla's date centres upon the issue of whether the person who composed *aṭṭhakathā* (commentaries) upon texts from the *KN* is the same as the person who wrote *ṭīkā* (subcommentaries) upon works of Buddhaghosa's. The tradition attributes

both sets of works to a 'Dhammapāla'. Other external evidence suggests that the *aṭṭhakathā* may date from the sixth century or so and the *ṭīkā* from the ninth and tenth centuries. This creates obvious problems in attributing both sets of works to the same individual, and the usual solution is to suggest that there were two Dhammapālas. Discussions may be found in Buddhadatta [1957:189–197], Saddhatissa [1965:2ff], Cousins [1972], Pieris [1978] and Norman [1983]. A subsidiary problem concerns whether the later of these Dhammapālas (or the only one for those who think there was only one) is the same as the Indian Dharmapāla (to use the Sanskrit form of his name) who was mentioned by the Chinese Buddhist pilgrim Izing as being active in Nālandā around the seventh century. The thesis that Dhammapāla, author of the *ṭīkā* literature, and Dharmapāla were one and the same was examined and rejected by Hardy [1897] long ago, though recently resurrected and powerfully argued for (along with the thesis that there is only one Dhammapāla, thus reducing a possible three individuals—Dhammapāla author of the *aṭṭhakathā*, Dhammapāla author of the *ṭīkā* and Dharmapāla, monk from Nālandā—to one; this is at least economical) by De Silva [1970:ii–lxxxiii]. Despite De Silva's arguments and the seductive delights of Occam's razor (why postulate three individuals if you can get away with one?), it seems to me that the historical evidence, while by no means decisive and evidencing some confusion from within the tradition, suggests that we should separate the two Dhammapālas both from one another and from Dharmapāla. I shall assume, then, though not without some misgiving, that my Dhammapāla (author of *VMT*) was active not earlier than the ninth century AD.

[8]Stephan Beyer approaches rather closely to this odd view about the proper functions of the Western student of Buddhism: '. . . a Buddhologist does not deal with Buddhism so much as he deals with Buddhists.' [1973:xvi]. It's hard to know quite what this view means or how it could be defended. Certainly, Buddhists are an appropriate object of study, but so, presumably, are the texts which make up at least part of what is usually considered 'Buddhism'.

[9]For some discussion of this terminology, see Smart's [1965] classic study of the interpretation and assessment of accounts of mystical experience and Yandell's [1981] extensive critique of Smart's approach. By the phenomenological method here, I mean nothing more complex than the method outlined in Husserl's early works.

[10]A substantially parallel passage may be found at *SN* 4.293–295.

[11]*yvāyaṃ āvuso mato kālakato yo cāyaṃ bhikkhu saññā-vedayita-nirodhaṃ samāpanno imesaṃ kiṃ nānākaraṇan-ti | yvāyaṃ āvuso mato kālakato tassa kāyasankhārā niruddhā paṭippassaddhā | vacīsankhārā niruddhā paṭippassaddhā | cittasankhārā niruddhā paṭippassaddhā | āyu parikkhīṇo usmā vūpasantā indriyāni viparibhinnāni | yo cāyaṃ bhikkhu saññā-vedayita-nirodhaṃ samāpanno tassa pi kāyasankhārā niruddhā paṭippassaddhā | vacīsankhārā niruddhā paṭippassaddhā | cittasankhārā niruddhā paṭippassaddhā | āyu aparikkhīṇo usmā avūpasantā indriyāni vippasannāni | yvāyaṃ āvuso mato kālakato yo cāyaṃ bhikkhu saññā-vedayita-nirodhaṃ samāpanno idaṃ tesaṃ nānākaraṇanti |* [*MN* 1.296.11–23].

[12]The two offences cited here—killing of parents and killing of *arhats* —are two of the most serious possible according to the Theravādin ethical code. Their commission requires expulsion from the monastic order. On the *pārājika* offences, see *Vinayapiṭaka* 1.172; 2.101; 2.242.

[13]The hermeneutical principle cited here is intended to argue against a literalistic exegesis which draws absurd conclusions from the form of words found in a text. It stresses instead the importance of penetrating to the meaning of a text, which is clearly regarded as to some extent independent of the words in which it is framed. The Pali *paṭisaraṇa*—here translated, following Edgerton [1953:372] as 'point of reference'—is equivalent to the Sanskrit *pratisaraṇa,* and the sentence from the *MA* under discussion here is very similar to the first of the four 'points of reference' which are frequently discussed in Buddhist Sanskrit texts. A full discussion of this formula would take me beyond the scope of this work; it must suffice to say that this fourfold formula is at the root of most Buddhist hermeneutical philosophy. Extensive discussion may be found in Lamotte [1949] and Thurman [1978]; further Buddhist Sanskrit sources are listed in La Vallée Poussin [1971:V.246–248]. Compare Gregory [1983] for an account of a Chinese discussion of a similar issue.

[14]The phrase 'those things with which they come into contact' translates *ghaṭṭentesu* rather freely. A more literal translation would be 'those things which cause obstructions to them'. The general point is that external objects *(ārammaṇa)* are conceived by Theravādins as obstructing or getting in the way of the clarity and sensitivity of the sense-organs; this is what causes the phenomenon of perception.

[15]The Pali term *pasāda* (Skt. *prasāda)* generally means 'clarity', 'brightness' or 'purity'. Here it refers specifically to the capacity of the sense-organs to clearly perceive external objects. Note the reference to the 'five [sensory] clarities' *(pañca pasādā)* towards the end of the translated extract. 'Clarity' in this sense is usually conceived by the *ābhidharmikas* as a kind of subtle physical form; the *AKBh* gives the standard gloss: *rūpaśabdagandharasaspraṣṭavyavijñānānām āśrayabhūtā ye pañca rūpātmakāḥ prasādās te yathākramamṃ cakṣuḥśrotraghrāṇajihvākāyā veditavyāḥ | yathoktaṃ bhagavatā cakṣur bhikṣo ādhyātmikam āyatanaṃ catvāri mahābhūtāny upādāya rūpaprasādaḥ iti vistaraḥ* | (Pradhan reads . . . *mahābhūtāny upādāya rūpaprasādāś ca cakṣurādayaḥ*. I follow *AKV* [31.3] and Tib. *'byung ba chen po bzhi dag rgyur byas gzugs dad pa'o zhes rgyas par gzungs pa lta bu'o* | [P GU 31b2–3]).

[16]*kāyasankhārā ti assāsapassāsā | vacīsankhārā ti vitakkavicārā | cittasankhārā ti saññāvedanā | āyū ti rūpajīvitindriyaṃ | viparibhinnāni ti upahatāni vinaṭṭhāni | 'tattha keci nirodhaṃ samāpanassa cittasankhārā va niruddhā ti | vacanato cittaṃ aniruddhaṃ hoti tasmā sacittakā ayaṃ samāpattī ti vadanti | te vattabbā vacīsankhārā pi 'ssa niruddhā ti vacanato vācā aniruddhā hoti tasmā nirodhaṃ samāpannena dhammam pi kathentena sajjhāyam pi karontena nisīditabbaṃ siyā | yo cāyaṃ mato kālakato tassāpi cittasankhārā niruddhā ti vacanato cittaṃ aniruddhaṃ bhaveyya tasmā kālakate mātāpitaro vā arahante vā jhāpentena ānantariyakammaṃ kataṃ bhaveyya | iti byañjane abhinivesaṃ akatvā ācariyānaṃ naye ṭhatvā attho upaparikkhitabbo | attho hi paṭisaraṇaṃ*

na byañjanaṃ | indriyāni vippassannāni ti kiriyamayapavattasmiṃ hi vattamāne bahiddhā ārammaṇesu pasāde ghaṭṭentesu indriyāni kilamanti upahatāni makkhitāni viya honti vātādīhi uddhatarajena cātummahāpathe ṭhapitādāso viya | yathā pana thavikāya pakkhipitvā mañjūsādisu ṭhapito ādāso anto yeva virocati evaṃ nirodhasamāpannassa bhikkhuno antonirodhe pañca pasādā ativiya virocanti | tena vuttaṃ indriyāni vippasannānī ti | [*MA* 2.351.14–352.4].

[17]Compare: *assāsapassāsā kho āvuso visākha kāyasankhāro vitakkavicārā vacīsankhāro saññā ca vedanā ca cittasankhāro ti |* [*MN* 1.301.20–22]. It seems more likely from the definitions, both in the canon and in the *MA*, that we are supposed to regard the process of respiration *(assāsapassāsa)* as an example of physical activity rather than an exhaustive account of it. The same is true for the other definitions/examples. In the *Cūlavedallasutta* we are told that respiration is regarded as physical activity because inbreathing and outbreathing are activities which are 'physical and bound up with the body' *(kāyikā ete dhammā kāyapaṭibaddhā* [*MN* 1.301.25]). Similarly, reasoning and deliberation are said to be verbal activities only because after such activities speech occurs *(vitakketvā vicāretvā pacchā vācaṃ bhindati . . .* [*MN* 1.301.26–27]), and sensation and conceptualization are mental activities simply because they are 'mental and bound up with the mind' *(saññā ca vedanā ca cetasikā ete dhammā cittapaṭibaddhā tasmā saññā ca vedanā ca cittasankhāro ti |* [*MN* 1.301.28–29]).

[18]To properly understand this example of *reductio ad absurdum,* it is important to realize that sentience—the possession of *citta*—is, for the Buddhist, an enabling condition for the performance of action, since action depends primarily upon volition *(cetanā)* which is in turn dependent upon the existence of mind—*citta.* Buddhaghosa chooses the example of killing parents or *arhats* since these are instances of the worst possible class of moral offences in Buddhist ethical doctrine and thus provide the most striking illustration of the *reductio.*

[19]*āyu pan'āvuso kiṃ paṭicca tiṭṭhatīti | āyu usmaṃ paṭicca tiṭṭhatīti | usmā pan'āvuso kiṃ paṭicca tiṭṭhatīti | usmā āyuṃ paṭicca tiṭṭhatīti | idān'eva kho mayaṃ āvuso āyasmato sāriputtassa bhāsitaṃ evaṃ ājānāma | āyu usmaṃ paṭicca tiṭṭhatīti | idān'eva kho mayaṃ āyasmati sāriputtassa bhāsitaṃ evaṃ ājānāma | usmā āyuṃ paṭicca tiṭṭhatīti | yathā kathaṃ pan'āvuso imassa bhāsitassa attho daṭṭhabbo ti | tena h'āvuso upamante karissāmi upamāya p'idh-'ekacce viññū purisā bhāsitassa atthaṃ ājānanti | seyyathā pi āvuso telapadīpassa jhāyato acciṃ paṭicca ābhā paññāyati | ābhaṃ paṭicca acci paññāyati | evam eva kho āvuso āyu usmaṃ paṭicca tiṭṭhati usmā ca āyuṃ paṭicca tiṭṭhatīti | te va nu kho āvuso āyusankhārā te vedaniyā dhammā udāhu aññe āyusankhārā aññe vedaniyā dhammā ti | na kho āvuso te va āyusankhārā te vedaniyā dhammā | te ca āvuso āyusankhārā abhaviṃsu te vedaniyā dhammā na-y-idaṃ saññāvedayitanirodhaṃ samāpannassa bhikkhuno vuṭṭhānaṃ paññāyetha | yasmā ca kho āvuso aññe āyusankhārā aññe vedaniyā dhammā tasmā saññavedayitanirodhaaṃ samāpannassa bhikkhuno vuṭṭhānaṃ paññāyatīti |* [*MN* 1.295.23–296.6].

[20]Buddhaghosa, in the *MA,* simply explains that 'vitality' is to be identified with the 'life-faculty' *(jīvitindriya)* and 'heat' with the 'energy

generated by action' *(kammajateja)* and stresses that the one cannot exist without the other.

[21]*eko puriso jālāpavatte ukkaṇṭhito udakena paharitvā jālaṃ appavattaṃ katvā chārikāya angare pidhāya tuṇhī nisīdati | yadā 'ssa puna jālāya attho hoti chārikaṃ apanetvā angare parivattetvā upādānaṃ datvā mukhavātaṃ vā tālavaṇṭavātaṃ vā dadāti | atha jālāpavattaṃ puna pavattati |* [*MA* 2.350.26–31].

[22]*rūpajīvitindriya,* here I think to be understood as equivalent to both vitality and heat, since both the canon and Buddhaghosa have already said that these two are radically interdependent.

[23]*chārikāya pihitangārā viya rūpajīvitindriyaṃ | purisassa puna jālāya atthe sati chārikāpanayanādīni viya bhikkhuno yathāparicchinna-kālāpagamanaṃ | aggijālāya pavatti viya puna arūpadhammesu uppannesu rūpārūpapavatti . . .* [*MA* 2.351.2–6].

[24]*tattha kā nirodhasamāpattī ti | yā anupubbanirodhavasena cittacetasikānaṃ dhammānaṃ appavatti |* [*VM* 1665.10–11(23.18)].

[25]*anupubbanirodhavasenā ti vipassanānugatā aṭṭhasamāpattiyo ārohantena taṃ taṃ paṭipakkhanirodhamukhena tiṇṇaṃ sankhārānaṃ anupubbato nirodhavasena | yathāparicchinnakālaṃ yā cittacetasikānaṃ appavatti ayaṃ nirod*hasamāpattī ti attho | [*VMT* 1665.23–25].

[26]The story occurs in *VM* 1676.9–18(23.36).

[27]The term 'enstatic' is derived from the Greek *en-stasis* meaning 'standing within', and etymologically is the opposite of 'ecstatic'—'standing without'. The term has, since the publication of Mircea Eliade's important study of the methods of yoga, become standard in studies of this kind (Eliade [1969:339 and passim]). It is used to denote techniques designed to withdraw the practitioner from contacts with the external world, to establish autonomy and ultimately to empty consciousness of all content. The *locus classicus* in Indian texts for a description of this type of technique is *Bhagavadgītā* II.58, describing a person whose 'wisdom is firm' *(sthitaprajñā):* When he entirely withdraws his senses from their objects like a tortoise his limbs, then his wisdom is firmly established. *(yadā saṃharate cāyaṃ kūrmo 'ngānīva sarva śaḥ | indriyāṇīndriyārthebhyas tasya prajñā pratiṣṭhitā ||).* See Zaehner [1969:151]; Van Buitenen [1981:78–79]. Eliade sometimes uses 'enstasy' as a translation for *samādhi* (not a practice that will be followed here; my standard translation for that term will be 'concentration', which is both etymologically and semantically preferable), and there are many errors, some of them egregious, in his comments on Buddhist psychotropic technique (for a discussion of some of which see Gombrich [1974]). But the basic distinction between enstatic technique and ecstatic technique remains invaluable.

[28]Poussin states the problem succinctly: 'On peut, sans imprudence, discerner dans les sources bouddhiques . . . deux théories opposées

. . . la théorie qui fait du salut une oeuvre purement ou surtout intellectuelle; la théorie qui met le salut au bout des disciplines ascétiques et extatiques.' [1937c:189–190]. There has been a reasonable amount of scholarly effort devoted to the issue in recent years, of which the most notable items are the following: Sopa [1979] has provided a brief study of a similar issue, the relationship between analytic and enstatic meditation from the perspective of his school of Tibetan Buddhism. King [1980:Chapters 3–5], while outlining the issue effectively, does little more by way of resolution than repeat the Theravādin orthodoxy as expressed by Buddhaghosa. Barnes [1980], in an article based upon his Oxford MPhil thesis, also contains some useful material, especially when he draws upon parallels from the *Mahābhārata.* My own [1981] study sets out the problem rather more fully than is possible here, though I there attempted no resolution of the issue. More recently, Nathan Katz [1982:55–95] is thorough and suggestive. Finally, in a fascinating, and at the time of writing still unpublished manuscript, Bronkhorst [unpublished] analyzes the issue in detail and illuminates it by adducing parallels from Jaina material. I am indebted to Dr. Bronkhorst for personal discussions and for allowing me to see a copy of this work.

29'Unsatisfactoriness' is, in general, not a bad translation for the basic Buddhist term *dukkha* (Skt. *duḥkha)* more often translated as 'suffering'.

30I'm indebted for some of these ideas to Stephan Beyer.

31See especially *Ṛgveda* I.164, where the poet as knower is celebrated, even if in somewhat obscure terms. O'Flaherty provides a useful discussion of this hymn as well as the best translation currently available in any Western language [1981:71–83]. *Ṛgveda* VI.9 also makes an explicit connection between knowledge and immortality.

32*aham annam aham annam aham annam | ahamannādo 'hamannādo 'hamannādaḥ | aham ślokakṛd ahaṃ ślokakṛd ahaṃ ślokakṛt | aham asmi prathamajā ṛtasya | pūrvaṃ devebhyo'mṛtasya nābhāyai | yo mā dadāti sa ideva mā 'vāḥ | aham annam annam adantamādyi | aham viśvaṃ bhavanamabhyabhavām* | Limaye and Vadekar [1958:60–61]

33This is, of course, a very schematic and imprecise analysis which leaves a great deal unaccounted for. I do not intend to claim that the view of salvation expressed by the *Taittirīya Upaniṣad* is identical with that expressed in those Buddhist texts which stress the importance of analytic technique and of knowledge and power. The Buddhist version is, of course, characteristically Buddhist and differs in many philosophical essentials from the *Upaniṣadic.* I intend simply to point out that there are some fascinating and deep rooted parallels between this *Upaniṣadic* view and the Buddhist view and to indicate that neither the Buddha nor Buddhists developed their views of salvation and soteriological method in isolation from what had preceded them in India. The stress on power as part of the soteriological goal is by no means foreign even to Theravāda texts and is still more obvious in Mahāyāna works. The great importance given in Theravāda texts to the attainment of various supernatural powers (for which there are a number of terms; the later standard became *abhiññā,* Skt. *abhijñā)* as a result of the practice of analytic techniques is the obvious example, but the effort put into describing the nature and range of the powers attributed to Buddhas and Bodhisattvas in later Mahāyāna texts also illustrates the significance of power as an integral part of the Buddhist soteriological goal.

[34]The unit of tradition describing this fivefold set of practices and resultant altered states of consciousness occurs in completely stereotyped form throughout the four *Nikāyā,* though in many different contexts. The text given in this note is from the *Mahāsīhanādasutta* of *DN,* and the context is a description of the eightfold series called the 'liberations' *(vimokkha): sabbaso rūpasaññānaṃ samatikkamā paṭighasaññānaṃ atthagamā nānattasaññānaṃ amanasikārā ananto ākāso ti ākāsānañcāyatanaṃ upasampajja viharati . . . sabbaso ākāsānañcāyatanaṃ samatikkamma anantaṃ viññāṇan ti viññāṇañcāyatanaṃ upasampajja viharati . . sabbaso viññāṇañcāyatanaṃ samatikkamma n'atthi kiñcīti ākiṇcaññāyatanaṃ upasampajja viharati . . . sabbaso ākiñcaññāyatanaṃ samatikkamma nevasaññānāsaññāyatanaṃ upasampajja viharati . . . sabbaso nevasaññānāsaññāyatanaṃ samatikkamma saññāvedayitanirodhaṃ upasampajja viharati* | [*DN* 2.71.2–17].

[35]*cattāro arūpā,* see, for example, the list at *DN* 3.224.10–19.

[36]Later Buddhist scholasticism goes into very elaborate detail in its discussions of the attributes of the divine beings who inhabit the different formless realms; while these distinctions are very important for a proper understanding of Buddhist cosmology, they will not concern me further in this study. The standard Indian Buddhist treatment of the issue may be found in the third chapter of the *AKBh,* translated and annotated extensively by La Vallée Poussin [1919 and 1971].

[37]This is indicated by the use in the description of the attainment of the first three formlessnesses of a *ti* clause in the Pali original—*ananto akāso ti* and so forth. This has been indicated in translation by the use of single quotation marks.

[38]The most significant occurrences in the four *Nikāyā* are *DN* 2.71, 2.112, 2.156, 3.261–262, 3.266, 3.288 and 3.290; *MN* 1.159–160, 1.174–175, 1.203–204, 1.207–209, 1.398–400, 1:454–456, 2.12–13, 3.25–26 and 3.42–45; *SN* 1.158, 2.210–212, 3.255–256, 4.217, 4.226–227, 4.262–265 and 5.318–319 and *AN* 1.41, 4.409, 4.418, 4.456 and 5.207–208.

[39]'Meditation' is frequently used in secondary sources as a translation for *jhāna* (Skt. *dhyāna).* This is either too general and vague (for those to whom its connotations are vaguely 'Eastern' and its denotation any set of psychotropic techniques) or too specific and misleading (for those to whom its denotation and connotation are precisely and specifically Christian). A good discussion of the problems involved in translating this term may be found in Cousins [1973]; compare Gunaratana [1980:5].

[40]The stereotyped formula describing the four *jhānā* occurs very frequently (86 times in clear and full form) throughout the first four *Collections*. I have provided elsewhere a detailed form-critical analysis of this unit of tradition together with a discussion of the meaning of the key terms involved [Griffiths 1983b]; compare Schmithausen [1976a], a study in which a somewhat similar approach. Gunaratana [1980] has provided a comprehensive survey of material on the four *jhānā* as it occurs in the *Collections*. The standard unit of tradition describing these altered states of consciousness runs thus: '(i) [The practitioner], separated from desire, separated from negative states of mind, attains to and remains in the first *jhāna* which possesses both reasoning and deliberation, originates from separation, and possesses both joy and happiness. (ii) Suppressing both reasoning and deliberation [the practitioner] attains to and remains in the second *jhāna* which possesses inner tranquillity and one-pointedness of mind, originates from concentration, is without reasoning and deliberation, and possesses both joy and happiness. (iii) By detachment from joy [the practitioner] remains in equanimity; mindful and aware he experiences physical happiness and attains to and remains in the third *jhāna* which the noble ones call 'remaining in equanimity, mindfulness and happiness.' (iv) By the abandonment of both happiness and sadness and by the disappearance of previous joy and sorrow, [the practitioner] attains to and remains in the fourth *jhāna* which possesses neither happiness nor sadness and which is characterized by that purity of mindfulness which is equanimity.' Text: (i) *vivicc'eva kāmehi vivicca akusalehi dhammehi savitakkaṃ savicāraṃ vivekajaṃ pītisukhaṃ paṭhamajjhānaṃ upasampajja viharati* | (ii) *vitakkavicārānaṃ vūpasamā ajjhattaṃ sampasādanaṃ cetaso ekodibhāvaṃ avitakkaṃ avicāraṃ samādhijaṃ pītisukhaṃ dutiyajjhānaṃ upasampajja viharati* | (iii) *pītiyā ca virāgā upekkhako ca viharati sato ca sampajāno sukhaṃ ca kāyena paṭisaṃvedeti yaṃ taṃ ariyā ācikkhanti upekkhako satimā sukhavihārī ti tatiyajjhānaṃ upasampajja viharati* | (iv) *sukhassa ca pahānā dukkhassa ca pahānā pubbeva somanassadomanassānaṃ atthagamā adukkhaṃ asukhaṃ upekhāsatiparisuddhiṃ catutthajjhānaṃ upasampajja viharati* || [*SN* 5.307.1–16 and passim.]

[41]The Pali terms are *anupubbanirodha* [*DN* 3.266; 3.290] for the successive attainments and *anupubbavihāra* [*DN* 3.265; 3.290] for the succesive abodes. It seems likely that these classificatory terms are a later development since it occurs only in the late proto-*abhidharma* list-suttas of the *Long Collection*.

[42]Thus the final stage of the ninefold series, the cessation of sensation and conceptualization, is described in the following terms: *idh-'ānanda bhikkhu sabbaso nevasaññānāsaññāyatanaṃ samatikkamma saññāvedayitanirodhaṃ upasampajja viharati* | *idaṃ kho ānanda etamhā sukhā aññaṃ sukhaṃ abhikkantataraññ ca paṇītataraññ ca* | [*MN* 1.400.11–14].

[43]*nirodho avedayitasukhavasena sukhaṃ nāma jāto* | *pañcakāmaguṇavasena hi aṭṭhisamāpattivasena ca vedayitasukhaṃ nāma* | *nirodho avedayitasukhaṃ nạma iti vedayitasukhaṃ vā hotu avedayitasukhaṃ vā taṃ nidukkhabhāvasankhātena sukhaṭṭhena ekaṃ sukham eva jātaṃ* | [*MA* 3.115.7–12].

[44]It is difficult to fully understand the eight liberations *(vimokkha* Skt. *vimokṣa)* without considering them in their relationship to two other important sets of techniques and altered states: the eight 'spheres of mastery' *(abhibhvāyatana)* and the 10 'spheres of totality' *(kaṣiṇāyatana* Skt. *kṛtsnāyatana).* In later Buddhist systematic works—though this is by no means so clear if we consider only material drawn from the *Nikāyā*—these three sets form a group, and when they are considered in this way the contention that the *vimokkhā* are, in part, a set of visualization exercises, becomes clearer. Discussion of these three sets may be found in almost all systematic Indian Buddhist texts, for example, the eighth chapter of the *AKBh,* the *AS* (D 112a2–112b7/P 132b3–133b3/ Pradhan [1950:95.4–96.14]) and the *ASBh* (Tatia [1976:124.18–127.26]). Compare the treatment given in the *MS* and its commentaries [Lamotte 1973:391]. Lamotte [1970–81:1281–1310] gives a collection and French translation of many of the significant Sanskrit texts; a partial study of these sets of practices in their Yogācāra context has been made by Hakamaya, Keenan and Griffiths [unpublished manuscript], and Hurvitz [1979] has devoted some effort to a study of the eight liberations as these are presented in Pali, Sanskrit and Chinese *abhidharma* texts.

[45]'Pericope' is a term derived from the Greek *perikope* meaning literally 'that which is cut around'; it has been a standard term in biblical studies since the end of the nineteenth century and is used to denote the individual units of tradition which the larger texts of the bible—or in this case of the Buddhist canonical collection—comprise. I have discussed this method and its possible applications to the Pali canon elsewhere [1983a and 1983b]. The important point is simply that the individual discourses which make up the *Collections* as they now stand are themselves for the most part composite works, patchwork affairs comprising numerous individually circulating pericopes.

[46]The additional material consists in the words: *paññāya c'assa disvā āsavā parikkhīṇā honti* [*MN* 1.204 and passim]; there are occasional variants. It's significant that a common commentarial gloss on this pericope is *maggapaññāya cattāri ariyasaccāni disvā cattāro āsavā parikkhīṇā honti* [*MA* 2.163.15–16 and passim]. The idea that the object of the practitioner's wisdom is the four truths makes very clear that this pericope moves firmly within the realm of analytic practice.

[47]There is, naturally enough, a clear awareness within the canonical collections themselves of the tension between these two types of practice and the soteriological goals that go with them. One of the several attempts to resolve the issue can be seen in the development of the categories of *cetovimutti* (liberation of the mind), *paññāvimutti* (liberation by means of wisdom) and *ubhatobhāgavimutti* (liberation in both ways). The problems surrounding these categories and the more detailed classifications of the types of liberation and of liberated persons in the context of which they are usually expounded (see, for example, the *Kīṭāgirisutta, MN* 1.177ff) are complex; all I can say here is that the category of *paññāvimutto,* one who is liberated by means of wisdom,

seems to envisage the possibility of the attainment of *nibbāna* without complete mastery over the enstatic practices, and that the category of *cetovimutto,* one whose mind is liberated, centres especially upon mastery of the enstatic practices. To give a single example, *AN* 1.161 defines *cetovimutti* as consisting in freedom from passion and *paññāvimutti* as consisting in freedom from ignorance *(rāgavirāgā cetovimutti avijjāvirāgā paññāvimutti),* a difference which is not unexpected in the light of the remarks made earlier about the different perceptions of the basic human problem belonging to the enstatic and the analytic soteriological techniques. More detailed discussions of the issue may be found in De Silva [1978] (I am grateful to Mr Bruce Burrill for bringing this piece to my attention); Gunaratana [1980:363–387]; Katz [1982:78–83]. De Silva is especially good on this, drawing heavily upon the commentarial literature and decisively correcting the common misapprehension that *ubhatobhāgavimutti* is simply a combination of *cetovimutti* and *paññāvimutti.* The 'both' refers instead to the physical *(rūpa)* on the one hand and the mental *(nāma)* on the other: *ubhatobhāgavimutto ti dvīhi bhāgehi vimutto arūpasamāpattiyā rūpakāyato vimutto maggena nāmakāyato vimutto ti* [*DA* 2.514]. See De Silva [1978:141–143]; Gunaratana [1980:369 Note 1 where the reference is given incorrectly].

[48]It isn't possible to give a comprehensive review here of all the textual evidence in the *Collections* which leads to the stated conclusions. The main text-places have already been listed in Note 38. Briefly, there is an invariant core to the tradition describing the fivefold set of practices leading to the attainment of cessation; this invariant core has been translated in Section 1.3.2, and the text given in Note 34. This invariant core occurs in combination as part of both the ninefold series *(anupubba-vihāra* or *anupubba-nirodha,* though these terms are not always used) and the eightfold series *(vimokkha).* In none of the major instances in *DN* [2.71; 2.112; 2.156; 3.261–262; 3.266; 3.288; 3.290] does it occur in conjunction with the *paññā* pericope, the text of which is given in Note 46. The major occurrences in *MN* [1.159–160; 1.174–175; 1.203–204; 1.207–209; 1.398–400; 1.454–456; 2.12–13; 3.25–26; 3.42–45] are more mixed, though most of the occurrences of the fivefold attainment-of-cessation unit do include the *paññā* pericope (all, in fact, except 1.398–400; 1.454–456; 2.12–13). The *SN*'s lengthy discussion of the techniques leading to the attainment of cessation frequently uses the invariant core of the tradition without the *paññā* pericope [e.g., *SN* 1.158; 2.210–212; 4.226–227; 5.318–319], as also does the *AN* [e.g., 1.41].

[49]Many of the canonical Pali texts divide those who have begun the practice of the path into four classes *(cattāro ariyapuggalā):* the first of these is the *sotāpanno* (Skt. *śrotrāpanna)* or 'stream-enterer', an individual whose eventual enlightenment is guaranteed; the second is the *sakadāgāmī* (Skt. *sakṛdāgāmī),* the 'once-returner' who has only one life to undergo subsequent to the present one before attaining enlightenment; third, there is the *anāgāmī,* the 'never-returner' who will attain enlightenment without a subsequent earthly birth (though the person may well have to undergo another life, or part thereof, in some *devaloka);* and finally the *arhat,* who attains enlightenment before death in

this present earthly life. The standard *sutta* text describing these four noble individuals occurs very frequently, usually in stereotyped form (see, for example, *Sampasādaniyasutta* in *DN*). These four noble individuals were later often multiplied into eight by dividing each stage into two: path and fruit. See, for example, *AN* 4.292–293.

[50]I omit, as of no great philosophical significance, Buddhaghosa's detailed description [*VM* 1676.1–1679.7 (23.35–42)] of the kinds of preparatory duties that need to be done by the practitioner between attaining the sphere of nothingness (the third formless state and the seventh attainment) and that of neither conceptualization nor nonconceptualization (the fourth formless state and the eighth attainment, that altered state which immediately precedes the attainment of cessation itself). These are interesting because they illustrate with what seriousness the possibility of reaching cessation was taken: the practitioner is instructed, and must ensure, before entering cessation (i) that nothing borrowed from another will come to harm (from rats, fire or flood) during the temporary unconciousness; (ii) that the monastic community will not require the practitioner's presence for the taking of a communal decision during the trance; (iii) that the Buddha will not require the presence of the practitioner while unconscious (not perhaps an especially pressing consideration during these degenerate days when there seems to be a striking lack of Buddhas) and (iv) that the practitioner is not likely to die while in the attainment of cessation.

[51]*kathañcassā samāpajjanaṃ hotī ti | samathavipassanāvasena ussakkitvā katapubbakiccassa nevasaññānāsaññāyatanaṃ nirodhayato evamassa samāpajjnaṃ hoti | yo hi samathavaseneva ussakkati so nevasaññānāsaññāyatanasamāpattiṃ patvā tiṭṭhati | yo pana vipassanāvaseneva ussakkati so phalasamāpattiṃ patvā tiṭṭhati | yo pana ubhayavaseneva ussakkitvā pubbakiccaṃ katvā nevasaññānāsaññāyatanaṃ nirodheti so taṃ samāpajjatī ti ayam ettha sankhepo | | ayaṃ pana vitthāro | idha bhikkhu nirodhaṃ samāpajjitukāmo katabhattakicco sudhotahatthapādo vivitte okāse supaññattamhi āsane nisīdati pallankaṃ ābhujitvā ujuṃ kāyaṃ paṇidhāya parimukhaṃ satiṃ upaṭṭhapetvā | so paṭhamaṃ jhānaṃ samāpajjitvā vuṭṭhāya tattha sankhāre aniccato dukkhato anattato vipassati | | . . . nevasaññānāsaññāyatanaṃ samāpajjati | athekaṃ vā dve vā cittavāre atikkamitvā actittako hoti nirodhaṃ phusati | kasmā panassa dvinnaṃ cittānaṃ uparicittāni na pavattantī ti | nirodhassa payogattā | idaṃ hi imassa bhikkhuno dve samathavipassanādhamme yuganaddhe katvā aṭṭhasamāpatti-ārohanaṃ anupubbanirodhassa payogo na nevasaññānāsaññāyatanasamāpattiyā ti nirodhassa payogattā dvinnaṃ cittānaṃ upari na pavattanti |* [*VM* 1673.8–1674.9; 1679.2–7 (23.31–32; 43)].

[52]The term 'attainment of fruition' *(phalasamāpatti)* refers to another altered state of consciousness classified by Buddhaghosa as one of the 'benefits of cultivating wisdom' *(paññābhāvanānisaṃsa)* in the final chapter of the *VM*. Both Buddhaghosa and Dhammapāla explain this in detail [*VMT* 1654.7–1664.24]; the only point that needs to be noted here is that this altered state differs from the attainment of cessation in that it has an object—*nibbāna*—and therefore is not devoid of all mental events. The attainment of fruition also differs depending upon the stage of development of the individual reaching it; it is open to anyone

of the four (or eight) classes of *ariyapuggalā* (for a discussion of which see Note 49).

[53]*samathavipassanāvasenā ti yuganaddhānaṃ viya aññamaññūpakāritāya sahitānaṃ vasena | . . . nevasaññānāsaññāyatanasamāpattiṃ patvā tiṭṭhati taduddhaṃ suddhasamathavipassanāya abhāvato | yo vipassanāvaseneva ussakkati sace ariyo phalasamāpattatthiko so attano phalasamāpattiṃ patvā tiṭṭhati | . . . nirodhaṃ phusatī ti acittakabhāvam evāha | nirodhassa payogattā ti cittanirodhāya payogabhāvato baladvayasambharaṇādipayogassa cittanirodhattā ti attho | samathavipassanābalasamannāgamo ñāṇasamādhicariyāvasabhāvo cettha aññamaññānativattanavaseneva icchitabbo ti āha dve samathavipassanādhamme yuganaddhe katvā ti | anupubbanirodhassa payogo ti paṭhamajjhānādīnaṃ tadanupassanānāñca anupubbato nirodhanassāyaṃ payogo |* [*VMT* 1673.23; 1674.16–19; 1679.15–19].

[54]Scholars who have made in-depth studies of these matters are not in agreement. Among contemporary expositors from within the tradition there is ambiguity, if not open contradiction, about the value of enstatic practice and the soteriological goals that go with it. Vajirañāṇa comes close to contradicting himself on the issue [1962.18 and 343]. Compare Rahula [1967:68] and Nyanaponika [1962:102]. From outside the tradition, Winston King presents a fairly strong case for the integral unity of the *jhānic* and *vipassanic* (as he prefers to call them) modes of practice [1977; 1980:103–115] in the production of the *nirodhasamāpatti,* while I have myself stated a much more negative view of the possibilities of combining the two modes into a coherent system [1981].

[55]The works of Nyanaponika [1962] and Vajirañāṇa [1962] are perhaps the best examples of late twentieth-century Sinhalese Theravādin orthodoxy on the problem of meditational practice. These works reflect splendidly the stress placed on *satipaṭṭhāna* ('mindfulness', a species of observational analysis, dramatically opposed in both theory and practice to enstatic practice) on the one hand, and the synthesis of Buddhaghosa on the other. An interesting review of the practical methods employed by some contemporary Theravādin meditation-teachers may be found in Kornfield [1977]. This work also shows that the majority of meditation-teachers stress *vipassanā* at the expense of *samatha* though there are exceptions and many of the teachers do try and create some sort of synthesis.

[56]The discourse in question is the *Cūlasāropamasutta.* The answer to the question *katame ca brāhmaṇa dhammā ñāṇadassanena uttaritarā ca paṇītatarā ca* [*MN* 1.203.24–25] is a listing of the four *jhānā* of form, the four formless attainments and the attainment of cessation [*MN* 1.203–204].

[57]*kathaṃ ime paṭhamajjhānādidhammā ñāṇadassanena uttaritarā jātā ti | nirodhapādakattā | heṭṭhā paṭhamajjhānādidhammā hi vipassanāpādakā ime nirodhapādakā tasmā uttaritarā ti veditabbā |* [*MA* 2.234.25–28].

[58]See *AN* 4.454 and *MN* 1.209.

[59]See *MN* 1.456.

[60]*kasmā samāpajjantī ti | sankhārānaṃ pavattibhede ukkaṇṭhitvā diṭṭhe vā dhamme acittakā hutvā nirodhaṃ nibbānaṃ patvā sukhaṃ viharissāmā ti samāpajjanti* [*VM* 1673.5–7(23.30)].

[61]*sukhaṃ ti niddukkhaṃ* [*VMT* 1673.22]. Compare *MA* 3.115.7–12 (commenting upon *MN* 1.398–400) where the attainment of cessation is described as possessing that happiness which consists in absence of sensation.

[62]*ucchedadiṭṭhi,* usually opposed to *sassatadiṭṭhi,* the 'eternity view'. *SN* 2.20, 3.98 and passim.

[63]There are a number of dialectical soft-shoe-shuffles which can be used to get round this. The most common in Buddhist texts is to say that this view—that all views about Nirvana (or in some schools about anything at all) are false—is not itself a view but (something like) a meta-linguistic and meta-philosophical pointer to the truth, which, naturally, transcends views and verbalization. If this move is to work —and ultimately I don't think it can—we need some fairly tight criteria for what 'views' are and why such things as the proposition 'all views are false' isn't one. Such criteria are not usually given in Buddhist texts. If an attempt were made to generate some criteria which would exclude 'all views are false', the probable result would be to empty such statements of all philosophical power. Suppose we suggest as a necessary (and possibly sufficient) condition for any proposition P to be considered a 'view' that P and its contradictory cannot both be true; if the proposition 'all views are false' isn't a view given this condition, then it's hard to know what it is or why anyone would want to assert it or even what it could mean to assert it. Can one assert a proposition P which does not logically exclude not-P? Some related issues springing from the question of ineffability have been usefully discussed by Keith Yandell [1979]. But the whole issue needs much more space than can be given it here.

[64]The relevant Pali terms are *anupādisesanibbāna* (Nirvana without remainder) and *sa-upādisesanibbāna* (Nirvana with remainder). The historical problems involved in assessing why this distinction came to be thought necessary and what its effects should be on our view of the nature of Nirvana are immense, and there is as yet no scholarly orthodoxy on the issue. The literature on the meaning of Nirvana is immense. A good place to start is with Welbon's [1968] historical study of the understandings of Nirvana which have been common in the West. Two more recent discussions of specific issues close to that which has arisen in our study are Masefield [1979] and Kalansuriya [1979].

[65]*nibbānaṃ patvā ti anupādisesanibbānaṃ patvā viya* | [*VMT* 1673.22].

[66]This formula occurs frequently with only minor variations in the Pali canonical texts. The standard form is *imasmiṃ sati idaṃ hoti* | *imassa uppādā idaṃ uppajjati* || *imasmiṃ asati idaṃ na hoti* | *imassa nirodhā idaṃ nirujjhati* || [*MN* 1.262–264; *SN* 2.28; passim]. I agree with C. A. F.

Rhys-Davids [1908–26:672] and Kalupahana [1975:90] that although the Pali version (and many Buddhist Sanskrit versions) uses one and the same pronoun throughout (in the neuter nominative and locative) it is nevertheless appropriate, indeed required, to translate by two different terms (x and y in my version) when using English. It's perhaps also worth noting that the grammar of this standard formula does not permit us to distinguish between a constant conjunction view of causality and one that postulates a stronger metaphysical relationship. The ablative case *(uppādā* and *nirodhā)* will support either interpretation.

[67]This is Jayatilleke's view [1963:449]. Kalupahana [1975:96–109] thinks, in contrast, that we do not have an instance of *parallelismus membrorum* here, but that the second halves of both the first and second lines—those that talk of 'arising' and 'ceasing'—add something to the first halves, and that this something is 'a deliberate effort to include the idea of productivity in the statement of causation.' [1975:96]. This interpretation is linked with Kalupahana's view that, according to early Theravāda Buddhism (by which he usually means pre-Buddhaghosa Theravāda), this verse and other more extended statements of the universality of causality suggest that it consists not merely in the facts of the constant conjunction of x and y but also in some kind of (metaphysical) relationship between them, a relationship which can, moreover, be directly perceived. It doesn't seem to me that this view of the causal process—as an additional fact over and above constant conjunction in the Humean sense—is clearly expressed in the pre-Buddhaghosa Pali texts of Theravāda Buddhism, though neither, it must be admitted, is a strict Humean view. On the exegetical level, then, Kalupahana thinks the texts are less ambiguous than I take them to be. Whether his view can be justified philosophically, whether it is a defensible view of causality and what exactly it might mean to directly perceive a causal relation between x and y, are different and large questions which, fortunately, are not of direct relevance for this study. See also Silburn [1955:165–228] for a more detailed discussion of early Buddhist notions of causation.

[68]The universality of application of the principle of causation is clearly implied by the famous formula: *sabbe sankhārā aniccā | sabbe sankhārā dukkhā | sabbe dhammā anattā* [*SN* 3.132–134; *AN* 1.286; passim]. Lamotte [1962:165 Note 51] has collected references to this formula in Buddhist Sanskrit literature. I take *dhammā* here to be a universal category and all things to be included under the rubric of *paṭiccasamupannadhammā* (causally arisen things). There is a problem, as so often, with the status of Nirvana, but leaving that aside there can be no doubt that the universality of principle (1) is intended by the texts.

[69]Kalupahana [1975:99].

[70]Leibniz [1714:paragraph 32].

[71]I am dependent here on the formulations of William L. Rowe [1984:362–364]. Compare Hill [1982] for a somewhat different perspective. Much useful discussion pertaining to this issue will be found in Swinburne [1979].

72 See, for some preliminary discussion, Jaini [1974] and Bühnemann [1980].

73 *saññāvedayitanirodhasamāpattiyā vuṭṭhahantassa bhikkhuno evaṃ hoti | ahaṃ saññāvedayitanirodhasamāpattiyā vuṭṭhahissanti vā | ahaṃ saññāvedayitanirodhasamāpattiyā vuṭṭahamīti vā | ahaṃ saññāvedayitanirodhasamāpattiyā vuṭṭhito ti vā | atha khvāssapubbe va tathā cittaṃ bhāvitaṃ hoti yaṃ taṃ tathattāya upanetīti* || [*MN* 1:302].

74 *kathaṃ ṭhānaṃ ti | evaṃ samāpannāya pan'assā kālaparicheda-vasena c'eva antarā āyukkhayasanghapaṭimānanasatthupakkosanābhāvena ca ṭhānaṃ hoti | kathaṃ vuṭṭhānaṃ ti | anāgāmissa anāgāmiphaluppattiyā | arahato arahattaphaluppattiyā ti evaṃ dvedhā vuṭṭhāna hoti* | [*VM* 1681.6–9(23.48–49)] My translation is based partly upon Dhammapāla's glosses [*VMT* 1681:18–19], which are here merely formal.

75 See, for example, Henepola Gunaratana's paraphrase of Buddhaghosa [1980:360] and Vajirañāṇa [1962:464–466].

76 Thus I take Buddhaghosa's description of the practitioner's mind tending towards Nibbāna upon leaving the attainment of cessation, *vuṭṭhitassa kiṃninnaṃ cittaṃ hotī ti nibbānaninnaṃ | vuttaṃ hetaṃ saññāvedayitanirodhasamāpattiyā vuṭṭhitassa kho āvuso visākha bhikkhuno vivekaninnaṃ cittaṃ hoti vivekapoṇaṃ vivekapabbhāraṃ ti* || *VM* 1681.10-12(23.50)], as simply unpacking what is meant by experiencing the fruitions of Arhatship and Non-Returnership. Dhammapāla's comment supports this view: *vivekaninnaṃ ti nissaraṇavivekaninnaṃ· pageva sankhāravimukhitāya phalacittuppattiyā cā ti veditabbaṃ* | [*VMT* 1681.20–21].

77 The most influential summaries of the meanings of *dhamma* from within the tradition are those by Buddhaghosa [see especially *DhsA* 33 and *DA* 1.99]. In these summaries five senses of the term are distinguished. The first is *desanā,* or 'teaching', meaning simply the Buddha's doctrine. The second is *pariyatti,* referring to the canonical texts in which that doctrine is set forth. The third sense is *dhamma* as *guṇa* or 'good quality', something which causes people to 'attain a good destiny' *(dhammo pāpeti sugatiṃ—DhsA* 33 and *DA* 1.99, quoting *Theragāthā* 304), in other words, to get a good rebirth. Buddhaghosa also refers to another meaning of *dhamma* considered as *guṇa,* the Buddha's unique good qualities. The fourth, *dhammā* (plural) refers to all non-sentient and non-living existents; these are the basic existents/events of the Theravāda metaphysical system. The fifth is *hetu* or 'cause', here *dhamma* is considered under its aspect as producing results. The two most thorough examinations of the semantic range of this term in the Pali literature are Geiger and Geiger [1920] and Carter [1978]. The two works complement one another, that of the Geigers being more thorough in its analysis of the textual material, and Carter's covering in addition material from the non-Pali Sinhalese tradition. See also Hirakawa [1980:163–167] for a brief discussion. A. K. Warder's sevenfold listing of possible meanings [1974:398–399] overlaps somewhat with Buddhaghosa's list, though he appears to have revised his list later [1971; 1980]. Fumimaro Watanabe [1983:9–17], basing himself

largely upon Warder, distinguishes four basic meanings/uses for *dhamma*.

78For example in Buddhaghosa's discussion of the importance of ascertaining that one's life has at least seven days to run before one enters the attainment of cessation, an important matter since imminent death will apparently force premature withdrawal from the attainment. [*VM* 1678.13–20(23.42)].

79This is certainly implied in the extract from *VM* translated earlier in Section 1.5.

80The standard account of the perceptual process in Theravāda shows clearly that a form of mind–body interactionism is envisaged: 'Visual consciousness occurs in dependence upon the eye and material objects; the meeting of these three is 'contact'. Sensation is conditioned by contact, and what one senses one conceptualizes; what one conceptualizes one reasons about; what one reasons about one proliferates intellectually . . . *cakkhuñca paṭicca rūpe ca uppajjati cakkhuviññānaṃ | tiṇṇaṃ sangati phasso | phassapaccayā vedanā | yaṃ vedeti taṃ sañjānāti | yaṃ sañjānāti taṃ vitakketi | yaṃ vitakketi taṃ papañceti* . . .[*MN* 1.111 passim]. Interesting and often conflicting interpretations of this may be found in Sarathchandra [1958:4ff]; Jayatilleke [1963:435ff] and Nāṇananda [1976:3ff].

81It is not quite true that there is no suggestion of a purely physical cause for the re-emergence of consciousness. Such may in fact be suggested by the possibility of the practitioner's death (a physical event) directly causing the re-emergence of consciousness (on which see Section 1.5). But this is not a possibility treated with much seriousness by the tradition.

82This fundamental division is indicated by the division of the individual person into *nāma* (literally 'name', a term used to denote all mental functions including the four *khandhā); vedanā* (sensation), *saññā (conceptualization), viññāṇa* (consciousness) and *sankhārā* (volitional actions). Opposed to *nāma* is *rūpa,* physical form. This division is the most fundamental among all the Buddhist analyses of the person, all the others depend upon it. See Chapter Four.

83The standard Theravāda discussions of *bhavanga* are found in Buddhaghosa's *DhsA* [72, 140, 212, 276] and in *VM* 1020.1ff(14.111ff). See also Sarathchandra [1958:75–96] for a valuable discussion.

84Though the term is used in an early post-canonical work [*Miln* 299ff].

85The rebirth process and the links between the terms *bhavangasota, bhavangacitta* and *paṭisandhiviññāṇa* are discussed in detail at *VM* 1021.1ff(14.114ff).

86*iminā bhikkhunā addhānaparicchede sukusalena bhavitabbaṃ | attano āyusankhārā sattāhaṃ pavattissanti na pavattissantī ti āvajjitvā va samāpajjitabbaṃ | sace hi sattāhabbantare nirujjhanake āyusankhāre anāvajjitvā va samāpajjati* *nāssa nirodhasamāpatti maraṇaṃ paṭibāhituṃ sakkoti | antonirodhe maraṇassa natthitāya antarā va samāpattito vuṭṭhāti |* [*VM* 1678.13–18(23.42)]

[87]*antonirodhe maraṇaṃ natthi carimabhavangena mīyanato* . . . [*VMT* 1678.25].

[88]Some discussion of these problems may be found in Griffiths [1982 and 1984] and White [1983].

NOTES TO CHAPTER TWO

[1]The much-discussed historical problems surrounding the origin of the Buddhist schools in India and exactly what is meant by a 'school' cannot be entered into in any detail here. Briefly, my views on this matter are heavily dependent on those of Frauwallner [1952 and 1956] and Bechert [1961]; I follow these scholars in thinking that, given that there are no *vinaya* rules about the matter, the very concept of a schism in the pan-Indian Buddhist *saṃgha* was not present at least until after the Aśokan period, and that the references to *saṃghabheda* in the so-called 'schism edict' of Aśoka are primarily to splits in specific monastic communities caused by (or manifested in) a failure of the members of such a community to celebrate *uposatha* jointly and therefore have nothing to do with the situation of the pan-Indian monastic community, the *'bhikkhusaṃgha* of the four quarters'. Of course there were fundamental intellectual disagreements among the doctrinal systems developed by the various schools, and many polemical tests were produced by the intellectual elite of each. However, it seems likely that these disagreements were in many cases due simply to independent intellectual developments based upon geographical separation. Discussions of the complex materials upon which any history of scholastic Buddhism in India must be based may be found in all the standard surveys. The most useful general studies are Lamotte [1958] and Bareau [1947; 1954; 1955a; 1955b]. Bechert [1973] contains some useful methodological remarks.

[2]Chinese pilgrims began to make journeys to India in search of teachings and texts from the third century AD onwards. The travel-accounts that some of them left us suggest that it was commonplace for monks of differing philosophical persuasions to share the same *saṃghārāma* and to celebrate *uposatha* together. See, for example, Legge [1965:45–47].

[3]These dates are, of course, somewhat arbitrary; they reflect at the lower limit the probable date of the *Mahāvibhāṣā* and at the upper limit

the probable date of the *AKBh* and the 'orthodox' Vaibhāṣika responses to it. I take the former text to define the Vaibhāṣika tradition as a sub-school within the Sarvāstivāda and the latter group of texts to provide a comprehensive and subsequently normative statement of Vaibhāṣika doctrine.

4The name 'Sarvāstivāda' means 'the doctrine *(vāda)* that everything *(sarvam)* exists *(asti)*' and refers to one key idea of the school, namely that there is a sense in which any existent, simply in virtue of its capacity to be the referent of a proposition, exists always, i.e., in past, present and future. For an excellent recent exposition of the philosophical dynamics of this position, see Williams [1981]. All major works of the Sarvāstivādin tradition contain a discussion of the meaning of this key doctrine, and it has received a great deal of attention in the West. Perhaps the most easily available English translation of one such discussion (from the *AKBh)* may be found in Stcherbatsky [1923]. The Sarvāstivāda, like the Theravāda (see Section 1.1), possessed its own tripartite canonical collection, and the Vaibhāṣika school—which may appropriately be regarded as a sub-school of the Sarvāstivāda—bases itself upon the third part of the Sarvāstivādin tripartite collection, namely the *Abhidharmapiṭaka,* a collection of seven semi-systematic philosophical works. While the early history of the Sarvāstivādin canon remains obscure, the tradition itself claims that the texts were written down (in Sanskrit) at the time of Kaniṣka and that they are based upon earlier orally preserved traditions. These canonical texts largely exist only in Chinese translations. More detailed discussions of the Sarvāstivādin canon may be found in Banerjee [1952; 1957] and Frauwallner [1964:70–99 for the seven canonical works; 1971:69–102 for the early post-canonical works, especially the **AH* (which Frauwallner likes to reconstruct as **Abhidharmasāra);* and 1973 for a systematic overview, including a detailed study of the *AKBh's* structure]. See also Takakusu Junjiro [1904–5] for a systematic survey of the *abhidharma* literature of the Sarvāstivāda.

5Details of editions and translations of this text—in fact there is more than one work bearing the name—may be found in the short essay devoted to it in the Bibliography.

6As, for example, in the *AKBh* itself: 14.4; 31.8; 32.18.

7Details of editions and translations of these texts may be found in the essays devoted to them in the Bibliography. Frauwallner [1971:73ff] has some useful comments to make about the influence of the **AH* upon the *AKBh.* De Jong's [1980a] critical review of the two translations of the **AH* is also useful.

8The two texts by Saṃghabhadra are the **Nyāyānusāra* and the **Samayapradīpika,* both extant only in Chinese, and that by the anonymous author is the *Abhidharmadīpa (AD),* uniquely extant only in Sanskrit. For further details on these texts, refer to the relevant bibliographical entries.

[9]I use Vasubandhu's name here as author of the *AKBh* in accordance with the unanimous witness of the traditions, Indian, Tibetan and Chinese. There is, notoriously, an intractable set of historical problems connected with the date of the *AKBh* and with the precise identity of the person denoted by the name 'Vasubandhu'. A comprehensive review of the issues would run to monograph length itself and I do not intend to attempt this here. Very briefly, then, I follow the traditions, both Tibetan and Chinese, which identify the author of the *AKBh* with the (half)-brother of another famous Indian Buddhist intellectual, Asanga. The earliest and most important source which contains an unambiguous statement of this position is Paramārtha's *Life of Vasubandhu* (written in Chinese but translated into English by Takakusu [1904]), written in the mid-sixth century AD (on the dates of Paramārtha, see Ch'en [1964:134–135] and more recently Paul [1982 and 1984], but it is confirmed in essentials by the standard Tibetan *chos 'byung* [Obermiller 1932:142–147; Chattopadhyaya and Chimpa 1970:155ff]. This is not, of course, very much help in establishing anything other than a relative dating for Vasubandhu, and the complex evidence from Chinese sources which is often used in an attempt to give an absolute date is, to say the least, ambiguous and difficult to assess. The best review of the Chinese evidence remains Péri [1911], although his conclusion—that Vasubandhu should be placed in the fourth century AD—cannot, for a variety of reasons, any longer be followed. Essentially, the Chinese evidence contradicts itself, and these contradictions led, in the early part of this century, to two contradictory conclusions: that Vasubandhu, author of the *AKBh* and many Mahāyāna works, lived in the fourth century (especially Péri [1911]) and that he lived in the fifth century (especially Takakusu [1905 and 1929]). Frauwallner's [1951] radical answer was to suggest that there were in fact two different Vasubandhus, one ('the elder') from the fourth century, Asanga's (half)-brother and the author of the Mahāyāna works in question, and the other ('the younger') from the fifth century, the author of the *AKBh*. Frauwallner's thesis is not finally persuasive (for his own later thoughts, see Frauwallner [1961]) and has been criticized from a number of perspectives since the publication of his monograph [1951] on the issue. See especially Jaini [1958; 1977a:introduction], Wayman [1961:25ff], Anacker [1970], Hirakawa et al. [1973:ivff], Dowling [1976] and Hall [1983:13–21]. Neither the contradictory Chinese evidence nor the putative references to a Vasubandhu other than the kośakāra found in the *AKV* (for more detailed discussions of which see Griffiths [1983a:184–187] and Hall [1983:19–20]) require, or even strongly support, Frauwallner's radical conclusion. This is especially the case when it is realized that Yaśomitra's attribution of certain views to a Vasubandhu who may be someone other than the author of the *AKBh* is not always followed by other commentators to the *AKBh*. To take just one example, in his comment on a discussion about what causes the nonexistence of existents, Yaśomitra tells us that the opinion that a given existent ceases to exist because its 'durative cause' (*avasthānahetu*) no longer exists was held by 'those headed by the Elder Vasubandhu' (*sthaviravasubandhuprabhṛti*, *AKV* 571.15). Frauwallner [1951:21] took this as one piece of evidence for the existence of a Vasubandhu other

than the *kośkāra*. Despite the fact that this text (and the others that Frauwallner quotes) is not unambiguous, it becomes even less convincing when we look at Sthiramati's comment on the same passage and see that he identified this opinion as one belonging to *slob dpon dpal len/ācārya śrīlāta* [*AKT* P THO 124a7–8], quite a different person! It is true that in other cases [*AKV* 45.29/*AKT* TO 71a1] there is agreement between Yaśomitra and Sthiramati in attributing a view to a 'previous teacher' Vasubandhu (see also Pūrṇavardhana, *AKTL* JU 42b1), but the agreement is not universal. Much more could be said; the issue is not finally resolved—full consideration of evidence from the commentaries to *AKBh* will help to resolve it—and is not in any case of key importance for the philosophical purposes of this work. The provisional perspective of this study, not fully argued for in this note, will be that the *AKBh* is the work of a Vasubandhu active in the fifth century (c. 400–480), a man active under, and probably patronized by, the Gupta monarchs Vikramāditya and Balāditya; that this Vasubandhu clearly possessed an encyclopaedic knowledge of the *abhidharma* traditions of the Sarvāstivāda/Vaibhāṣika; and that he was very probably the (half-) brother of Asanga and also the author of a substantial number of Mahāyāna works.

10Stcherbatsky [1923:3–5] supports this statement with his descriptions of the use of the *AKBh* in some key monastic institutions of Central and Inner Asia (including Mongolia) in the late nineteenth and early twentieth centuries. I have myself benefited from a reading of portions of the sixth Dalai Lama's commentary to the *AKBh* under the direction of Geshe Lhundup Sopa at the University of Wisconsin—Madison in 1982. There is a caveat here: it appears to be the case that very frequently the Tibetan and Central Asian scholastics were content to approach the *AKBh* through the medium of commentarial digests rather than by a direct reading of the text itself; the Western investigator therefore needs to use the very valuable materials preserved by these thinkers with some care. There is also, of course, the linguistic problem. Tibetan scholastics do not, for the most part, have more than a nodding acquaintance with Sanskrit; native Tibetan commentaries on the *AKBh* therefore need to be used with the care appropriate to all discussions of a work in translation.

11Of primary importance among the seven is Yaśomitra's *AKV* which survives in full in both Tibetan and Sanskrit. The other six survive only in Tibetan translation, with the possible exception of Saṃghabhadra's (or Vinitabhadra's) *AKSBh* (P 5592/Tōhoku 4091) which may be the same as Taishō (1563). The longest and most important of these is Sthiramati's *AKT*. The others are Pūrṇavardhana's *AKTL* (in two versions, one long and one short: P 5594/Tōhoku 4093 and P 5597/Tōhoku 4096), Dignāga's *AKVr* (P 5596/Tōhoku 4059) and Śamathadeva's (possibly Śāntisthiradeva's) *AKTU* (P 5595/Tōhoku 4094). Further details on these texts may be found in the Bibliography.

12This statement needs the modification only that the *AKV* survives in Sanskrit as well as Tibetan and that some other commentaries to the

AKBh also survive partially or entirely in other Central Asian languages—as, for example, the Uigur translation of Sthiramati's *AKT*, for which see Tekin [1970]. But the generalization holds for practical purposes.

[13]*kāśmīravaibhāṣikanītisiddhaḥ prāyo mayā'yaṃ kathito'bhidharmaḥ | yad durgṛhītaṃ tadihāsmadāgaḥ saddharmanītau munayaḥ pramāṇam || 40 || prāyeṇa hi kāśmīravaibhāṣikāṇāṃ nityā* (Pradhan reads *nityādi;* I follow Tibetan . . . *tshul du grub pa* [P NGU 93b2–3] and *AKV* [1187.3]) *siddha eṣo'smabhir abhidharma ākhyātaḥ | yad atrāsmābhir durgṛhītaṃ so'smākam aparādhaḥ | saddharmanītau tu punar buddhā eva buddhaputrāś ca |* [*AKBh* 459.16–460.3]. Yaśomitra's comments have some historical interest and provide an excellent illustration of the commentarial style: 'A detailed exposition of the words 'established according to the interpretations of the Vaibhāṣikas of Kaśmīr' follows: 'Kaśmīr' means those who live in Kaśmīr. 'Vaibhāṣikas' means those who praise the *Vibhāṣā*—this has already been explained. There are [Buddhist] inhabitants of Kaśmīr who are not Vaibhāṣikas, for example, experts in the texts on monastic discipline and Sautrāntikas such as the Bhadanta [Vasumitra]. There are also Vaibhāṣikas who are not inhabitants of Kaśmīr, namely those Vaibhāṣikas who are called 'outsiders'. Such is the specifying function of each term [in the phrase 'Vaibhāṣikas of Kaśmīr']. It is the metaphysical system established by their interpretation which for the most part I [viz: Vasubandhu, the author of the *AKBh*] have taught here [in this text]. What has been said here [Yaśomitra now speaks with his own voice] explains the meaning [of the words used by Vasubandhu; in reality Vasubandhu] has also taught [in the *AKBh*] doctrines established according to other interpretations [than the Vaibhāṣika]. '—*kāśmīravaibhāṣikanītisiddhaḥ iti vistaraḥ | kaśmīre bhavāḥ kāśmīrāḥ | vibhāsayā dīvyanti vaibhāṣikāḥ iti vyākhyātam etat | santi kāśmīrā na vaibhāṣikāḥ ye vinayavidādayaḥ sautrāntikāḥ bhadantādayaḥ | santi vaibhāṣikā na kāśmīrā ye bahirdeśakā vaibhāśikāḥ ity ubhayaviśeṣaṇaṃ | teṣāṃ nītyā yaḥ siddho'bhidharmaḥ sa prāyeṇeha mayā deśitaḥ | arthād uktaṃ bhavati | anyanītisiddho'pi deśita ita |* [*AKV* 1186.21–26].

[14]See Hirakawa [1980] and Watanabe [1980 and 1983]. There are also extensive discussions in the major Japanese works on *adhidharma* known to me: Sasaki [1958], Sakurabe [1969] and Yoshimoto [1982].

[15]*ko 'yaṃ abhidharmo nāma | prajñā 'malā sānucarā 'bhidharmaḥ tatra prajñā dharmapravicayaḥ | amale'ty anāsravā | sānucare'ti saparivārā | evam anāsravaḥ pañcaskandhako 'bhidharma ity uktaṃ bhavati | eṣa tāvat pāramārthiko 'bhidharmaḥ | sāṃketikas tu tatprāptaye yā 'pi ca yac ca śastram | yā 'pi ca śrutacintābhāvanāmayī sāsravā prajño'papattipratilambhikā ca sānucarā | yac ca śāstram asyāḥ prāptyartham anāsravāvāḥ prajñāyās tad api tat saṃbhārabhāvād abhidharma ity ucyate | nirvacanaṃ tu svalakṣaṇadhāraṇād dharmaḥ | tad ayaṃ paramārthadharmaṃ vā nirvāṇaṃ dharmalakṣaṇaṃ vā pratyabhimukho dharma ity abhidharmaḥ |* [*AKBh* 2.2–11]. Yaśomitra in the *AKV* makes still clearer what is meant by defining a dharma as 'that which bears its defining characteristic' when he glosses 'defining characteristic' (*lakṣaṇa)* thus: ' 'Defining characteristic' means particular defining characteristic, as in the hardness of earth, and general defining

characteristic, as in impermanence and unsatisfactoriness [which apply to all existents].' *(dharmalakṣaṇaṃ veti | svasāmānyalakṣaṇam khakkhaṭalakṣaṇaḥ pṛthivīdhātuḥ anityaṃ duḥkham ity evam ādi |* [*AKV* 12.29–30]. The term *lakṣaṇa* therefore includes both the uniquely individuating characteristic of any existent and the characteristics which, in virtue of being an existent, it shares with all other existents. It should be noted that *svabhāva* and *svalakṣaṇa* are frequently used interchangeably in the *AKBh*. For example, in a discussion of the nature of *kāya*, Vasubandhu says *svabhāva evaiṣāṃ svalakṣaṇam* [341.11–12], and Yaśomitra frequently glosses *svabhāva* with *svalakṣaṇa* and *vice-versa*. If there is any distinction (and certainly there's no consistently held or precisely defined difference between the two), it might be that a dharma's *svalakṣaṇa* is more closely connected with what it effects—with its *kāritra*, its efficacy—and its *svabhāva* with what it essentially is. Support for this tentative suggestion is found in the fact that when Vaibhāṣika theorists speak of a dharma as existing in the past, they frequently designated it as *sasvabhāvamātra* ('merely possessing svabhāva') but never as *sasvalakṣaṇamātra* [see Williams 1981:236ff]. This seems to be because a past dharma does not possess causal efficacy *(kāritra)* even though it exists, and it at least sugggests that there is a closer connection between the possession of *svalakṣaṇa* and causal efficacy than there is between the possession of *svabhāva* and such efficacy. However, I have not yet located a specific statement to this effect, and it's clear that *svabhāva* and *svalakṣaṇa* are frequently synonymous.

[16]*dharmāṇāṃ pravicayam antareṇa nāsti kleśānāṃ yata upaśāntaye 'bhupāyaḥ | kleśaiś ca bhramati bhavārṇave 'tra lokas taddhetor ata uditaḥ kilaiṣa śāstrā || yato na vinā dharmapravicayenāsti* (*AKV* 15.1: *yato vinā dharmapravicayena nāsti;* compare Tibetan *gang gi phyir chos rab tu rnam par byed pa med pa* [P GU 29a3]) *kleśopaśamābhyupāyaḥ | kleśāś ca lokaṃ bhramayanti saṃsāra mahārṇave 'smin | atas taddhetor tasya dharmapravicayasyārthe śāstrā kila buddhenābhidharma uktaḥ | na hi vinā 'bhidharmopedeśena śiṣyaḥ śakto dharmān pravicetum iti |* [*AKBh* 2.20–3.2].

[17]What follows is based mostly upon the extracts from Saṃghabhadra's **Nyāyānusāra* translated from Chinese into French by La Vallée Poussin [1937a:27ff]. See also Williams [1981].

[18]This exact term frequently used by Saṃghabhadra to describe the kind of existence that dharmas have (at least this is so if La Vallée Poussin's reconstruction of the Sanskrit from the Chinese is correct, something which is by no means certain; see La Vallée Poussin [1937a:27 Note 1]), does not occur in the *AKBh*, though there are close analogues. See Hirakawa et al. [1973:193]. Refer especially to the discussion between Vaibhāṣikas and Sautrāntikas on the question of whether, and in what sense, atoms *(paramāṇu)* are substantial *(dravya)* [*AKBh* 53.19ff].

[19]I follow here (with some slight alterations) La Vallée Poussin's French translation of the relevant section of the **Nyāyānusāra* [1937a:28].

[20]This requires the qualification that it applies only to conditioned *(saṃskṛta)* dharmas and not to the three unconditioned *(asaṃskṛta)* dharmas, *ākāśa, pratisaṃkhyānirodha,* and *apratisaṃkhyānirodha,* expounded at *AKBh* 3.21–4.22. These do not possess the four general characteristics *(sāmānyalakṣaṇa)* of *jāti* (origination), *jarā* (decay), *sthiti* (endurance) and *anityatā* (impermanence): *etāni hi saṃskṛtasya catvāri lakṣaṇani | yatraitāni bhavanti sa dharmaḥ saṃskṛto lakṣyate | viparyayād asaṃskṛtaḥ* [*AKBh* 75.20–21]. The 'general characteristics' (*sāmānyalakṣaṇa) are also called 'conditioned characteristics' (saṃskṛtalakṣaṇa)*—see *AKBh* ad II.23b. For more on the unconditioned dharmas, see La Vallée Poussin [1930b], wherein the *Mahāvibhāṣā's* discussions of these dharmas are translated into French. Compare *AS(G)* 21.16–20: *kathaṃ saṃskṛtaṃ kati saṃskṛtāni kim arthaṃ saṃskṛtaparīkṣā | yasyotpādo 'pi prajñāyate vyayo 'pi sthityanyathātvam api tat sarvaṃ saṃskṛtaṃ draṣṭavyam | sarvāṇi saṃskṛtāni sthāpayitvā dharmadhātvāyatanaikadeśam | anityātmābhiniveśatyājanārtham* (Gokhale reads *anityābhiniveśatyājanārtham;* I follow *AS(P)* 18.8 and Tibetan *bdag mi rtag pa . . .* [D 59a4]) || *katham asaṃskṛtam katyasaṃskṛtāni kim artham asaṃskṛtaṃ parīkṣā | saṃskṛtaviparyāyeṇāsaṃskṛtam | dharmadhātvāyatanaikadeśaḥ | nityātmābhiniveśatyājanārtham ||*

[21]The best recent account is Williams [1981]. See *AKBh* ad II.46 and AK V.24–26.

[22]Vasubandhu here adds the illustration 'like the wielder of a club' *(daṇḍikavat)* to point to the fact that *kṣaṇika* is an adjectival form—'momentary'—rather than a nominal form.

[23]*ko 'yaṃ kṣaṇo nāma | ātmalābho 'nantaravināśī | so 'syāstīti kṣaṇikam* (Sāstrī [1981:569.1] reads *kṣaṇikaḥ*) . . . *sarvaṃ hi saṃskṛtam ātmalābhād ūrdhvaṃ na bhavatīti yatraiva jātaṃ tatraiva dhvasyate |* [*AKBh* 193.1–2]. The context here is the beginning of a debate as to whether physical motion is a logical possibility. It should be noticed that momentariness is predicated in this extract only of 'conditioned things'. In Vaibhāṣika theory this means everything except three things, the three *asaṃskṛtadharmāḥ* defined and described in the first chapter of the *AKBh.*

[24]See especially the lengthy Vaibhāṣika–Sautrāntika debate on the nature of momentariness and the philosophical problems involved therein in *AKBh* ad II.46, especially: . . . *athāpyevaṃ brūyāt eṣa eva hi naḥ kṣaṇo yāvataitat sarvaṃ samāpyata iti* [*AKBh* 78.24]. Yaśomitra comments: *eṣa eva hi naḥ kṣaṇa iti kāryaparisamāptilakṣaṇaḥ na tūtpattyanantaravināśalakṣaṇa ity arthaḥ |* [*AKV* 264.21–22].

[25]*balavat puruṣācchaṭamātreṇa pañcaṣaṣṭiḥ kṣaṇā atikramantīty ābhidharmikāḥ* [*AKBh* 176.13–14]. The *ābhidharmikas* here are probably the Vaibhāṣikas. The whole of the debate immediately following this brief attempted measure becomes extremely complex and is indeed, as Stcherbatsky put it, a series of 'mere attempts to seize the infinitesimal' [1923:37].

[27]Standard expositions of Vaibhāṣika thought which also contain easily accessible lists of the 75 dharmas together with comments on

them are Stcherbatsky [1923], Hirakawa et al. [1973] and (for a rather more extensive summary of the content of the *AKBh* without much interpretive discussion) Chaudhuri [1983].

27*sarva ime dharmāḥ pañca bhavanti | rūpaṃ cittaṃ caitasikāś cittaviprayuktāḥ saṃskārā asaṃskṛtaṃ ca* | [*AKBh* 52.20–21].

28On this *(avijñapti-rūpa)* see especially Dowling [1976].

29I refer here to the 'four stations of mindfulness' *(smṛtyupasthāna),* given classical expression within the Theravāda tradition by the *Mahāsatipaṭṭhānasutta* of the *Long Collection.* See Nyanaponika [1962] for a detailed discussion; also Griffiths [1981] for some philosophical suggestions.

30The standard definition of *vijñāna* is found in the first chapter of *AKBh:* 'Consciousness is a specific communication. That is, the aggregate of consciousness is described as apprehension which is communication relating to specific sense-objects.' *(vijñānaṃ prativijñaptiḥ | viṣayaṃ viṣayaṃ prativijñaptir upalabdhir vijñānaskandha ity ucyate | sa punaḥ ṣaḍ vijñānakāyāḥ cakṣurvijñānaṃ yāvan manovijñānam iti* | [*AKBh* 11.6–8 | | P GU 36a2–3]). Yaśomitra glosses *upalabdhi* with *vastumātragrahaṇa* [*AKV* 51.25], thus stressing that *vijñāna* apprehends bare particulars, and contrasts this with sensation *(vedanā)* and conceptualization *(saṃjñā),* which, respectively, react affectively to, and classify conceptually, the bare particulars cognized by consciousness.

31The distinction made here is not in fact rigidly followed by the tradition. It is notorious that Vasubandhu himself not infrequently explicitly states that *citta* and *vijñāna* (not to mention *manas,* another key term not mentioned here) are synonymous, for example in *AK* II.34: *cittaṃ mano 'tha vijñānam ekārtha. . . .* Compare Vasubandhu's *VVr* ad *V* 1. Nevertheless, the distinction will do as a generalization: there is no doubt that for the most part *citta* is a wider concept than *vijñāna,* and the description given will be heuristically useful.

32I base this judgement largely upon the standard (though folk) etymology given to *rūpa* by which it is derived from the root *rup-*, meaning 'to strike, break, injure'. Vasubandhu's long discussion of this [*AKBh* 9.10–10.6] stresses that this root *rup-* should be understood to mean 'oppression, restriction' (root *bādh-)* and 'resistance' *(pratigha)* —largely in the mundane sense that form gets in the way of things. There is also considerable emphasis on changeability (compare here *AS: gzugs kyi phung po'i mtshan nyid ci zhe na | gzugs su yod pa rnam pa gnyis kyis gzugs su yod pa'i mtshan de | reg pas gzugs su yod pa dang | yul dpyad pas gzugs su yod pa'o* | [D Sems-Tsam RI 45a5–6]), but since this is a characteristic shared with the other four (non-physical) aggregates, it need not be dwelt upon here.

33The three *asaṃskṛtadharmāḥ* are *ākāśa* (space), *pratisaṃkhyanirodha* (cessation caused by realisation) and *apratisaṃkhyanirodha* (cessation not caused by realization). These are defined and discussed at *AKBh* 3.21–4.22.

[34]The terms are *āryapudgala* and *pṛthagjana*. The Vaibhāṣika definitions of these terms do not differ significantly from the Theravāda ones, already discussed in Chapter One.

[35]*asaṃjñisamāpattau kasmād ucchedabhayaṃ na bhavati | tatra rūpasadbhavāt | rūpe hyātmasaṃjñām abhiniveśya tā samāpadyante | nirodhasamāpattau tv ārūpyabhūmikatvād rūpam api nāstīti sarvātmabhāvābhāvaṃ paśyanto na tā samāpattum utsahante* [*AKV* 237.18–20]. The non-existence of the body in the attainment of cessation is not so clearly stated in the texts of the Theravāda tradition examined in Chapter One. Indeed, some stories about it—such as that of the elder Mahānāga quoted in *VM* (see Section 1.2 and notes thereto)—make it very clear that the body of one in the attainment of cessation apparently does continue to exist. Nevertheless, what is said by Yaśomitra here is not in contradiction with the more precise and scholastic statements about the continued existence of *āyu, uṣma* and *jīvitindriya* for one in the attainment of cessation.

[36]All quotations from *AK, AKBh, AKT* and *AKV* in what follows are taken from the translation given in Appendix B. Readers are referred to that translation for the full debate, for technical clarifications and for the text.

[37]See also the extract from the *Mahāvibhāṣā* translated by Hakamaya [1975:36–37] which makes this point unambiguously clear.

[38]See the notes to the translation of this section of the *AKBh* in Appendix B. Vasubandhu's explanation of *samanantarapratyaya* as a *karmadhāraya* compound reveals a folk etymology rather than a true one. If *samanantara* were really derived from *sama*-plus-*anantara, samānantara* rather than *samanantara* would be expected. Yaśomitra recognizes this and says *samānārthe samśabdaḥ* [*AKV* 342.16]. The Tibetan translators standardly translate the *sam-* prefix to *samanantara* as though it were *sama-* or *samāna-*, using *mtshungs pa*.

[39]'With the exception of the last [thoughts] of an *arhat,* all arisen mental events and events associated with mind are immediately antecedent and similar conditions . . . why are the arhat's final mental events and events associated with mind not immediately antecedent and similar conditions? Because they are not followed by other mental events.' (*arhataḥ paścimān apaśyotpannāś cittacaittāḥ samanantarapratyayaḥ . . . kasmād arhataś caramāś cittacaittā na samanantarapratyayaḥ | anyacittāsaṃbandhanāt (AKV* reads *saṃbandhāt)* | [*AKBh* 98.10; 99.16]). Yaśomitra comments: *kasmād arhataś caramāḥ iti | acaramāḥ iti vacanādayaṃ praśna āgataḥ | anyacittāsaṃbandhād iti | yasmāt tadanantaram anyacittaṃ na sambadhnanti* | [*AKV* 346.18–19].

[40]See Section 2.2 and the excellent discussion in Williams [1981].

[41]The complete tetralemma as given in the *AKBh* reads thus: 'Do those dharmas which have a mental event as their immediately antecedent and similar condition also occur without a temporal interval between [themselves] and that mental event? There are four alternatives:

(i) That consciousness which emerges [from the mindless attainments] together with the second and subsequent moments of those attainments [which possess X and not Y]; (ii) The characteristics of origination and so forth which belong to the first moment of the [mindless] attainments and to all those conditions characterized by mind [which possess Y and not X]; (iii) The first moment of the [mindless] attainments and those conditions characterized by mind [which possess both X and Y]; (iv) The characteristics of origination and so forth which belong to the second and subsequent moments of the [mindless] attainments and to that consciousness which emerges [from those mindless attainments, which possess neither X nor Y].' *(ye dharmāś cittasamanantarāś cittanirantarā api te | catuṣkoṭikaḥ | prathamā koṭir acittakāyāḥ samāpatter (AKV* [347.13] reads *samāpattivyutthānacittaṃ) vyutthānacittaṃ dvitīyādayaś ca samāpattikṣaṇāḥ | dvitiyā koṭiḥ (AKV* [347.17] omits *koṭi;* Tibetan: *mu gnyis pa ni* [P GU 115b8]) *prathamasya samāpattikṣaṇasya sacittakāyāś cāvasthāyā (AKV* [347.19] reads *sacittakāvasthāyāṃ ca;* the Tibetan translators apparently read a genitive: *sems dang bcas pa'i gnas skabs kyi* [P GU 115b8]) *jātyādayaḥ | tṛtīyā koṭiḥ prathamaḥ samāpattikṣaṇaḥ sacittakā cāvasthā | caturtho koṭiḥ (AKV* [347.25] omits *koṭiḥ;* Tibetan *mu bzhi pa ni* [P GU 116a1]) *dvitīyādīnāṃ samāpattikṣaṇānāṃ (AKBh* [99.26] adds *jātyādayo* here; I follow *AKV* [347.26] and Tibetan [P GU 116a1]) *vyutthānacittasya ca jātyādayaḥ* | [*AKBh* 99.21–26].

42*katham idānīṃ dūrāntaravicchinnaṃ vyutthānacittaṃ samāpatticittasya samanantaram ity ucyate | cittāntarāvyavahītatvāt* | [*AKBh* 100.1–2].

43This extract is taken from Vasubandhu's *KSP*, extant only in Tibetan (see the entry on this text in the Bibliography): *de yang ci'i phyir mtshams 'byor | snyoms par 'jug pa'i sems ni de'i de ma thag pa'i rkyen yin pas de las mtshams 'byor ro zhe na* | [*KSP* 193.8–10].

44This image of the *tulādaṇḍa*, used by Yaśomitra at *AKV* 245.25ff., is a common one in Buddhist texts. See, for example, Prajñākaramati's *Bodhicaryāvatārapañjikā*, ed. La Vallée Poussin [1904–1914:483], where the rise and fall of a *tulādaṇḍa* is used to explain the temporal relations between death and rebirth.

45See, for example, the text from the *KSP* (Lamotte [1935b:235–236]). Lamotte, in his translation of this section attributes it to the Dārṣṭāntikas, but this is simply a synonym for 'Sautrāntika'.

46See, for example, the discussion of *sabhāgatā* in the *AKBh: atha keyaṃ sabhāgatā | sabhāgatā sattvasāmyam | sabhāgatā nāma dravyam | sattvānāṃ sādṛśyaṃ nikāyasabhāga ity asyāḥ śāstre saṃjñā | sā punar abhinnā bhinnā ca | abhinnā sarvasattvānāṃ sattvasabhāgatā | pratisattvaṃ sarveṣu bhāvāt | bhinnā punas teṣām eva sattvānāṃ dhātubhūmigatiyonijātistrīpuruṣopāsakabhikṣuśaikṣāśaikṣyādi bhedena pratiniyatā dharmasabhāgatā* | [*AKBh* 67.13–18]. There follow extensive debates on the details surrounding this category.

47*kha cig na re de'i sa bon dbang po gzugs can la gnas pa las te* | [*KSP* 193.14]

[48]*sems ni rnam pa gnyis te | de gcig ni de'i sa bon rnams bsags pa yin no | gnyis pa ni de'i dmigs pa dang | rnam pa dang | bye brag tha dad pa dag gis sna tshogs pa yin no | sems gnyis pa ma tshang ba'i phyir sems med pa yin te | dper na khri rkang pa gcig pa la rkang pa gzhan ma tshang ba'i phyir | rkang pa med pa zhes bya ba lta bu'o |* [*KSP* 197.20–25]. See also the notes to the translation of the *AKBh* on Vasumitra's view in Appendix B.

[49]For the standard exposition, see *AKBh* 143.2ff and the clear discussion by Stcherbatsky [1962:2.311–312].

[50]*akāryatvād abhāvasya* [*AKBh* 193.17]. The context here is a debate between Vaibhāṣikas and Vātsiputrīyās as to whether motion *(gati)* is possible, and whether the destruction of existents is spontaneous *(ākasmika)* or the result of causes *(hetu)*.

NOTES TO CHAPTER THREE

[1]The term Yogācāra means 'practitioner of spiritual discipline'. It was used to describe a definite school with well-defined philosophical positions by Vasubandhu in the *AKBh* (for example at *AKBh* 197.5, where an opinion on a scriptural text which describes three kinds of *rūpa* is attributed to the Yogācārins) and thus had become established as a school-name by the fourth century AD at the latest, and probably much earlier than that. Alternative names for this school are *vijñānavāda* (consciousness doctrine), *vijñaptimātratā* ([the doctrine that] there is nothing but representation) and *cittamātratā* ([the doctrine that] there is nothing but mind).

[2]There is, naturally, a much more complex dynamic underlying the development of Yogācāra thought than I have indicated here. There are, for example, links to and reactions against the *satyadvaya* doctrines of the early Madhyamaka, for discussions of which see Nagao [1978a; 1978b; 1979; 1982]; there are also important connections with early Tathāgatagarbha thought, brought out especially by Takasaki [1966]. An excellent discussion of the issues raised in what I am calling the 'pre-systematic' and 'early systematic' phases of Indian Yogācāra may be found in Keenan [1982].

[3]The usual version of this (in Sanskrit) is *cittamātram idaṃ yad idaṃ traidhātukam.*

[4]For the early uses of the phrase in the **Bhadrapālasūtra*, see Schmithausen [1976b:246ff] and Willis [1979:26ff]. The next substantial occurrence is in the *Daśabhūmikasūtra,* see Rahder [1926:49,74]. The most important passages of the *Saṃdhinirmocanasūtra* may be found in Lamotte's edition [1935a:90–91]. Compare May [1971:279ff] for a discussion of a relevant passage in the *Samādhirājasūtra;* also Régamey [1938:92 Note 202]. Matilal [1974] has some illuminating comments to make on these passages and provides an (English) translation of the relevant passages from the *Saṃdhinirmocana.*

[5]There are, of course, many other works which could be considered as representative of this stage of the Yogācāra tradition, including especially the *RGV*, for a study of which see Takasaki [1966]. But a close and careful reading of these works will provide, I think, a reasonably adequate picture of the world-view developed by Yogācāra thinkers in India circa 350 AD.

[6]There is a detailed entry on the *YBh* in the Bibliography.

[7]The date of Asanga is, as might be expected, problematic. Paramārtha's *Life of Vasubandhu* tells us that Asanga was Vasubandhu's eldest brother (Takakusu [1904:273–274]), and that Asanga was instrumental in converting his younger brother to the Mahāyāna (Takakusu [1904:-290–292]). Xuanzang's account of his travels in India repeats many of these motifs and adds specifics as to the texts received by Asanga from the celestial *bodhisattva* Maitreya (Beal [1981:1.226–227]). Similar details are given by the Tibetan historians (see, for example, Tāranātha's account in Chattopadhyaya and Chimpa [1970:154ff]. Following the almost unanimous witness of the traditions (which is not without its problems but, without entering upon a full-scale historical study, will do for the purpose of this investigation), the perspective taken here will be that Asanga was an elder (perhaps half-) brother of Vasubandhu; that he was born towards the end of the fourth century AD in Gandhara; that he entered the Buddhist saṃgha as a young man, possibly within the Mahiśāsaka school (for more on this see Wayman [1961:25ff]; Willis [1979:5ff]; Bareau [1955a:182]); that he later became enamoured of the emerging doctrines that we now call Yogācāra or Vijñaptimātratā; that he composed a number of seminal treatises in this area and that he died around the middle of the fifth century AD.

[8]I follow here Schmithausen's important study [1969b]: Schmithausen thinks of the *YBh* as an 'allmählich gewachsenes Schulwerk' [1969b:812]., The details, though fascinating, are too complex to enter into here.

[9]The standard Buddhist accounts of Asanga's life from both the Tibetan and Chinese traditions make much of Asanga's encounters with the celestial Maitreya. The Tibetan tradition, as I have suggested, even attributes five books to Maitreya, making Asanga merely the recipient and transcriber of these works (though it appears that this view is quite a late development even within the Tibetan traditions, since in the earliest Tibetan catalogues of Buddhist texts—as for example the *ldan kar ma* catalogue—the texts which later became the 'five books of Maitreya' are not so classified. The question of Maitreya's historicity has provoked a great deal of debate since the beginning of the twentieth century; the earliest writers on the issue (for example, Ui [1929] and Tucci [1930]) were inclined to demythologize Maitreya and see him as a human teacher rather than a celestial Bodhisattva with semi-divine powers. La Vallée Poussin [1930a] early expressed doubts about this rationalist interpretation, and Demiéville [1954:381n.4] argued that the attribution of the five books to Maitreya was simply an attempt to authenticate the basic works of the Yogācāra school, an attempt to ground them in the sacred rather than the profane. Tucci

appears to have changed his mind on the basis of Demiéville's arguments [1956:14 note 1] and Wayman [1961:33] also follows Demiéville here. For contrasting views see Willis [1979:53 Note 42] and Shukla [1973:1xi]. It does not seem to me that the historical data are such as to allow a definite resolution of this question without detailed internal analyses of the style and content of the works in question: only in this manner (and Schmithausen is really the only Western scholar who has yet begun this undertaking) can some useful data on the relations between these texts be arrived at.

10There are important commentaries to the *MSA* by Vasubandhu (though this attribution is far from certain), Sthiramati and Asvabhāva. Both Vasubandhu and Sthiramati also wrote commentaries to the *MV*. Further details will be found under 'Texts' in the Bibliography.

11Both the *MS* and the *AS* are extremely important texts. For further details, see the Bibliography under 'texts'.

12For further details on *V, VVr, T, TBh* and *TSN*, see, Bibliography under 'Texts'. It should be noted that the attribution of *MSABh* and *MVBh*, referred to in passing in this paragraph, to Vasubandhu is not uncontroversial.

13Neither Asvabhāva's commentary to the *MSA (MSAT)* nor that to the *MS (MSU)* have been fully translated into any Western language. Some bibliographical details on these texts will be found in the Bibliography under 'Texts'.

14The text of *V* and *VVr* 1–2, upon which much of the discussion in the next few pages is based, reads as follows (the verses of *V* are translated in upper case and the prose commentary of *VVr* is translated in lower case): 'In the [doctrine of] the Great Vehicle the three-realmed [cosmos] is established to be nothing but representation, for a sacred text says: 'O Sons of the Conqueror, this three-realmed [cosmos] is nothing but mind.' The terms 'mind', 'mental consciousness' and 'representation' are synonyms [so any of them could have been used in the sacred text quoted]. The term 'mind' [in the sacred text quoted] refers also to what is associated with mind. The term 'nothing but' [in the sacred text quoted] indicates the denial of external objects. THIS [THREE-REALMED COSMOS] IS NOTHING BUT REPRESENTATION BECAUSE OF THE APPEARANCE OF NON-EXISTENT OBJECTS; IN JUST THE SAME WAY A MAN WITH FAULTY VISION SEES SUCH THINGS AS UNREAL HAIRS AND MOONS.(1) Here it is asked: IF REPRESENTATIONS ARE WITHOUT [CORRESPONDING] EXTERNAL OBJECTS THEN THERE COULD BE NO: (i) LIMITATION [OF THEIR APPEARANCE] TO [ONE] PLACE AND TIME; (ii) NON-LIMITATION [OF THEIR APPEARANCE] TO [ONE] MENTAL CONTINUUM; (iii) PERFORMANCE OF FUNCTION.(2) What does this mean? If representations of things such as physical form occur without external objects consisting in physical form, then [such representations] do not occur because of [the presence of] external objects consisting in physical form. [If this is so then the following questions arise]: (i) Why do [such representations] arise in a particular place and not just anywhere? (ii) Why do [such representations] arise in that place at a particular time and not at just any time? (iii) Why do [such representations] arise in the continuua of all those who are in a particular place at a particular time, and not just in one (as is the case, for example, for the appearance of such things as hairs in the continuua of those with faulty vision, since [such things do not appear in the continuua] of others)? (iv) Why do such things as hairs and insects seen by those with faulty vision not perform the functions of [real] hairs and so forth? For it isn't the case that other things [i.e., real hairs and so forth] do not perform [their proper functions]. Also, things seen in a dream—for example food, drink, clothing, poison, weapons—do not perform their proper functions (viz., of being eaten and so forth), whereas other [real instances] of such things do perform [their proper functions]. The same is true, for example, of an unreal city, such as that in which the *Gandharvas* live: this does not perform the functions of a city, whereas other [real cities] do perform [such functions]. So, if there are no external objects [corresponding to representations] it would not be proper to assert (i) limitation to [a single] time and place; (ii) non-limitation to [a single] continuum; and (iii) performance of [the appropriate] function.' (The text that follows is cited from Lévi [1925:-3.1–16]; this is a Sanskrit reconstruction, made by Lévi with the help of the Chinese and Tibetan versions. I have not had an opportunity to check these myself and so have simply translated the Sanskrit that follows): *mahāyāne traidhātukaṃ vijñaptimātraṃ vyavasthāpyate | cittamātraṃ bho jinaputrā yaduta traidhātukam iti sutrāt | cittaṃ mano vijñānaṃ vijñaptiś ceti paryāyāḥ | cittam atra sasaṃprayogam abhipretam | mātram ity arthapratiṣedhārthaṃ || vijñaptimātram evaitad asadarthāvabhāsanāt | yathā taimirikasyāsatkeśacandrādidarśanam || 1 || atra codyate | yadi vijñaptir anarthā niyamo deśakālayoḥ | saṃtānasyāniyamaś ca yuktā kṛtyakriyā na ca || 2 || kim uktaṃ bhavati | yadi vinā rūpādyarthena rūpādivijñaptir utpadyate na rūpādyarthāt | kasmāt | kvacid deśa utpadyate na sarvatra | tatraiva ca deśe kadācid utpadyate na sarvadā | taddeśakālapratiṣṭhānāṃ sarveṣāṃ saṃtāna utpadyate na kevalam ekasya | yathā taimirikāṇāṃ saṃtāne keśādyābhāso nānyeṣāṃ | kasmād yat taimirikaiḥ keśabhramarādi dṛśyate tena keśādi kriyā na kriyate na ca tadanyair na kriyate | yadannapānavastraviṣāyudhādi svapne dṛśyate tenānnādikriyā na kriyate na ca tadanyair na kriyate | gandharvanagareṇāsattvān nagarakriyā na kriyate na ca tadanyair na kriyate | tasmād arthābhāve deśakālaniyamaḥ saṃtānāniyamaḥ kṛtyakriyā ca na yujyate ||*

It will be noted that I disagree with Kochumuttom's recent translation of *mahāyāne traidhātukaṁ vijñaptimātraṃ vyavasthāpyate* as: ' . . . in the Mahāyāna system it has been established that those belonging to the three worlds are mere representations of consciousness . . .' [1982:-165]. Kochumuttom agrues (rightly) that *traidhātuka* is an adjectival form and (wrongly) that it is meant to qualify *cittacaitta*. It is clear from the many other contexts in which this phrase occurs that *traidhātuka* is meant to qualify an (understood but not expressed) *loka*—world or cosmos. For translations of the same passage as quoted in the *MS*, see Lamotte [1973:1.93] and Nagao [1982:288].

[15]For an extremely detailed exposition of (one of) the standard Indian Buddhist cosmologies, see the third chapter of *AKBh;* also Kloetzli [1983].

[16]It's significant that Vasubandhu uses here the Sanskrit term *asadartha,* clearly indicating that he intends objects which simply do not exist.

[17]Such, for example are the eight *vimokṣāḥ,* the eight *abhibhvāyatanāni* and the 10 *kṛtṣnāyatanāni*. The four *smṛtyupasthānāni* can also be understood under this rubric. See Griffiths [1983a], Hurvitz [1979] and Schmithausen [1976a] for some discussion along these lines. All the standard works on Buddhist meditation contain some discussion of these techniques.

[18]My account here is heavily dependent upon Schmithausen's excellent discussion of the relationship between 'spiritual practice' and 'philosophical theory' in Buddhism [1976b]. There he says: 'Thus, the result of our examination of the oldest materials of the Yogācāra school clearly speaks in favour of the theory that Yogācāra idealism primarily results from a *generalization* of a fact observed in the case of meditation-objects, i.e., in the context of a *spiritual* practice.' Schmithausen [1976b:241].

[19]See, for example Matilal who thinks that it is appropriate to apply the term 'idealism'—meaning a denial of the common-sense view that material external objects exist independently of the mind [1974:139]—to this variety of the Yogācāra. Compare May [1971:266], who has more reservations. A constrasting view is held, for example, by Ueda, who differentiates Yogācāra thought on this question into two 'streams'. He defines one as a 'theory of reality' [1967:164–165], in which the duality of subject and object *(grāhaka/grāhya)* is abandoned and all there really is is the non-duality of subject and object. This Ueda identifies with that introduced into China by Paramārtha, based upon the texts of what I am calling the 'classical period' of Indian Yogācāra. Ueda's 'second stream' is the more strictly 'idealistic' view made popular in China by Dharmapāla and Xuanzang. Alex Wayman [1961] and his pupil Janice Dean Willis [1979] are both wary of applying the term 'idealism' to Vasubandhu's version of Yogācāra, Wayman apparently because he thinks that the Yogācāra theorists of the classical period do not deny the object and affirm the subject (as, presumably, an idealist would), but rather stress the constructively deceptive activities of the mind while acknowledging that ultimately everything is emptiness *(śūnyatā).* Willis is more circumspect, admitting that Vasubandhu in his philosophical moods sounds like a idealist but wanting to explain such texts as the *VVr* as diagnostic rather than strictly philosophical [1979:33ff]. Kochumuttom [1982] has recently tried to show that the classical Indian Yogācāra is not idealistic in any meaningful sense, and that we find in, say, *V,* is a 'critique of the correspondence theory of knowledge' [1982:228ff]. I cannot follow Kochumuttom in this view, though to demonstrate exactly why would extend this note into a monograph in its own right.

[20]*svapne dṛgviṣayābhāvaṃ nāprabuddho 'vagacchati || evaṃ vitathavikalpābhyāsavāsanānidrayā prasupto lokaḥ svapna ivābhūtam arthaṃ paśyan na prabuddhas tad abhāvaṃ yathāvan nāvagacchati | yadā tu tatpratipakṣalokottaranirvikalpajñānalābhāt prabuddho bhavati tadā tatpṛṣṭhalabdhaśuddhalaukikajñānasaṃmukhībhāvād viṣayābhāvaṃ yathāvad avagacchatīti samānam etat* | [*VVr* ad *V* 17cd. Lévi, 1925:9.12–16]. Kochumuttom [1982:187] gives both an incorrect text and an incorrect translation.

[21]The Sanskrit term *trisvabhāva* is more often translated 'three natures'. It is the same term, as I have shown in Section 2.2 and the notes thereto, as that used by the Vaibhāṣika theoreticians in their discussions of the sense in which dharmas may properly be said to exist. To translate *svabhāva* in the context of classical Yogācāra theories of consciousness as 'nature' or 'essence' or 'own-being', though, would connote an inappropriately substantialist view. As I hope the following exposition will make clear, we are in fact dealing here with a set of categories designed to explain how consciousness functions, the three modes under which it operates. This is in part an epistemological notion and in part a descriptive-phenomenological notion, and 'aspect' therefore seems an appropriate translation for svabhāva. Stephan Beyer also used this translation in a privately circulated typescript translation of the *TSN*.

[22]*kalpitaḥ paratantraś ca pariniṣpanna eva ca | trayaḥ svabhāvā dhīrāṇāṃ gaṃbhīraṃ jñeyam iṣyate || yat khyāti paratantro 'sau yathā khyāti sa kalpitaḥ | pratyayādhīnavṛttitvāt kalpanāmātrabhāvataḥ || tasya khyātur yathākhyānaṃ yā sadāvidyamānatā | jñeyaḥ sa pariniṣpannaḥ svabhāvo 'nanyathātvataḥ* || *TSN* 1–3. Tola and Dragonetti [1983:249].

[23]As, for example, in *TSN* 4–6, where 'what appears' is identified with the 'imagination of what is unreal', and this in turn is said to be 'mind'. Mind in turn is described as twofold: the 'store-consciousness' (discussed at length in Section 3.2.3) and the 'functioning consciousnesses': *tatra kiṃ khyāty asatkalpaḥ kathaṃ khyāti dvayātmanatā | tasya kā nāstīti tena yā tatrādvayadharmatā || asatkalpo 'tra kaś cittaṃ yatas tat kalpyate yathā | yathā ca kalpayaty arthaṃ tathātyantaṃ na vidyate || tad dhetuphalabhāvena cittaṃ dvividham iṣyate | yad ālayākhyavijñānaṃ pravṛttyākhyaṃ ca saptadhā* || *TSN* 4–6. Tola and Dragonetti [1983:249].

[24]*gal te rnam par rig pa tsam don snang ba'i gnas gzhan gyi dbang gi ngo bo nyid yin la | de ji ltar na gzhan gyi dbnag yin la | ci'i phyir na gzhan gyi dbang zhes bya zhe na | rang gi bag chags kyi sa bon las skyes pa yin pas de lta bas na rkyen gyi gzhan dbang yin no | skyes nas kyang skad cig las lhag par bdag nyid gnas par mi nus pas na gzhan gyi dbang zhes bya'o* || *MS* II.15A. Nagao [1982:73]. Lamotte [1973:2.107].

[25]*bag chags zhes bya ba 'di ci zhig | bag chags zhes brjod pa 'di'i brjod par bya ba ni ci zhe na | chos de dang lhan cig 'byung ba dang | 'gag pa la brten nas de 'byung ba'i rgyu mtshan nyid gang yin pa de ni brjod par bya ba ste | dper na til dag la me tog gis bsgos pa til dang me tog lhan cig 'byung zhing 'gags*

kyang til rnams de'i dri gzhan 'byung ba'i rgyu mtshan nyid du 'byung ba dang | 'dod chags la sogs pa la spyod pa rnams kyi 'dod chags la sogs pa'i bag chags 'dod chags la sogs pa dang lhan cig 'byung zhing 'gags kyang sems ni de'i rgyu mtshan nyid du 'byung ba dang | mang du thos pa rnams kyi mang du thos pa'i bag chags kyang thos pa de yid la byed pa dang lhan cig tu 'byung zhing 'gags kyang sems ni de brjod pa'i rgyu mtshan nyid du 'byung ste | bag chags des yongs su zin pas chos 'dzin pa zhes bya ba ltar kun gzhi rnam par shes pa la yang tshul de bzhin du blta bar bya'o || *MS* I.15. Nagao [1982:23]. Lamotte [1973:2.33]. Compare the useful discussion of *bīja* and *vāsanā* in La Vallée Poussin [1928–29:100–123].

26*abhūtam asmin dvayaṃ parikalpyate 'nena vety abhūtaparikalpaḥ | abhūtavacanena ca yathā 'yaṃ parikalpyate grāhyagrāhakatvena tathā nāstīti pradarśayati | parikalpavacanena tv artho yathā parikalpyate tathārtho na vidyate iti pradarśayati | evam asya grāhyagrāhakavinirmuktaṃ lakṣaṇaṃ paridīpitaṃ bhavati ||* *MVT* ad *MV* I.2. Pandeya [1971:11.30–34].

27*kaḥ punar asau | atītānāgatavartamānā hetuphalabhūtās traidhātukā anādikālikā nirvāṇaparyavasānāḥ saṃsārānurūpāś cittacaittā aviśeṣeṇābhūtaparikalpaḥ | viśeṣeṇa tu grāhyagrāhakavikalpaḥ | tatra grāhyavikalpo 'rthasattvapratibhāsaṃ vijñānam | grāhakavikalpa ātamvijñaptipratibhāsam ||* *MVT* ad *MV* I.2 Pandeya [1971:11.34–12.2]

28See *TSN* 4cd and compare *TSN* 25: *tato dvayābhāvabhāvo niṣpanno 'tra praviśyate | tathā hy asāv eva tadāsti nāstīti cocyate ||* Tola and Dragonetti [1983:250]. See also *MSABh* ad *MSA* XI.13: *satataṃ dvayena rahitaṃ tattvaṃ parikalpitaḥ svabhāvo grāhyagrāhakalakṣaṇenātyantam asattvāt | bhrānteḥ saṃniśrayaḥ paratantras tena tatparikalpanāt | anabhilāpyam aprapañcātmakaṃ ca pariniṣpannaḥ svabhāvaḥ | tatra prathamaṃ tattvaṃ parijñeyaṃ dvitīyaṃ praheyaṃ tṛtīyaṃ viśodhyaṃ . . .* Bagchi [1970:59.16–18]. That the perfected aspect of experience is not accessible to language is an important point which there has not been space to discuss in the body of this study.

29*gal te de gtan med pa'i mtshan nyid yongs su grub pa'i ngo bo nyid yin na | de ji ltar na yongs su grub pa nyid yin la | ci'i phyir na yongs su grub pa zhes bya zhe na | gzhan du mi 'gyur ba'i phyir yongs su grub pa'o | rnam par dag pa'i dmigs pa yin pa dang | dge ba'i chos thams cad kyi mchog yin pa'i phyir mchog gi don gyis yongs su grub pa zhes bya'o ||* *MS* II.15C. Nagao [1982:-74]. Lamotte [1973:2.107–108]. For more on the *pariniṣpannasvabhāva,* see La Vallée Poussin [1928–29:527–533] and the extensive discussion in the second chapter of *MS,* immediately following the extract quoted.

30In what follows I am indebted to the sensitive and learned treatment of Nagao [1983:11ff]. See also Kochumuttom [1982:111–119].

31See, for example, *MSABh* ad *MSA* XI.15ff, Bagchi [1970:59.27ff]; *MVT* ad *MV* I.2, Pandeya [1971:11.30].

32*māyākṛtaṃ mantravaśāt khyāti hastyātmanā yathā | ākāramātraṃ tatrāsti hastī nāsti tu sarvathā || svabhāvaḥ kalpito hastī paratantras tadākṛtiḥ | yas* *tatra hastyabhāvo 'sau* (Tola and Dragonetti read *'sāu* here) *parinispanna iṣyate* || *asatkalpas tathā khyāti mūlacittād dvayātmanā* | *dvayam atyantato nāsti tatrāsty ākṛtimātrakam* || *mantravan mūlavijñānaṃ kāṣṭhavat tathatā matā* | *hastyākāravad eṣṭavyo vikalpo hastivad dvayam* || *TSN* 27–30. Tola and Dragonetti [1983:250–251].

[33]'Reality' here translates *tathatā*, one of the many important Buddhist *termini technici* denoting the way things really are *(yathābhūta)*. A more literal (and in fact quite common) translation would be 'suchness'.

[34]See Nagao [1983:12–13]; Kochumuttom [1982:115ff]. *MSABh* ad *MSA* XI.15–17 (Bagchi [1970:60.1–14]) gives a full description and discussion of this image.

[35]I have devoted some philosophical discussion to this question elsewhere: Griffiths [1982; 1984]. See also White [1983].

[36]See especially Jaini [1959b]; La Vallée Poussin [1934:151–152; 1928–29:100ff].

[37]See notably *MS* I.2–3 and *MSBh* and *MSU* thereto: Lamotte [1934:-175–176]; Nagao [1982:10,111–116]. *MS* I.14 and *MSBh* and *MSU* thereto: [Lamotte 1934:221–225]; Nagao [1982:22–23,133–135]. *KSP* 33: Lamotte [1935b:198–199,247–249]. *TBh* ad *T* 2cd: Lévi [1925:18.22–19.2]. This *TBh* passage reads (verses in upper case, prose commentary in lower case): "HERE THE MATURATION [OF ACTION] IS THAT CONSCIOUSNESS WHICH IS CALLED 'STORE': IT HOLDS ALL SEEDS(2cd) . . . here, the term 'store' is used because [the store-consciousness] acts as a receptacle for the seeds of all defiled things. 'Receptacle' and 'store' are synonymous. Alternatively, the term 'store' [in the expression 'store-consciousness'] means: (i) that considered as effect, all things are stored in or dependent upon that; (ii) considered as cause it is stored in or dependent upon all things . . . The term 'maturation' is used because [the store-consciousness] has the quality of effecting the maturation of good and bad actions in all cosmic spheres, destinies, wombs and births [viz., in every possible kind of rebirth]. The term 'holds all seeds' is used because [the store-consciousness] possesses the quality of being the basis for the seeds of all things." *(tatrālayākhyāṃ vijñānaṃ vipākaḥ sarvabījakam* | . . . *tatra sarvasaṃkleśikadharmabījasthānatvād ālayaḥ* | *ālayaḥ sthānam iti paryāyau* | *atha vālīyante upanibadhyante 'smin sarvadharmāḥ kāryabhāvena* | *tad vālīyate upanibadhyate kāraṇabhāvena sarvadharmeṣv ity ālayaḥ* | . . . *sarvadhātugatiyonijātiṣu kuśalākuśalakarmavipākatvād vipākaḥ* | *sarvadharmabījāśrayatvāt sarvabījakam* |*)*.

[38]Much of the first part of the first chapter of *MS* (I.1–13) and its commentaries is devoted to an exploration of the scriptural witness to the existence of the *ālayavijñāna*.

[39]This is especially clear in *KSP* 34, where it is asked (rhetorically) how rebirth can be explained without postulating the *ālaya: gal te de*

yang mi 'dod na gzhan gang zhig lus zin par 'gyur | de las gzhan pa'i rnam par shes pa ni ji srid 'tsho ba'i bar du lus mi gtong ba 'am khyab par 'dug pa ni med do | Lamotte [1935b:198]. *MS* I.4–5 and its commentaries may usefully be compared. In *MS* I.34–42 a detailed argument is presented to explain why *janma-saṃkleśa* (defilement by (re)-birth) would not be possible without the store-consciousness. The basic point is that rebirth with the appropriate karmic inheritance would not be possible without the store-consciousness, since it is only this which can carry the seeds and tendencies which make such rebirth possible: Nagao [1982:36–41,191–212]; Lamotte [1973:2.54–63].

40For a detailed presentation of this argument, see *MS* I.30–33: Nagao [1982:32–36,179–188]; Lamotte (1973:2.49–54].

41Classically by the tenth century Naiyāyika Udayana in his *Atmatattvaviveka,* Dvivedin and Dravida [1907–39:778ff].

42See, for example, *MSU* ad *MS* I.2 in which the difference between the (impermanent) *ālaya* and the (permanent) *pradhāna* of the Sāṃkhya theorists is underlined by Asvabhāva (Lamotte [1934:174–175]). *TBh* ad *T* 4d is also relevant here: there the image of the *ālayavijñāna* flowing like a stream is used: *tac ca vartate srotasaughavat | tac cety ālayavijñānam eva saṃbadhyate | tatra sroto hetuphalayor nairantaryeṇa pravṛttiḥ | udakasamūhasya pūrvāparabhāgāvicchedena pravāha augha ity ucyate | yayā hy oghas tṛṇakāṣṭhagomayādīnākarṣayan gacchati evam ālayavijñānam api puṇyāpuṇyāneñjyakarmavāsanānugataṃ sparśamanaskārādīnākarṣayat srotasāsaṃsāvam avyuparataṃ pravartata iti |* Lévi [1925:21.26–22.5].

43This relationship of cause and effect is clearly stated in TSN 6: *tad dhetuphalabhāvena cittaṃ dvividham iṣyate | yad ālayākhyavijñānaṃ pravṛttyākhyaṃ ca saptadhā ||* Tola and Dragonetti [1983:249].

44Thus, for example, in *AKBh* ad *AK* I.16a the *vijñānaskandha* is defined as an apprehension or representation of specific objects *(viṣayaṃ viṣayaṃ prativijñaptir upalabdhir vijñānaskandha ity ucyate |* [*AKBh* 11.7]). It is interesting that Sthiramati in his *TBh* says, in similar vein, that the *ālayavijñāna* is called 'consciousness' because it cognizes *(vijānātīti vijñānam,* Lévi [1925:18.26]).

45Thus, for example, Vasubandhu in the *KSP (KSP* 36, Lamotte [1935b:199]). Sthiramati in the *TBh* explicitly asks how something with undefined *(aparicchinna)* objects and modes of functioning can properly be called 'consciousness'. His answer to this interestingly uses the example of the attainment of cessation: he says that the consciousness belonging to the store-consciousness has indistinctly cognized and undefined objects, but that in this it is not different from that consciousness which exists in the attainment of cessation. Sthiramati clearly also thinks that both reason and scripture demonstrate that the attainment of cessation is a state in which there is consciousness of a sort, and, though he does not say so at this point in the *TBh,* he also identifies this consciousness with the *ālayavijñāna: sa*(i.e., *ālayavijñāna) apy aparicchinnālambanākārapravṛttatvād asaṃviditety ucyate | kathaṃ vijñānam aparicchinnālambanākāraṃ bhaviṣyatīti | anyavijñānavādinām api nirodhasamāpattyādyavasthāsu tulyam etan na ca nirodhasamāpattyādyavasthāsu vijñānaṃ naivāstīti śakyate pratipattuṃ | yuktivirodhāt sūtravirodhāc ceti |* Lévi [1925:19.22–25].

46Some terminological clarification at this point is appropriate: I am translating *citta* by 'mind', *manas* by 'thought' and *vijñāna* by 'consciousness'. In the Theravāda and Vaibhāṣika traditions, no consistent distinction was made between these terms; see, for example, *AKBh* and *AK* II.34cd. The nicer distinctions made by the theorists of the classical Yogācāra are precisely set forth in Asanga's *AS* and Sthiramati's *ASBh.* In the *AS, citta* is identified with *ālayavijñāna, manas* with the object *(ālambana)* of the *ālaya* and *vijñāna simpliciter* with the six sense-consciousnesses: *vijñānaskandhavyavasthānaṃ katamat | yac cittaṃ manovijñānam api | tatra cittaṃ katamat | skandhadhātvāyatanavāsanāparibhāvitaṃ sarvabījakam ālayavijñānam | vipākavijñānam ādānavijñānam api tat tadvāsanācitatām upādāya | manaḥ katamat | yan nityakālaṃ manyanātmakam ālayavijñānālambanaṃ caturbhiḥ kleśaiḥ saṃprayuktam ātmadṛṣṭyātmasnehenāsmimānenāvidyayā ca | tac ca sarvatragaṃ kuśale 'py akuśale 'py avyākṛte 'pi sthāpayitvā mārgasaṃmukhībhāvaṃ nirodhasamāpattim aśaikṣabhūmiñ ca yac ca ṣaṇṇāṃ vijñānānāṃ samanantaraniruddhaṃ vijñānam | vijñānaṃ katamat | ṣaḍ vijñānakāyāḥ |* Gokhale [1947b:19.12–17]. Sthiramati's commentary on this passage of the *AS* contains his version of the eightfold proof of the existence of the *ālayavijñāna,* to be discussed in Section 3.3.

47The version in the *YBh,* extant only in Tibetan, may be found in P Sems-Tsam ZI2b1–4a4. The version in the *ASBh,* extant in the original Sanskrit, may be found in Tatia [1976:11.15–13.20]. The only study of which I am aware in any Western language is McDermott [1973]. The standard study in Japanese is Hakamaya [1978]; I am heavily indebted to Hakamaya's work in the remarks that follow and would like to express here my gratitude to him for his gracious willingness to communicate to me his profound learning in this area. A complete text and translation of the eightfold argument will be found in Appendix C.

48For example, the first chapter of the *MS* contains detailed arguments for the existence of the *ālaya,* many of which overlap with the eightfold form found in *ASBh* and *YBh.* I shall draw upon these where relevant. See also La Vallée Poussin [1928–29:182–220] for some detailed sets of proofs.

49*mahata udakaughasya vahataḥ saced ekasya tarangasyotpattipratyayaḥ pratyupasthito bhavaty ekam eva tarangaṃ pravartate | saced dvayos trayāṇāṃ saṃbahulānāṃ tarangāṇām utpattipratyayaḥ pratyupasthito bhavati | yāvat saṃbahulāni tarangāṇi pravartante | na ca tasyodakaughasya srotasā vahataḥ samucchittir bhavati | na paryupayogaḥ prajñāyate | evam eva viśālamate | tad oghasthānīyam ālayavijñānaṃ saṃniśritya pratiṣṭhāya saced ekasya vijñānasyotpattipratyayaḥ pratyupasthito bhavati | evam eva cakṣurvijñānaṃ pravartate | saced dvayos trayāṇāṃ sacet pañcānāṃ vijñānānām utpattipratyayaḥ pratyupasthito bhavati |* Lévi [1925:33.26–34.1].

[50] I refer here to the important technical term *dhātu,* which in Buddhist theory refers both to psychological realms—altered states of consciousness—and to cosmological realms, places in which the practitioner can exist or be reborn. To attain a particular altered state of consciousness is also to (temporarily) exist in the corresponding cosmological realm and (if other things are equal) to be reborn in that realm. There is thus an intimate link between the psychological and the cosmological, a link which sounds odd to most Western ears.

BIBLIOGRAPHY: TEXTS

Here are listed, alphabetically by title following English alphabetical order, all the texts given significant mention in the body of the monograph or in the notes. I have not included details of texts merely referred to once or twice in passing without being quoted.

I give initially information about editions and follow this with information about translations, and, in some cases, useful studies. Unless some other language is mentioned, reference to a translation should be understood as reference to an English translation.

All references given, whether to editions, translations or studies, are given simply by author (editor/translator) and date; full bibliographical details will be found under 'Works Cited'. In no case should it be assumed that the bibliographical information given here either is or is intended to be exhaustive.

Where appropriate, abbreviations for text-names used in the notes are given with the text-titles. A full listing of abbreviations is given separately. Personal or text-names preceded by an asterisk (*) are reconstructions into Sanskrit from some other language.

Abhidharmadīpavṛtti (Vibhāṣāprabhā) ADV

A lengthy orthodox Vaibhāṣika text whose main goal is the refutation of the Sautrāntika views expressed by Vasubandhu in the *AKBh*. The work was originally written in Sanskrit in the standard verse-plus-commentary form. Strictly speaking, the title *AD* refers only to the *kārikā;* the prose commentary is called the *Vibhāṣāprabhā*. Uniquely, there are no surviving translations of the *AD* into either Chinese or Tibetan or evidence that any were made. The work survives only in one incomplete Sanskrit manuscript, discovered by Sānkṛtyāyana in 1936 (Sānkṛtyāyana [1937:54]) and edited by Jaini [1977a]. The single manuscript appears to represent about 40 percent of the original work—62 leaves from an original 150 (Jaini [1977a:1–3]). There is no clear indication of the author's name. Jaini [1977a:129–136] suggests that it might be Vimalamitra; De Jong [1966] tentatively identifies the Dīpakāra with Iśvarasena, a pupil of Dignāga. The text has not been translated in its entirety into any modern language. The most useful studies are those of Jaini [1959a; 1959b; 1977a; 1977b] on specific philosophical issues in Vaibhāṣika theory, drawing heavily upon the *AD*, and those of Yoshimoto [1982; 1983], which approach most closely to a systematic study of the text as a whole.

***Abhidharmahṛdaya AH**

A short systematic proto-Vaibhāṣika text, whose author was probably named *Dharmaśrī. The creative organizational structure developed by this author was to be highly influential upon subsequent Vaibhāṣika thinkers. The text was originally written in Sanskrit but now only extant in Chinese translation (Taishō 1550). Both the title and the author's name are somewhat tentative Sanskrit reconstructions from the Chinese. Translated into English (Willemen 1975) and French [Armelin 1978]. Both these translations contain useful critical introductions. De Jong's critical review of these translations [1980a] and Frauwallner's remarks on the influence of this text on subsequent intellectual developments within the school [1971:73ff], are both useful.

Abhidharmakośabhāṣya AKBh

This work consists of a series of mnemonic verses *(AK)* together with an extensive prose commentary *(AKBh)*, originally composed in Sanskrit. The verses circulated independently of the prose commentary, though the prose commentary does not appear to have circulated independently of the verses. Prior to Sānkṛtyāyana's journeys to Tibet in the mid-1930's, only fragmentary manuscripts of the verses were available, one of which was described by La Vallée Poussin [1971:I.iii], but in 1936 a virtually complete manuscript of *AK* (missing only 16 verses from a total of 613) was discovered and photographed in Ngor monastery by Sānkṛtyāyana. The find was reported by him shortly after the discovery [1937:54], and the manuscript was shortly thereafter edited by V. V. Gokhale [1946 & 1947a]; this edition of the *AK* remains the most reliable and useful. A complete manuscript of the Sanskrit text of the *AKBh* was similarly discovered and photographed by Sānkṛtyāyana [1937:18,53–54]. This is the only complete Sanskrit manuscript of the *AKBh* now extant. The photographs of both it and the manuscript of the *AK* are in the Bihar Research Society Collection in Patna Museum. An edition of the manuscript of the *AKBh* was published by Pradhan in 1967 and reprinted with some alterations and a slightly different pagination in 1975. References in this study to the *AKBh* are to page/line of Pradhan [1975] unless otherwise noted. There is also an edition of both *AK* and *AKBh* included in the edition of *AKV* by Sāstrī [1981].

The *AKBh* was translated into Chinese twice, first by Paramārtha in 564–567 AD (Taishō 1559) and then by Xuanzang in 651–654 AD (Taishō 1558). A single Tibetan translation survives, produced by Jinamitra and Dpal brtsegs [Tōhoku 4090 Mngon-pa KU 26b1-KHU

258a7; Peking 5591 Mngon-pa GU 27b6-NGU 109a8; N Mngon-pa GU 29a7-NGU 110b4; C Mngon-pa KU 26b1-KHU 97b5]. Reference to this Tibetan translation will be made on occasion and will be to folio and line of the xylographs just noted. The only complete modern translation of the *AKBh* into any language is that into French by La Vallée Poussin [1971]. This translation was made before the recovery of the Sanskrit text and is based largely upon Xuanzang's Chinese version, though including Sanskrit reconstructions and occasional reference to the Tibetan translation.

The most valuable critical tool for the study of the *AKBh* is the three-volume index to the entire text (Sanskrit–Tibetan–Chinese; Chinese–Sanskrit; Tibetan–Sanskrit) edited by Hirakawa Akira and others [Hirakawa et al. 1973; 1977; 1978]. Another useful study is that of Chaudhuri [1983], which provides a synopsis of the content of the entire text (in English). Among Japanese scholars Sasaki [1958] and Yoshimoto [1982] provide much useful background information, though neither of them are concerned exclusively with *AKBh*. Kimura [1937], though dated and difficult to read, is still useful. Oshio [1934] produced some beautiful and useful charts representing visually the complex organizational and doctrinal schemata of the *AKBh*. Sakurabe [1969] published a very accurate and useful translation (into Japanese) of the first two chapters of the *AKBh* and more recently [1981] a complete translation of the *AK* together with his own commentary, based upon the *AKBh*.

***Abhidharmakośabhāṣyaṭīkā (Tattvārthā) AKT**

A very long and extemely useful commentary to the *AKBh* by Sthiramati, originally written in Sanskrit but now extant only in Tibetan translation (P 5875, Ngo-mtshar TO lal-THO 565b8; Tōhoku 4421, Sna-tshogs THO 1b2-426a7). References are to folio/line of P or D.

***Abhidharmakośaśāstrakārikābhāṣya AKSBh**

A commentary to *AKBh* by Saṃghabhadra (or possibly Vinītabhadra; the Tibetan 'dul bzang is not unambiguous), originally written in Sanskrit and now extant in Tibetan translation (P 5592/Tōhoku 4091) but with a possible partial Chinese version (Taishō 1563).

Abhidharmakośaṭīkā (Lakṣaṇānusāriṇī) AKTL

A lengthy commentary upon *AKBh* by Pūrṇavardhana, originally written in Sanskrit but now extant only in Tibetan translation (P 5594/Tōhoku 4093). There are many connections between this text and *AKT;* lengthy parallel passages, verbally identical and common to both texts, are common. There is also a shorter version of this work (P 5597/Tōhoku 4096) which I have not consulted.

Abhidharmakośaṭīkā (Upāyikā) AKTU

A commentary to *AKBh* by Śamathadeva (or possibly Śāntisthiradeva; Tibetan zhi gnas lha) originally written in Sanskrit but now extant only in Tibetan translation (P 5595/Tōhoku 4094).

Abhidharmakośavṛtti (Marmapradīpa) AKVr

A relatively short summary of the content of the *AKBh* by Dignāga, originally written in Sanskrit but now extant in Tibetan translation (P 5596/Tōhoku 4095).

Abhidharmakośavyākhyā (Sphuṭārthā) AKV

A long commentary to *AKBh* by Yaśomitra, largely concerned to defend the Sautrāntika positions often enspoused by Vasubandhu in the text against the neo-Vaibhāṣika orthodoxy of Saṃghabhadra et al. This text is unique among the Indian commentaries to *AKBh* in that it is fully extant in both Sanskrit (several manuscripts) and Tibetan, though not in Chinese. The Sanskrit text has been edited in bits and pieces several times (see Narendra Law [1949] for the first three chapters; Law and Dutt [1957] for the fourth chapter; Stcherbatsky et al. [1970] for the first two chapters; La Vallée Poussin [1919] for the third chapter) and in its entirety twice (Wogihara [1932–36] and Sāstrī [1981]). I shall refer to page/line of Sāstrī's edition unless otherwise noted. References to the Tibetan text are to folio/line of P or D (P 5593/Tōhoku 4092).

There is no complete translation into any modern language, although many extracts have been translated and studied in a variety of critical works; La Vallée Pousin [1919] provides a complete translation of the third chapter.

***Abhidharmāmṛta AA**

A short proto-Vaibhāṣika text attributed to Ghoṣaka. Originally written in Sanskrit, now extant only in Chinese translation (Taishō 1553). Translated into French by Van Den Broeck [1977]. It remains unclear whether this text was written before or after the *AH* and whether the Ghoṣaka who wrote it is the same as the Ghoṣaka frequently quoted in the *AKBh*. Van Den Broeck [1977:81] thinks that Ghoṣaka was consciously revising *Dharmaśrī's work; Frauwallner [1971:71] also considers that the *AA* is later than the *AH* Both Sakurabe [1969:57–59] and De Jong [1980b:279] think that the order should be reversed. This latter view is probably correct since the *AH* shows evidence of a more systematic organization than does the *AA*. But such judgements must remain to some extent subjective. The text has also been re-translated from Chinese into Sanskrit by Sastri [1953]; this rendering is interesting but unlikely to be an accurate guide to the lost original.

Abhidharmasamuccaya AS

A short, tersely phrased text by Asanga. A single incomplete manuscript of the Sanskrit original was recovered by Sānkṛtyāyana [1937] in 1936. Descriptions of this manuscript have been given by Gokhale [1948] and Pradhan [1948], and an edition of the fragments was published by Gokhale [1974b]. This is still the most reliable way of access to what we have of the original. I quote it as *AS(G)* by page and line. Pradhan's [1950] edition/reconstruction is not reliable. There are translations into Tibetan (Tōhoku 4049), Chinese (Taishō 1605) and French (Rahula 1971).

Abhidharmasamuccayabhāṣya ASBh

A lengthy commentary to *AS*, probably by Sthiramati. The question of authorship is discussed by Pradhan [1949]. I quote the text by page and line of Tatia's [1976] edition of the sole surviving Sanskrit manuscript.

Anguttaranikāya AN

I have used the standard PTS romanized edition of the Pali text produced by R. Morris, E. Hardy, Mabel Hunt, A. K. Warder and C. A. F. Rhys-Davids [1885–1910]. References are to volume, page and line of this edition. The standard translation is that by F. L. Woodward and R. M. Hare [1951–55].

Dhammasangaṇi Dhs

I have used the standard PTS romanized edition of the Pali text, edited by Muller [1885]; references are to page and line of this edition. There is also an edition by Bapat and Vadekar [1940] to which I have not had access, though it is reputed to give a better text. The standard English translation is that by C. A. F. Rhys-Davids [1900].

Dhammasangaṇi-aṭṭhakathā (Atthasālinī) DhsA

I have used the edition by Bapat and Vadekar [1942] in the Bhandarkar Oriental Series; references are to chapter and paragraph number of this edition, which is considerably more reliable than the 1897 PTS edition. The standard translation is that by Pe Maung Tin [1920–21].

Dīghanikāya DN

I have used the standard PTS romanized edition of the Pali text produced by T. W. Rhys-Davids and J. Estlin Carpenter [1890–1911]. References are to volume, page and line of this edition. The standard translation is that by T. W. Rhys-Davids and C. A. F. Rhys-Davids [1899–1921].

Dīghanikāya-aṭṭhakathā (Sumangalavilāsinī) DA

I have used the standard PTS romanized edition of the Pali text produced by T. W. Rhys-Davids, J. Estlin Carpenter and W. Stede [1886–1932]. References are to volume, page and line of this edition.

Karmasiddhiprakaraṇa KSP

This work is almost certainly attributable to Vasubandhu. It discusses the central theoretical problems connected with the mechanisms of karma. It exists only in Tibetan and Chinese translations. I have used the edition of the Tibetan text by Lamotte [1935b]; this work also includes a translation (largely based on the Chinese) into French.

Madhyāntavibhāga MV

The *MV* itself is a verse-text. There are two important Indian commentaries: the *MVBh* (probably by Vasubandhu) and the *MVT* (probably by Sthiramati). I have usually quoted Pandeya's edition [1971] of all three texts, though this is not the most reliable. Yamaguchi's [1934–37] has not been available to me.

***(Abhidharma)Mahāvibhāṣā**

The largest and most comprehensive single text in the Vaibhāṣika Abhidharma tradition, that from which the name Vaibhāṣika is derived. Originally written in Sanskrit but now extant only in Chinese, translated by Xuanzang (Taishō 1545). There are two other texts in the Chinese Tripiṭaka (Taishō 1546–1547) which bear the name *Vibhāṣā;* it is probable that 1546 is an earlier translation (by Buddhavarman) of the same Sanskrit original, though there are substantial differences between Buddhavarman's version and Xuanzang's, consisting largely in the fact that Xuanzang's version is longer and contains more detail on key doctrinal issues. Taishō 1547 is an altogether different text, though the exact nature of the relationships between these three texts remains obscure. There is no complete translation of the *Mahāvibhāṣā* into any Western language, though short sections have been translated and commented upon by La Vallée Poussin [1930b; 1932; 1937a; 1937b]. There is a great need for further study and clarification of this important text.

Mahāyānasaṃgraha MS

Asanga's most important prose work, perhaps the most influential systematic exposition of Yogācāra theory produced in India. Extant only in Tibetan and Chinese translations. I have usually quoted the edition of the Tibetan text produced by Lamotte [1973]. There are important commentaries by Vasubandhu *(MSBh)* and Asvabhāva *(MSU);* these too are lost in their original Sanskrit versions.

Mahāyānasūtrālaṃkāra MSA

A Yogācāra verse-text of central importance. Commentaries by Vasubandhu *(MSABh* though there is some debate about this; some Japanese scholars think that Asanga wrote this text) and Asvabhāva *(MSAT).* Only the *MSABh* survives in its original Sanskrit; I have quoted Bagchi's edition by page and line. The commentary by Asvabhāva is extant only in Tibetan (Tōhoku 4029).

Majjhimanikāya MN

I have used the standard PTS romanized edition of the Pali text produced by V. Trenckner, Robert Chalmers and C. A. F. Rhys-Davids (ed), [1888–1925]. References are to volume, page and line of this edition. The standard translation is that by I. B. Horner [1954–59].

Majjhimanikāya-aṭṭhakathā (Papañcasūdanī) MA

I have used the standard PTS romanized edition of the text produced by J. H. Woods, D. Kosambi and I. B. Horner [1922–1938]. References are to volume, page and line of this edition. There is no English translation.

Milindapañha Miln

A fairly early and very influential post-canonical Theravāda text. There are numerous translations into other Buddhist canonical languages and into modern languages. I have referred to the romanized edition by Trenckner [1880] and to the translation by Horner [1963–64].

***Nyāyānusāra**

A lengthy attempted refutation of the *AKBh* by Saṃghabhadra, reproducing many of the verses of that text but usually explaining their meaning differently. The work was originally written in Sanskrit but is now extant only in Chinese translation (Taishō 1562). The most useful discussion of the epistemological aspects of Saṃghabhadra's work is Sasaki [1958:343ff].

***Samayapradīpika**

A shorter digest of Saṃghabhadra's views, less obviously polemical than the Nyāyānusāra. Extant only in Chinese (Taishō 1563) and scarcely worked on as yet by Western scholarship. The Sanskrit reconstruction of the title given here is far from certain.

Samyuttanikāya SN

I have used the standard PTS romanized edition of the Pali text, produced by Léon Feer [1884–1904]. References are to volume, page and line of this edition. The standard English translation is that by C. A. F. Rhys-Davids and F. L. Woodward [1917–1930].

Samyuttanikāya-aṭṭhakathā (Sāratthappakāsinī) SA

I have used the standard PTS romanized edition of the Pali text, produced by F. L. Woodward [1929–37]. References are to volume, page and line of this edition. There is no complete English translation.

Triṃśikā T

Vasubandhu's work in 30 verses expounding the key tenets of Yogācāra ontology and psychology. This work survives in its original Sanskrit, together with Sthiramati's prose commentary *(TBh)*. I have quoted the edition by Lévi [1925].

Trisvabhāvanirdeśa TSN

Vasubandhu's short verse-text expounding the Yogācārin three-aspect theory. The edition/translation by Tola and Dragonetti [1983] is convenient and accurate. I quote the text either by verse number or by page and line of Tola and Dragonetti.

Viṃśatikā V

Vasubandhu's 20-verse text together with his own prose commentary *(VVr)*. Most of this work survives in Sanskrit; I quote the edition by Lévi [1925].

Visuddhimagga VM

A systematic presentation of Theravādin orthodoxy in the form of a synthetic presentation of the doctrines contained in the tripartite canon. Written by Buddhaghosa in Pali and still extant in that language. The most commonly used edition in the West is the romanized one by Warren [1950]. While I have consulted this edition, I have relied mostly upon the Devanāgarī edition produced by Rewatadhamma [1969–72] and included by him as part of his edition of *VMT*. References in the notes are given initially to page/line of Rewatadhamma followed by chapter/section of Warren for ease of cross-reference. There is also a romanized edition produced by the Pali Text Society [C. A. F. Rhys-Davids 1920–21] which I have not used. There are two complete translations into English: Pe Maung Tin [1923–31] and Nyanamoli [1976]. The latter is by far the best, both in terms of accuracy and English style; I am greatly indebted to Nyanamoli's renderings for my understanding of much Theravādin technical terminology.

Visuddhimaggaṭīkā (Paramatthamañjūsā) VMT

An extensive and often illuminating commentary to *VM*. The only complete edition of this text available to me has been Rewatadhamma [1969–72] (see previous entry). There is no translation into any modern language.

Yogācārabhūmi YBh

The *YBh* was originally written or compiled in Sanskrit and appears to have had five major divisions. The first of these, called *Bahubhūmikavastu*, is the basic division, approximately equal in length to the other four parts, and is itself subdivided into 17 sections, corresponding to the 17 stages of the practice of a Bodhisattva according to the Yogācāra school. A manuscript of the Sanskrit text of this first division was recovered by Rahula Sānkṛtyāyana during his second search for Sanskrit manuscripts in Tibet [Sānkṛtyāyana 1937:6], and some parts of this manuscript have appeared in editions of varying quality since then: see Vidushekara Bhattacharya [1957] for stages 1–5; Wayman [1960] for stages 8, 9 and 14; Shukla [1973] for stage 13 (for a very critical review of this edition, see De Jong [1976]); the fifteenth stage, that of the bodhisattva is of special importance and appears to have circulated independently both in Inida and later in China and Tibet; there are also independent Sanskrit manuscripts of this part of text. It has been edited in Sanskrit by Wogihara [1971] and Nalinaksha Dutt [1978] (for some observations on Dutt's edition and an edition of the first chapter of this section see Roth [1976]). Wayman [1961] gives an analysis of the *Śrāvakabhūmi* section. Schmithausen [1982] provides some remarks on the concluding sections of this same section. Demiéville [1957] gives a French translation of the chapter on *dhyāna;* Willis [1979] translates the *tattvārtha* chapter. Finally, the *YBh* is extant in Chinese in a translation by Xuanzang (Taishō 1599) and substantially in Tibetan (Tōhoku 4035–4042). The only significant study of any portion of the *YBh* outside the *Bahubhūmikavastu* is Schmithausen [1969a].

BIBLIOGRAPHY: WORKS CITED

Adikaram, E. W.

1946 *Early History of Buddhism in Ceylon.* Migoda: D. S. Puswella.

Anacker, Stefan

1970 *Vasubandhu: Three Aspects. A Study of a Buddhist Philosopher.* PhD Dissertation, University of Wisconsin—Madison.

Armelin, I.

1978 (tr) *Le Coeur de la loi suprême. Traité de Fa-Cheng. Abhidharmahṛdayaśāstra.* Paris: Geuthner.

Aronoff, Arnold

1982 *Constrasting Modes of Textual Classification: The Jātaka Commentary and its Relationship to the Pali Canon.* PhD Dissertation: University of Chicago.

Bagchi, S.

1970 (ed) *Mahāyānasūtrālankāra of Asanga.* Buddhist Sanskrit Texts Number 13. Darbhanga: Mithila Institute.

Banerjee, Anukul C.

1952 'Abhidharma Texts in Tibetan.' *Indian Historical Quarterly,* 28:372–378.

1957 *Sarvāstivāda Literature.* Calcutta: Calcutta University Press.

Bapat, P. V. and Vadekar, R. D.

1940 (eds) *Dhammasangaṇi.* Bhandarkar Oriental Series No.2. Poona: Bhandarkar Oriental Research Institute.

1942 (eds) *Atthasālinī.* Bhandarkar Oriental Series No.3. Poona: Bhandarkar Oriental Research Institute.

Bareau, André

1947 'Les sectes bouddhiques du Petit Véhicule et leurs Abhidharmapiṭaka.' *Bulletin de l'école française d'Extrême-Orient,* 44:1–11.

1954 (tr) 'Trois traités sur les sectes bouddhiques attribués a Vasumitra, Bhavya, et Vinītadeva (1).' *Journal Asiatique,* 229–266.

1955a *Les Sectes bouddhiques du Petit Véhicule.* Saigon: Ecole française d'Extrême-Orient.

1955b *Les Premières conciles bouddhique.* Paris: Presses Universitaires de France.

1956 (tr) 'Trois traités sur les sectes bouddhiques attribués a Vasumitra, Bhavya, et Vinītadeva (2).' *Journal Asiatique,* 167–299.

1963 *Recherches sur la biographie du Bouddha dans les Sūtrapiṭaka et les Vinayapiṭaka anciens: de la quête de l'eveil à la conversion de Sāriputra et de Maudgalyāyana.* Publications d'école française d'Extrême-Orient Vol. 53. Paris: Ecole française d'Extrême-Orient.

1971 *Recherches sur la biographie du Bouddha dans les Sūtrapiṭaka et les Vinayapiṭaka anciens: les derniers mois, le Parinirvāṇa et les funerailles.* Publications d'école française d'Extrême Orient Vol. 77. Paris: Ecole française d'Extrême Orient.

Barnes, Michael

1980 'The Buddhist Way of Deliverance.' *Studia Missionalia,* 223–277.

Barnes, Barry and Bloor, David

1982 'Relativism, Rationalism and the Sociology of Knowledge.' In Martin Hollis and Steven Lukes (eds), *Rationality and Relativism,* Oxford: Basil Blackwell, pages 21–47.

Beal, Samuel

1981 (tr) *Si-Yu Ki: Buddhist Records of the Western World.* Two volumes bound as one. Separate pagination. Delhi: Motilal Banarsidass. First edition, London 1884.

Bechert, Heinz

1961 'Aśokas "Schismenedikt" und der Begriff Saṃghabheda.' *Wiener Zeitschrift für die Kunde Sud- und Ostasiens,* 5:18–52.

1973 'Notes on the Formation of Buddhist Sects and the Origins of Mahāyāna.' In *German Scholars on India* (1), Varanasi: Chowkhamba Sanskrit Series, pages 6–18.

Berger, Peter and Luckmann, Thomas

1966 *The Social Construction of Reality: A Treatise in the Sociology of Knowledge.* Garden City: Doubleday.

Betty, L. Stafford

1976 'A Death-Blow to Sankara's Non-Dualism? A Dualist Refutation.' *Religious Studies,* 12:281–290.

1978 *Vadirāja's Refutation of Sankara's Non-Dualism: Clearing the Way for Theism.* Delhi: Motilal Banarsidass.

1983a 'Nāgārjuna's Masterpiece: Logical, Mystical, Both, or Neither?' *Philosophy East and West,* 33:123–138.

1983b 'Is Nāgārjuna a Philosopher? Response to Professor Loy.' *Philosophy East and West,* 33:447–450.

Beyer, Stephan

1973 *The Cult of Tārā: Magic and Ritual in Tibet.* Berkeley: University of California Press.

1974 *The Buddhist Experience: Sources and Interpretations.* Encino–Belmont, California: Dickenson.

Bronkhorst, Johannes
Two Traditions of Meditation in Ancient India. Unpublished manuscript.

Buddhadatta, A. P.
1957 *Corrections of Geiger's Mahāvaṃsa.* Ambalangoda: Ananda Book Company.

Bühnemann, Gudrun
1980 *Der Allwissende Buddha: Eine Beweis und Seine Probleme. Ratnakīrtis Sarvajñasiddhi.* Wiener Studien zur Tibetologie und Buddhismuskunde, Heft 4. Wien: Arbeitskreis für Tibetische und Buddhistische Studien Universität Wien.

Carrithers, Michael
1983 *The Buddha.* Oxford: Oxford University Press.

Carter, John Ross
1978 *Dhamma: Western Academic and Sinhalese Buddhist Interpretations. A Study of a Religious Concept.* Tokyo: The Hokuseido Press.

Ch'en, Kenneth
1964 *Buddhism in China: A Historical Survey.* Princeton: Princeton University Press.

Chattopadhyaya, Alaka and Chimpa (Lama)
1970 (tr) *History of Buddhism in India.* Simla: Indian Institute of Advanced Study.

Chaudhuri, Sukomal
1983 *Analytical Study of the Abhidharmakośa.* Calcutta: Firma KLM Private Limited. First edition Calcutta: Sanskrit College, 1976.

Cousins, Lance S.
1972 'Dhammapāla and the Ṭīkā Literature.' *Religion,* 2:159–165.
1973 'Buddhist Jhāna: Its Nature and Attainment According to the Pali Sources.' *Religion,* 3:115–131.

Coward, Harold
1985 *Pluralism: Challenge to World Religions.* New York: Orbis Books.

De Jong, J. W.
1966 'L'Auteur de l'Abhidharmadīpa.' *T'oung Pao,* 52:305–307.
1976 Review of Shukla [1973]. *Indo-Iranian Journal,* 18:307–310.
1980a Review of Armelin [1978] and Willemen [1975]. *Eastern Buddhist,* 13:151–158.
1980b Review of Van Den Broeck [1977]. *T'oung Pao,* 66:277–282.

de Man, Paul
1978 'The Epistemology of Metaphor.' *Critical Enquiry,* 5:13–30.

De Silva, Lily
1970 (ed) *Dīghanikāyaṭṭhakathāṭīkā. Līinatthavaṇṇanā.* Three volumes. London: Pali Text Society.
1978 'Cetovimutti Paññāvimutti and Ubhatobhāgavimutti.' *Pali Buddhist Review,* 3:118–145.

Demiéville, Paul
1954 (tr) 'La Yogācārabhūmi de Sangharakṣa.' *Bulletin de l'Ecole Française d'Extrême Orient* 44:339–436.
1957 (tr) 'Le Chapitre de la *Bodhisattvabhūmi* sur la Perfection du Dhyāna.' *Rocznik Orientalistyczny,* 21:109–128.
Dharmasiri, Gunapala
1974 *A Buddhist Critique of the Christian Concept of God: A Critique of the Concept of God in Contemporary Christian Theology and Philosophy of Religion from the point of view of Early Buddhism.* Colombo: Lake House.
Dowling, Thomas L.
1976 *Vasubandhu on the Avijñapti-Rūpa: A Study in Fifth-Century Abhidharma Buddhism.* PhD Dissertation, Columbia University.
Dutt, Nalinaksha
1978 *Bodhisattvabhūmiḥ.* Tibetan-Sanskrit Works Series Volume 7. Patna: Kashi Prasad Jayaswal Research Institute.
Dvivedin, V. P. and Dravida, L. S.
1907–39 (eds) *Atmatattvaviveka.* Calcutta: Bibliotheca Indica, No. 170.
Edgerton, Franklin
1953 *Buddhist Hybrid Sanskrit Grammar and Dictionary.* Two volumes. New Haven: Yale University Press.
Eliade, Mircea
1969 *Yoga: Immortality and Freedom.* Second revised edition, New York: Bollingen Foundation.
Feer, Léon
1884–1904 (ed) *Samyutta-Nikāya.* Six volumes (including index volume). London: Pali Text Society.
Feyerabend, P. K.
1974 *Against Method.* London: New Left Books.
Frauwallner, Erich
1951 *On the Date of the Buddhist Master of the Law Vasubandhu.* Serie Orientale Roma No.3. Rome: Instituto italiano per il Medio ed Estremo Oriente.
1952 'Die buddhistischen Konzile.' *Zeitschrift der Deutschen Morgendlandischen Gesellschaft,* 102:240–261.
1956 *The Earliest Vinaya and the Beginnings of Buddhist Literature.* Serie Orientale Roma No.8. Rome: Instituto italiano per il Medio ed Estremo Oriente.
1961 'Landmarks in the History of Indian Logic.' *Wiener Zeitschrift für die Kunde Sud- und Ostasiens,* 5:125–148.
1963 'Abhidharma-Studien (1).' *Wiener Zeitschrift für die Kunde Sud- und Ostasiens,* 7:20–36.
1964 'Abhidharma-Studien (2).' *Wiener Zeitschrift für die Kunde Sud- und Ostasiens,* 8:59–99.
1971 'Abhidharma-Studien (3).' *Wiener Zeitschrift für die Kunde Sud- und Ostasiens,* 15:69–121.
1972 'Abhidharma-Studien (4).' *Wiener Zeitschrift für die Kunde Sud- und Ostasiens,* 16:95–152.

1973 'Abhidharma-Studien (5).' *Wiener Zeitschrift für die Kunde Sud- und Ostasiens,* 17:97–121.

Gadamer, Hans-Georg
1975 *Truth and Method.* London: Weidenfeld. Translated from the 2d German edition.

Geertz, Clifford
1983 *Local Knowledge.* New York: Basic Books.

Geiger, Wilhelm
1956 *Pali Literature and Language.* English translation by Batakrishna Ghosh, second edition, Calcutta: University of Calcutta Press. First published in German: *Pali Literatur und sprache.* Strassburg: Trübner, 1916.

Geiger, Wilhelm and Geiger, Magdalene
1920 *Pali Dhamma: vornehmlich in der kanonischen Literatur.* Munich: Bavarian Academy of Sciences.

Gimello, Robert M.
1978 'Mysticism and Meditation.' In Steven T. Katz (ed), *Mysticism and Philosphical Analysis,* New York: Oxford University Press, pages 170–199.
1983 'Mysticism in its Contexts.' In Steven T. Katz (ed), *Mysticism and Religious Traditions,* New York: Oxford University Press, pages 61–88.

Gokhale, V. V.
1946 (ed) 'The Text of the Abhidharmakośakārikā of Vasubandhu.' *Journal of the Bombay Branch of the Royal Asiatic Society,* New Series, 22:73–102.
1947a 'An Emendation in the Text of the Abhidharmakośakārikā, IV, 74.' *Journal of the Bombay Branch of the Ṛoyal Asiatic Society,* New Series, 23:12.
1947b 'Fragments from the Abhidharmasamuccaya of Asaṃga.' *Journal of the Bombay Branch of the Royal Asiatic Society,* New Series, 23:13–38.
1948 'A Rare Manuscript of Asanga's *Abhidharmasamuccaya.*' *Harvard Journal of Asiatic Studies,* 2:207–213.

Gombrich, Richard F.
1974 'Eliade on Buddhism.' *Religious Studies,* 10:225–231.

Gregory, Peter N.
1983 'Chinese Buddhist Hermeneutics: The Case of Hua-Yen.' *Journal of the American Academy of Religion,* 51:231–249.

Griffiths, Paul
1981 'Concentration or Insight: The Problematic of Theravāda Buddhist Meditation-Theory.' *Journal of the American Academy of Religion,* 49:606–624.
1982 'Notes Towards a Critique of Buddhist Karmic Theory.' *Religious Studies,* 18:277–291.
1983a *Indian Buddhist Meditation-Theory: History, Development and Systematization.* PhD Dissertation: University of Wisconsin —Madison.
1983b 'Buddhist Jhāna: A Form-Critical Study'. *Religion,* 13:55–68.

1983c 'On Being Mindless: The Debate on the Reemergence of Consciousness from the Attainment of Cessation in the Abhidharmakośabhāṣyam and its Commentaries.' *Philosophy East and West*, 33:379–394.
1984 'Karma and Personal Identity: A Response to Professor White.' *Religious Studies*, 20:481–485.

Griffiths, Paul and Lewis, Delmas
1983 'On Grading Religions, Seeking Truth and Being Nice to People: A Reply to Professor Hick.' *Religious Studies*, 19:75–80.

Gunaratana, Henepola
1980 *A Critical Analysis of the Jhānas in Theravāda Buddhist Meditation*. PhD Dissertation: American University.

Hakamaya Noriaki
1974 'On a Verse Quoted in the Tibetan Translation of the Mahāyānasaṃgrahopanibandhana.' *Indogaku Bukkyōgaku Kenkyū (Journal of Indian and Buddhist Studies)*, 22:(17)–(21).
1975 'Nirodhasamāpatti: Its Historical Meaning in the Vijñaptimātratā System.' *Indogaku Bukkyōgaku Kenkyū (Journal of Indian and Buddhist Studies)*, 23:(33)–(43).
1978 'Araya-shiki sonzai no hachi ronshō ni kansuru shobunken.' *Komazawa Daigaku Bukkyōgakubu Kenkyū Kiyo*, 36:1–26.

Hakamaya Noriaki, Keenan, John and Griffiths, Paul
The Realm of Enlightenment: A Translation and Study of the Tenth Chapter of the Mahāyānasaṃgraha and its Commentaries. Unpublished manuscript.

Hall, Bruce Cameron
1983 *Vasubandhu on 'Aggregates, Spheres and Components': Being Chapter One of the 'Abhidharmakośa'*. PhD Thesis, Harvard University.

Hardy, E.
1897 'Ein Betrag zur Frage, ob Dhammapāla im Nālandāsaṃghāramā seine Kommentare geschrieben.' *Zeitschrift der Deutschen Morgenlandischen Gesellschaft*, 51:105–127.

Hick, John
1981 'On Grading Religions.' *Religious Studies*, 17:451–467.
1983 'On Conflicting Religious Truth-Claims.' *Religious Studies*, 19:485–491.

Hill, Christopher
1982 'On A Revised Version of the Principle of Sufficient Reason.' *Pacific Philosophical Quarterly*, 63:236–242.

Hirakawa Akira
1980 'The Meaning of "Dharma" and "Abhidharma".' In *Indianisme et Bouddhisme: Mélanges offerts a Mgr. Etienne Lamotte*. Publications de l'Institut Orientaliste No.23. Louvain-la-Neuve: Institut Orientaliste, pages 159–175.

Hirakawa Akira et al.
1973 *Index to the Abhidharmakośabhāṣya. Part One: Sanskrit–Tibetan–Chinese*. Tokyo: Daizo Shuppan Kabushikikaisha.
1977 *Index to the Abhidharmakośabhāṣya. Part Two: Chinese–Sanskrit*. Tokyo: Daizo Shuppan Kabushikikaisha.

1978 *Index to the Abhidharmakośabhāṣya. Part Three: Tibetan–Sanskrit.* Tokyo: Daizo Shuppan Kabushikikaisha.

Hoffman, Frank J.

1982 'The Buddhist Empiricism Thesis.' *Religious Studies,* 18:151–158.

Horner, I. B.

1954–59 (tr) *The Collection of the Middle Length Sayings.* Three volumes. London: Pali Text Society.

1963–64 (tr) *Milinda's Questions.* Sacred Books of the Buddhists Nos.22–23. London: Pali Text Society.

Hurvitz, Leon

1979 'The Eight Liberations.' In A. K. Narain (ed), *Studies in Pali and Buddhism,* Delhi: B. R. Publishing, pages 121–169.

Jaini, Padmanabh S.

1958 'On the Theory of Two Vasubandhus.' *Bulletin of the School of Oriental and African Studies,* 21:48–53.

1959a 'The Vaibhāṣika Theory of Words and Meanings.' *Bulletin of the School of Oriental and African Studies,* 22:95–107.

1959b 'The Sautrāntika Theory of Bīja.' *Bulletin of the School of Oriental and African Studies,* 22:236–249.

1959c 'The Development of the Theory of the Viprayukta-Saṃskāras.' *Bulletin of the School of Oriental and African Studies,* 22:531–547.

1974 'On the Sarvajñatva (Omniscience) of Mahāvīra and the Buddha.' In L. Cousins et al. (eds), *Buddhist Studies in Honour of I. B. Horner,* Dordrecht: Reidel, pages 71–90.

1977a (ed) *Abhidharmadīpa with Vibhāṣāprabhāvṛtti.* Tibetan Sanskrit Works Series, Volume 4. Second edition. Patna: Kashi Prasad Jayaswal Research Institute. First edition 1959.

1977b 'Prajñā and dṛṣṭi in the Vaibhāṣika Abhidharma.' In Lewis Lancaster (ed) *Prajñāpāramitā and Related Systems,* Berkeley Buddhist Studies Series No.1, Berkeley: University of California Press, pages 403–415.

Jayatilleke, K. N.

1963 *Early Buddhist Theory of Knowledge.* London: Allen and Unwin.

Kalansuriya, A. D. P.

1979 'Two Modern Sinhalese Views of Nibbāna.' *Religion,* 9:1–12.

1981 'On the Notion of Verification in Buddhism and in Logical Positivism: A Brief Philosophical Study.' In Nathan Katz (ed) *Buddhist and Western Philosophy,* Delhi: Stirling, pages 287–305.

Kalupahana, David J.

1975 *Causality: The Central Philosophy of Buddhism.* Honolulu: University of Hawaii Press.

Katz, Nathan

1982 *Buddhist Images of Human Perfection: The Arahant of the Suttapiṭaka Compared with the Bodhisattva and the Mahāsiddha.* Delhi: Motilal Banarsidass.

Katz, Steven T.
1978 'Language, Epistemology and Mysticism.' In Steven T. Katz (ed), *Mysticism and Philosophical Analysis,* New York: Oxford University Press, pages 22–74.
1982 'Models, Modeling and Mystical Experience.' *Religion,* 12:247–275.
1983 'The "Conservative" Character of Mysticism.' In Steven T. Katz, (ed), *Mysticism and Religious Traditions,* New York: Oxford University Press, pages 3–60.
Keenan, John
1982 'Original Purity and the Focus of Early Yogācāra.' *Journal of the International Association of Buddhist Studies,* 5/1:7–18.
Keith, Arthur Berriedale
1936 'Pre-Canonical Buddhism.' *Indian Historical Quarterly,* 12:1–20.
Kimura Taiken
1937 *Abidatsumaron no Kenkyū.* Tokyo: Meiji Shōin.
King, Winston L.
1977 'The Structure and Dynamics of the Attainment of Cessation in Theravāda Meditation.' *Journal of the American Academy of Religion,* (Supplements), 45:707–725.
1980 *Theravāda Meditation: The Buddhist Transformation of Yoga.* Pennsylvania: Pennsylvania State University Press.
Kloetzli, Randy
1983 *Buddhist Cosmology: From Single World-System to Pure Land. Science and Theology in the Images of Motion and Light.* Delhi: Motilal Banarsidass.
Kochumuttom, Thomas
1982 *A Buddhist Doctrine of Experience: A New Translation and Interpretation of the Works of Vasubandhu the Yogācārin.* Delhi: Motilal Banarsidass
Kornfield, Jack
1977 *Living Buddhist Masters.* Santa Cruz: Unity Press.
Kuhn, T. S.
1962 *The Structure of Scientific Revolutions.* Princeton: Princeton University Press.
1970a *The Structure of Scientific Revolutions.* Second Edition. Princeton: Princeton University Press.
1970b 'Reflections on My Critics.' In I. Lakatos and A. Musgrave (eds), *Criticism and the Growth of Knowledge,* Cambridge: Cambridge University Press, pages 237–278.
La Vallée Poussin, Louis de
1904–14 (ed) *Bodhicaryāvatāra-Pañjikā With the Commentary of Prajñākaramati.* Seven fascicles, Bibliotheca Indica 983, 1031, 1090, 1126, 1139, 1305, 1399. Calcutta: Asiatic Society.
1917 *The Way to Nirvāṇa: Six Lectures on Ancient Buddhism as a Discipline of Salvation.* Cambridge: Cambridge University Press.
1919 (ed and tr) *Vasubandhu et Yaçomitra. Troisième chapitre de l'Abhidharmakoça, kārikā, bhāṣya et vyākhyā. Avec une analyse*

de la Lokaprajñapti et de la Karaṇaprajñapti de Maudgalyāyana. Memoires de l'Academie Royale de Belgique, Classe des Lettres et des Sciences morales et politiques, Second Series Volume 6. Brussels: Hayez.

1928–29 (tr) *Vijñaptimātratāsiddhi: La Siddhi de Hiuan-Tsang.* Eight Fascicles. Buddhica: Documents et travaux pour l'étude du Bouddhisme, Première Serie, Tomes I (fasc 1–4) and V (fasc 5–8). Paris: Geuthner.

1930a 'Maitreya et Asanga.' Notes bouddhiques XVI. *Academie royale de Belgique, bulletins de la classe des lettres et des sciences morales,* 16:9–19.

1930b (tr) 'Textes relatifs au Nirvāṇa et aux Asaṃskṛtas en gén éral.' Documents d'Abhidharma (1), Premiere Partie. *Bulletin de l'Ecole française d'Extrême-Orient,* 30:1–28.

1932 (tr) 'La Doctrine des refuges et le corps de l'Arhat.' Documents d'Abhidharma (2). *Mélanges Chinois et Bouddhiques,* 1:65–125.

1934 'Note sur l'Alayavijñāna.' *Mélanges Chinoise et Bouddhiques,* 3:145–168

1937a (tr) 'La Controverse du Temps.' Documents d'Abhidharma (3). *Mélanges Chinois et Bouddhiques, 5:7–158.*

1937b (tr) 'Les Deux verités.' Documents d'Abhidharma (4). *Mélanges Chinois et Bouddhiques,* 5:159–187.

1937c 'Musīla et Nārada: le chemin du nirvāṇa.' *Mélanges Chinois et Bouddhiques,* 5:189–222.

1971 (tr) *L'Abhidharmakośa de Vasubandhu.* Reprinted from the original six volume 1923–31 edition (Paris: Geuthner) as *Mélanges Chinois et Bouddhiques,* Volume 16. Original pagination and volume-division preserved. Quoted by volume (in roman numerals) and page.

Lamotte, Etienne

1934 (tr) 'L'Alayavijñāna (Le Receptacle) dans le Mahāyānasaṃgraha (Chapitre II).' *Mélanges Chinoise et Bouddhiques,* 3:169–255.

1935a (ed and tr) *Saṃdhinirmocanasūtra: L'Explication des Mystères.* Louvain: Universite de Louvain.

1935b (ed and tr) 'Le Traité de l'Acte de Vasubandhu.' *Mélanges Chinoise et Bouddhiques,* 4:151–263.

1949 'La critique d'interpretation dans le bouddhisme.' *Annuaire de l'Institut de philologie et d'histoire orientales et slaves,* 9:341–361.

1958 *Histoire du Bouddhisme indien: des origines à l'ère Śaka.* Bibliotheque du Muséon, Volume 43. Louvain-la-Neuve: Institut Orientaliste de Louvain.

1962 (tr) *L'Enseignement de Vimalakīrti (Vimalakīrtinirdeśa).* Bibliotheque du Muséon, Volume 51. Louvain-la-Neuve: Institut Orientaliste de Louvain.

1973 (ed and tr) *La somme du Grand Vehicule d'Asanga (Mahāyānasaṃgraha).* Two volumes. Publications de l'Institut Orientaliste de Louvain, No.8. Louvain-la-Neuve: Institut

Orientaliste de Louvain. The PIOL edition is a photographic reprint of the 1938 edition published as No.7 in the Bibliotheque du Muséon.
1970–81 (tr) *Le Traité de la grande vertue de sagesse.* Five volumes. Publications de l'Institut Orientaliste de Louvain Nos.2, 12, 24–26. Louvain-la-Neuve: Institut Orientaliste de Louvain. Volume 1 (currently PIOL 25) originally appeared in 1944 as No.18 of the Bibliotheque du Muséon; Vol.2 (currently PIOL 26) originally appeared in the same series in 1949. The PIOL editions of these volumes are photographic reproductions of the originals. Vols.3, 4 and 5 (PIOL Nos.2, 12 and 24, respectively) originally appeared in the PIOL series.

Law, B. C.
1974 *A History of Pali Literature.* Two volumes. Varanasi: Bharatiya Publishing House. 1st edition, London, 1933.

Law, Narendra Nath
1949 (ed) *Sphuṭārthā Abhidharmakośa-vyākhyā of Yaśomitra.* Calcutta Oriental Series No.31. London: Luzac. First three chapters only.

Law, Narendra Nath and Dutt, Nalinaksha
1957 (eds) *Sphuṭārthā Abhidharmakośa-vyākhyā of Yaśomitra.* Calcutta Oriental Series, No.31 (continued). Calcutta: Oriental Book Agency. Fourth chapter only.

Legge, James
1965 *A Record of Buddhistic Kingdoms: Being an Account by the Chinese Monk Fa-Hien of his Travels in India and Ceylon (A.D. 399–414) in search of the Buddhist Books of Discipline.* New York: Dover-Paragon. First edition, Oxford: Clarendon Press, 1896.

Leibniz
1714 *Monadology.* Many editions. Quoted by standard paragraph numbering.

Lévi, Sylvain
1925 (ed) *Vijñaptimātratāsiddhi. Deux Traités de Vasubandhu: Viṃśatikā et Triṃśikā.* Bibliotheque de l'Ecole des Hautes Etudes, Sciences Historiques et Philologiques, Fascicule 245. Paris: Librairie Ancienne Honoré Champion.

Limaye, U. P. (Acārya) and Vadekar, R. V.
1958 (ed) *Eighteen Principal Upaniṣads.* Poona: Vaidika Saṃśodhana Maṇḍala.

Loy, David
1983 'How Not to Criticize Nāgārjuna: A Response to L. Stafford Betty.' *Philosophy East and West,* 33:437–445.

Masefield, Peter
1979 'The Nibbāna-Parinibbāna Controversy.' *Religion* 9:215–230.

Matilal, Bimal Krishna
1974 'A Critique of Buddhist Idealism.' In L. Cousins, A. Kunst and K. R. Norman (eds), *Buddhist Studies in Honour of I. B. Horner,* Dordrecht: Reidel:139–169.

Maung Tin, Pe
1920–21 (tr) *The Expositor.* Two volumes. London: Pali Text Society.

May, Jacques
1971 'La Philosophie Bouddhique Idéaliste.' *Etudes Asiatique, 25:265–323.*

McDermott, A. Charlene S.
1973 'Asanga's Defense of *Alayavijñāna:* Of Catless Grins and Sundry Related Matters.' *Journal of Indian Philosophy,* 1:167–174.

Monier-Williams, Monier
1899 *A Sanskrit–English Dictionary Etymologically and Philologically Arranged with Special Reference to Cognate Indo-European Languages.* Oxford: Clarendon Press.

Morris, R., Hardy, E., Hunt, Mabel, Warder, A. K. and Rhys-Davids, C. A. F.
1885–1910 (eds) *Anguttara-Nikāya.* Six volumes (including index volume). London: Pali Text Society.

Muller, M.
1885 (ed) *Dhammasangaṇi.* London: Pali Text Society.

Nagao Gadjin
1978a *Chūkan to Yuishiki.* Tokyo: Iwanami Shoten.
1978b ''What Remains' in Sūnyatā: A Yogācāra Interpretation of Emptiness.' In Minoru Kiyota (ed) *Mahāyāna Buddhist Meditation: Theory and Practice.* Honolulu: The University Press of Hawaii: 66–82.
1979 'From Mādhyamika to Yogācāra: An Analysis of MMK, XXIV.18 and MV, I.1–2.' *Journal of the International Association of Buddhist Studies,* 2/1:29–43
1982 *Setsudaijōron: Wayaku to Chūkai.* Tokyo: Kodansha.
1983 'The Buddhist World-View as Elucidated in the Three-Nature Theory and Its Similes.' *Eastern Buddhist,* 16:1–18.

Nāṇananda (Bhikkhu)
1976 *Concept and Reality in Early Buddhist Thought.* Second edition, Kandy: Buddhist Publication Society. First edition, 1971.

Nelson, Andrew Nathaniel
1974 *The Modern Reader's Japanese-English Character Dictionary.* Second revised edition. Rutland, Vermont/Tokyo: Tuttle.

Norman, K. R.
1983 *Pali Literature, Including the Canonical Literature in Prakrit and Sanskrit of all the Hīnayāna Schools of Buddhism.* Volume 7 Fascicle 2 of Jan Gonda (ed) *A History of Indian Literature,* Wiesbaden: Otto Harrassowitz.

Nyanamoli (Bhikkhu)
1976 (tr) *The Path of Purification.* Two volumes. Berkeley & London: Shambhala Press (paperback reprint). First edition, Sri Lanka, 1956 and 1964.

Nyanaponika (Thera)
1962 *The Heart of Buddhist Meditation.* London: Rider.

Obermiller, E.
1932 (tr)*The History of Buddhism in India and Tibet.* Leipzig-Heidelberg: Harrassowitz.

O'Flaherty, Wendy Doniger
1981 (tr)*The Ṛgveda.* Penguin: Harmondsworth.

Oshio Dokusan
1934 *Abidatsuma Kusharon no Zuki.* Tokyo: Diayukaku.

Pandeya, R. C.
1971 (ed)*Madhyānta-Vibhāga-Sāstra. Containing the Kārikā-s of Maitreya Bhāṣya of Vasubandhu and Tīkā by Sthiramati.* Delhi: Banarsidass.

Paul, Diana
1981 'The Structure of Consciousness in Paramārtha's Purported Trilogy.' *Philosophy East and West,* 31:297–319.
1982 'The Life and Times of Paramārtha (499–569).' *Journal of the International Association of Buddhist Studies,* 5:37–69.
1984 *Philosophy of Mind in Sixth Century China: Parmārtha's 'Evolution of Consciousness'.* Stanford: Stanford University Press.

Péri, Noel
1911 'A propos de la date de Vasubandhu.' *Bulletin de l'école française d'Extrême Orient,* 11:339–390.

Piatigorsky, Alexander
1984 *The Buddhist Philosophy of Thought.* London: Curzon Press.

Pieris, Aloysius (S. J.)
1978 'The Colophon to the Paramatthamañjūsā and the Discussion on the Date of Acariya Dhammapāla.' In Heinz Bechert (ed), *Buddhism in Ceylon and Studies on Religious Syncretism in Buddhist Countries,* Symposien zur Buddhismusforschung, Volume 1. Gottingen: Vandenhoeck & Ruprecht, pages 61–77.

Pradhan, Pralhad
1948 'The MS of Asanga's *Abhidharmasamuccaya.' Indian Historical Quarterly,* 24:87–93.
1949 'A Note on *Abhidharma-samuccaya Bhāṣya* and its Author Sthiramati(?)' *Journal of the Bihar and Orissa Research Society,* 35:34–46.
1950 (ed)*Abhidharmasamuccaya of Asanga.* Santiniketan: Visvabharati.
1975 *Abhidharmakośabhāṣyam of Vasubandhu.* Tibetan–Sanskrit Works Series Volume 8. Second edition, Patna: Kashi Prasad Jayaswal Research Institute. First edition 1967.

Prebish, Charles
1973 'Theories Concerning the Skandhaka.' *Journal of Asian Studies,* 32:669–678.

Quine, Willard Van Orman
1969 *Ontological Relativity and Other Essays.* New York: Columbia University Press.

Rahder, Johannes
1926 (tr) *Daśabhūmikasūtra et Bodhisattvabhūmi: Chapitres Vihāra et Bhūmi*. Paris and Louvain.
Rahula, Walpola
1966 *History of Buddhism in Ceylon*. Colombo: M. D. Gunasena. First edition, 1956.
1967 *What the Buddha Taught*. Bedford (England): Gordon Fraser.
1971 (tr)*Le Compendium de la Super-Doctrine (philosophie) (Abhidharmasamuccaya) d'Asanga*. Paris: Ecole française d'Extrême-Orient.
Rawlinson, Andrew
1979 'Altered States of Consciousness.' *Religion*, 9:92–103.
Régamey, Constantin
1938 (ed and tr) *Three Chapters from the Samādhirājasūtra*. Warsaw.
1957 'Le probleme du bouddhisme primitif et les derniers travaux de Stanislaw Schayer.' *Rocznik Orientalistyczny*, 21:37–58.
Rewatadhamma
1969–72 (ed) *Buddhaghosācariya's Visuddhimaggo with Paramatthamañjūsāṭīkā of Bhadantācariya Dhammapāla*. Three volumes. Varanasi: Varanaseya Sanskrit Viśvavidyālaya.
Rhys-Davids, C. A. F.
1900 (tr) *A Buddhist Manual of Psychological Ethics*. London: Royal Asiatic Society.
1908–26 'Paṭiccasamuppāda.' Article in *Encyclopaedia of Religion and Ethics*, James Hastings (ed), New York: Charles Scribner's, Volume 6, pages 672–674.
1920–21 (ed) *Visuddhimagga*. Two volumes. London: Pali Text Society.
Rhys-Davids, C. A. F. and Woodward, F. L.
1917–30 (tr) *The Book of the Kindred Sayings*. Five volumes. London: Pali Text Society.
Rhys-Davids, T. W.
1890–94 (tr) *The Questions of King Milinda*. Sacred Books of the East, Nos.35–36. Oxford: Clarendon Press.
Rhys-Davids, T. W., Carpenter, J. Estlin and Stede, William
1886–1932 (ed) *Sumangalavilāsinī*. Three volumes. London: Pali Text Society.
Rhys-Davids, T. W. and Carpenter, J. Estlin
1890–1911 (ed) *Dīgha-Nikāya*. Three volumes. London: Pali Text Society.
Rhys-Davids, T. W. and Rhys-Davids, C. A. F.
1899–1921 (tr) *Dialogues of the Buddha*. Three volumes. London: Pali Text Society.
Roth, Gustav
1976 'Observations on the First Chapter of Asanga's *Bodhisattvabhūmi*.' *Indologica Taurinensia*, 4:403–412.

Rouner, Leroy S.
1984 (ed) *Religious Pluralism*. Boston University Studies in Philosophy and Religion, Volume 5. Notre Dame: University of Notre Dame Press.
Rowe, William L.
1984 'Rational Theology and some Principles of Explanation.' *Faith and Philosophy*, 1:357–369.
Saddhatissa, H.
1965 (ed) *Upāsakajanālankāra*. London: Pali Text Society.
Sakurabe Hajime
1969 *Kusharon no Kenkyū: Kai Konpon*. Kyoto: Hōzōkan.
1981 *Kusharon*. Bongo Butten No.18. Tokyo: Okura Shuppan
Sānkṛtyāyana, Rahula
1937 'Second Search of Sanskrit Palm-Leaf MSS in Tibet.' *Journal of the Bihar and Orissa Research Society*, 23:1–57.
Sarathchandra, E. R.
1958 *Buddhist Psychology of Perception*. Colombo: Ceylon University Press.
Sasaki Genjun
1958 *Abidatsuma Shiso Kenkyū*. Tokyo. Kobundo.
Sastri, Shanti (Bhikṣu)
1953 (tr) *Abhidharmāmṛta of Ghoṣaka*. Visvabharati Studies No.17. Santiniketan: Visvabharati.
Śāstrī, Dwārikādās (Swāmī)
1981 (ed) *Abhidharmakośa and Bhāṣya of Acārya Vasubandhu with Sphuṭārthā Commentary of Acārya Yaśomitra*. Two volume reprint (continuous pagination) of the four volume edition issued from 1970–73. Bauddha Bharati Series Nos. 5–8. Varanasi: Bauddha Bharati.
Schayer, Stanislaw
1935 'Precanonical Buddhism.' *Archiv Orientalni*, 8:121–132.
Schmithausen, Lambert
1969a *Der Nirvāṇa-Abschnitt in der Viniścayasaṃgrahaṇī der Yogācārabhūmiḥ*. Vienna: Osterreichische Akademie der Wissenschaften.
1969b 'Zur Literaturgeschichte der alteren Yogācāra Schüle.' *Zeitschrift der Deutschen Morgenlanischen Gesellschaft*, Supplementa 1, (XVII Deutscher Orientalistentag).
1972 'The Definition of Pratyakṣam in the *Abhidharmasamuccaya*.' *Wiener Zeitschrift für die Kunde Sud-Asiens*, 16:235–250.
1976a 'Die Vier Konzentrationen der Aufmerksamkeit: Zur geschichtlichen Entwicklung einer spirituellen Praxis des Buddhismus.' *Zeitschrift für Missionswissenschaft und Religionswissenschaft*, 60:241–266.
1976b 'On the Problem of the Relation of Spiritual Practice and Philosophical Theory in Buddhism.' In *German Scholars on India II*, Bombay: Nachiketa Publications:235–251.
1982 'Versenkungspraxis und erlosende Erfahrung in der *Śrāvakabhūmi*.' In *Epiphanie des Heils: Zur Heilsgegenwart in*

Indischer und Christlicher Religion, ed Gerhard Oberhammer, Vienna: Osterreichische Akademie der Wissenschaften, 59–85.

Sharma, Arvind
1984 'Playing Hardball in Religious Studies.' *Council on the Study of Religion: Bulletin.* 15:1,3–4

Shukla, Karunesha
1973 (ed) *Śrāvakabhūmi of Acārya Asanga.* Patna: K. P. Jayaswal Research Institute.

Silburn, Lilian
1955 *Instant et Cause: Le discontinue dans la pensée philosophique de l'Inde.* Paris: Libraire Philosophique.

Smart, Ninian
1965 'The Interpretation of Mystical Experience.' *Religious Studies,* 1:75–87.

Sopa, Lhundup (Geshe)
1979 'Samathavipaśyanāyuganaddha.' In Minoru Kiyota (ed), *Mahāyāna Buddhist Meditation: Theory and Practice,* Honolulu: University of Hawaii Press, pages 46–65.

Sperber, Dan
1985 *On Anthropological Knowledge.* Cambridge Studies in Social Anthropology 54. Cambridge: Cambridge University Press.

Stcherbatsky, Th.
1923 *The Central Conception of Buddhism and the Meaning of the Word 'Dharma'.* London: Royal Asiatic Society.
1962 *Buddhist Logic.* Two volumes. New York: Dover Publications. First published as Volume XXVI of Bibliotheca Buddhica, Leningrad 1930.

Stcherbatsky, Th. et al.
1970 (ed) *Sphuṭārtha Abhidharmakoçavyākhyā. The Work of Yaçomitra.* Bibliotheca Buddhica No.21. Osnabruck: Biblio Verlag. First edition, St. Petersburg, 1918–31. First two chapters only.

Swinburne, Richard R.
1979 *The Existence of God.* Oxford: Clarendon Press.

Takakusu Junjiro
1904 (tr) 'The Life of Vasubandhu.' *T'oung Pao,* 269–296.
1904–5 'On the Abhidharma Literature of the Sarvāstivādins.' *Journal of the Pali Text Society,* 67–146.
1905 'A Study of Paramārtha's Life of Vasubandhu and the Date of Vasubandhu.' *Journal of the Royal Asiatic Society,* 33–35.
1929 'The Date of Vasubandhu the Great Buddhist Philosopher.' In *Indian Studies in Honor of Charles Rockwell Lanman,* Cambridge, Mass.: Harvard University Press, pages 79–88.

Takasaki Jikido
1966 *A Study on the Ratnagotravibhāga (Uttaratantra): Being a Treatise on the Tathāgatagarbha Theory of Mahāyāna Bud-*

dhism. Serie Orientale Roma XXIII. Rome: Instituto Italiano per il Medio ed Estremo Oriente.

Tart, Charles T.

1969 (ed) *Altered States of Consciousness*. New York: John Wiley.

1971 'Scientific Foundations for the Study of Altered States of Consciousness.' *Journal of Transpersonal Psychology*, 3:93–124.

1972 'States of Consciousness and State-Specific Sciences.' *Science*, 176:1203–1210.

1975a (ed) *States of Consciousness*. New York: Dutton.

1975b (ed) *Transpersonal Psychologies*. New York: Harper & Row.

Tatia, Nathmial

1976 *Abhidarmasamuccayabhāṣyam*. Tibetan-Sanskrit Works Series, No. 17. Patna: Kashi Prasad Jayaswal Research Institute.

Tekin, Sinasi

1970 (ed)*Abhidharma-Kośa-Bhāṣya-Tīkā Tattvārtha-Nāma*. Text in facsimile with introduction. Sources of Oriental Languages and Literatures, Turkic Sources I. New York: Garland.

Thurman, Robert

1978 'Buddhist Hermeneutics.' *Journal of the American Academy of Religion*, 46:19–39.

Tin, Pe Maung

1923–31 (tr) *The Path of Purity*. Three volumes. London: Pali Text Society.

Tola, Fernando and Dragonetti, Carmen

1983 (ed and tr) 'The Trisvabhāvakārikā of Vasubandhu.' *Journal of Indian Philosophy*, 11:225–266.

Trenckner, V.

1880 (ed) *Milindapañha*. London: Williams and Norgate.

Trenckner, V., Chalmers, Robert and Rhys-Davids, C. A. F.

1888–1925 (ed) *Majjhima-Nikāya*. Four volumes (including index volume). London: Pali Text Society.

Tucci, Guiseppe

1930 *On Some Aspects of the Doctrines of Maitreya(nātha) and Asanga*. Calcutta: University of Calcutta Press.

1956 (ed) *Minor Buddhist Texts I*. Serie Orientale Roma IX.1. Rome: Instituto Italiano per il Medeo ed Estremo Oriente.

Ueda Yoshifumi

1967 'Two Main Streams of Thought in Yogācāra Philosophy.' *Philosophy East and West*, 17:155–165.

Ui Hakuju

1929 'Maitreya as a Historical Personage.' *Indian Studies in Honor of Charles Rockwell Lanman*, Cambridge: Harvard University Press:95–101.

Vajirañāṇa, (Mahāthera)

1962 *Buddhist Meditation*. Colombo: M. D. Gunasena.

Van Buitenen, J. A. B.
1981 (ed and tr) *The Bhagavadgītā in the Mahābhārata: A Bilingual Edition.* Chicago: University of Chicago Press.
Van Den Broeck, J.
1977 (tr) *La Saveur de l'immortel de Ghoṣaka.* Publications de l'Institut Orientaliste de Louvain No.15. Louvain-la-Neuve: Institut Orientaliste de Louvain.
Warder, A. K.
1971 'Dharmas and Data.' *Journal of Indian Philosophy,* 1:272–295.
1974 *Introduction to Pali.* Second edition, with additions and corrections. London: Pali Text Society.
1980 *Indian Buddhism.* Second edition. Delhi: Motilal Banarsidass. First edition 1970.
Warren, Henry Clarke
1950 (ed) *Visuddhimagga of Buddhaghosācariya.* Revised by Dharmānanda Kosambi. Harvard Oriental Series Volume 41. Cambridge: Harvard University Press.
Watanabe Fumimaro
1980 'The Conception of Abhidhamma in the Nikāyas and Agamas: Its Characteristics.' *Bukkyōgaku Kenkyū,* (Ryūkoku University, Kyoto), 1–23.
1983 Philosophy and its Development in the Nikāyas and Abhidhamma. Delhi: Motilal Banarsidass, 1983.
Watters, Thomas
1904–5 (tr) *On Yuan Chwang's Travels in India 629–645 AD.* London: Royal Asiatic Society.
Wayman, Alex
1960 'The Sacittikā and Acittikā Bhūmi and the Pratyekabuddhabhūmi (Sanskrit texts).' *Indogaku Bukkyōgaku Kenkyū,* 8:375–379.
1961 *Analysis of the Śrāvakabhūmi Manuscript.* Berkeley and Los Angeles: University of California Press.
Welbon, Guy Richard
1968 *The Buddhist Nirvāṇa and its Western Interpreters.* Chicago: University of Chicago Press.
White, J. E.
1983 'Is Karmic Theory False?' *Religious Studies,* 19:223–228.
Willemen, Charles
1975 (tr) *The Essence of Metaphysics.* Brussels: Publications de l'Institut Belge des Hautes Etudes Bouddhiques.
Williams, Paul M.
1981 'On the Abhidharma Ontology.' *Journal of Indian Philosophy,* 9:227–257.
Willis, Janice Dean
1979 (tr) *On Knowing Reality: The Tattvārtha Chapter of Asanga's Bodhisattvabhūmi.* New York: Columbia University Press.
Wittgenstein, Ludwig
1953 *Philosophical Investigations.* Bilingual edition, English translation G. E. M. Anscombe. New York: Macmillan.

Wogihara Unrai
1932–36 (ed) *Sphuṭārtha Abhidharmakośavyākhyā by Yaśomitra.* Two volumes. Tokyo: The Publishing Association of the Abhidharmakośavyākhyā. Reprinted 1971, Tokyo: Sankibo Buddhist Bookstore.
1971 (ed) *Bodhisattvabhūmi: A Statement of the Whole Course of the Bodhisattva.* Two volumes. Tokyo: Sankibo Buddhist Bookstore. First edition 1930–36.
Woods, J. H., Kosambi, Dharmānanda and Horner, I. B.
1922–38 (ed) *Papañcasūdanī.* Five volumes. London: Pali Text Society.
Woodward, F. L.
1929–37 (ed) *Sāratthappakāsinī.* Three volumes. London: Pali Text Society.
Woodward, F. L. and Hare, R. M.
1951–55 (tr) *The Book of the Gradual Sayings.* Five volumes. London: Pali Text Society.
Wylie, Turrell V.
1959 'A Standard System of Tibetan Transcription.' *Harvard Journal of Asiatic Studies,* 22:261–267.
Yamaguchi Susumu
1934–37 (ed and tr) *Madhyānatavibhāgaṭīkā de Sthiramati, Exposition Systematique du Yogācāravijñaptivāda.* Three volumes. Nagoya: Hajinkaku.
Yandell, Keith
1974 'Religious Experience and Rational Appraisal.' *Religious Studies,* 10:173–187.
1979 'Some Varieties of Ineffability.' *International Journal for the Philosophy of Religion,* 10:167–179.
1981 'Some Prolegomena to the Epistemology of Religion.' *International Journal for the Philosophy of Religion,* 12:193–215.
Yoshimoto Shingyō
1982 *Abidaruma Shisō.* Kyoto: Hōzōkan.
1983 'Abhidharmadīpa Nendaiki.' *Indogaku Bukkyōgaku Kenkyū (Journal of Indian and Buddhist Studies),* 31:890–885((94)–(99)).
Zaehner, Richard Charles
1969 (ed and tr) *The Bhagavadgītā with a Commentary Based on the Original Sources.* Oxford: Oxford University Press.

INDEX